Controlling Strategy

Controlling Strategy

Management, Accounting, and Performance Measurement

Edited by
CHRISTOPHER S. CHAPMAN

OXFORD
UNIVERSITY PRESS

OXFORD

UNIVERSITY PRESS

Great Clarendon Street, Oxford OX2 6DP

Oxford University Press is a department of the University of Oxford.
It furthers the University's objective of excellence in research, scholarship,
and education by publishing worldwide in

Oxford New York

Auckland Cape Town Dar es Salaam Hong Kong Karachi
Kuala Lumpur Madrid Melbourne Mexico City Nairobi
New Delhi Shanghai Taipei Toronto

With offices in

Argentina Austria Brazil Chile Czech Republic France Greece
Guatemala Hungary Italy Japan Poland Portugal Singapore
South Korea Switzerland Thailand Turkey Ukraine Vietnam

Oxford is a registered trade mark of Oxford University Press
in the UK and in certain other countries

Published in the United States
by Oxford University Press Inc., New York

British Library Cataloguing in Publication Data

Data available

Library of Congress Cataloguing in Publication Data

Data available

Typeset by SPI Publisher Services, Pondicherry, India
Printed in Great Britain
on acid-free paper by
Biddles Ltd., King's Lynn, Norfolk

ISBN 0-19-928323-0 978-019-928323-1
ISBN 0-19-928063-0 978-019-928063-6 (pbk.)

1 3 5 7 9 10 8 6 4 2

This book is humbly dedicated to

MY FATHER

for his encouragement, support, and wisdom over many years.

CONTENTS

LIST OF FIGURES

LIST OF TABLES

NOTES ON CONTRIBUTORS

Thomas Ahrens, University of Warwick

Christopher S. Chapman, University of Oxford

Robert H. Chenhall, Monash University & James Cook University

Tony Davila, Stanford University & IESE Business School

Allan Hansen, Copenhagen Business School

Christopher D. Ittner, University of Pennsylvania

Kim Langfield-Smith, Monash University

David F. Larcker, University of Pennsylvania

Peter B. Miller, London School of Economics and Political Science

Jan Mouritsen, Copenhagen Business School

Ted O'Leary, Manchester Business School & University of Michigan

Controlling Strategy

Christopher S. Chapman

The relationship between management control systems and strategy

The chapters that follow develop our understanding of the relationship between management control systems (MCS) and strategy through the synthesis of a considerable range of work in the fields of strategy and management accounting. As will be seen, such an easy labelling here belies the breadth and complexity of ideas underlying those labels (Miller 1998; Whittington 2003). A part of the motivation for this volume is to demonstrate something of the range of perspectives from which controlling strategy can be seen to be important. This volume does not attempt a complete inventory of possible perspectives, however. Instead, a common thread unites the diverse theoretical syntheses and analyses of field material presented in the contributions that follow. Both individually and collectively the chapters draw out in detail various ways in which MCS may actively build and sustain valuable strategic roles.

Except in highly controlled and stable environments it has become commonplace to think of MCS as at best irrelevant, more frequently as damaging (Chapman 1997). Yet, there is another view, taken forward in this volume, that MCS can enable innovative strategic responses in contemporary, unstable environments (e.g. Simons 1995; Chapman 1998; Ahrens and Chapman 2002, 2004). We hope this book will contribute to the emergence of a clearer and richer discussion of the strategic nature of MCS.

In the 1950s and 1960s management accounting techniques were seen as effective means of organizational coordination and control. Within firms and organizations, management accounting played a significant role through the disciplining effects of standard costing, variance analysis, and related systems (Anthony 1965). The increasing sophistication (aspirations) of corporate planning activities brought budgets greater prominence and prestige as the practical and effective toolkit for implementing organizational strategy. Whilst difficulties were clearly acknowledged (Argyris 1953; Ridgway 1956), discussions of strategic planning during this period were naturally couched in terms of accounting measurements and systems (Norman 1965). New technologies were expected to further enhance the role of management accounting (Diebold 1965).[1] By the 1980s, however, management accounting was subject to widespread and sustained critique (Hayes and Abernathy 1980; Johnson and Kaplan 1987).

Against the backdrop of the activities of organizations such as Slater Walker in the UK in the 1960s and 1970s it is easy to see why critiques of accounting were frequently couched not simply as a failure to consider new priorities, but as a more fundamental incompatibility with them. Hostile takeovers and asset-stripping had given an unattractive, even pathological, slant to the idea of financial management (e.g. Roberts 1990). In the 1980s it became increasingly unclear that 'managing by the numbers' was at all desirable (e.g. Ezzamel et al. 1990). Goold and Campbell (1987) in their influential book outlined three basic styles of corporate control: financial control, strategic planning, and strategic control. Whilst providing unequivocal targets and a clear framework for up-or-out management development, financial control was seen to generate a focus on the short run over the strategic, inhibiting integrated behaviour between business units, and ran the risk of engendering a plethora of dysfunctional behaviours.

At least a part of the problem seems to have lain in the professional organization of management accounting practice. Management accounting practitioners emerged during the twentieth century as a significant, professionally organized group with an increasingly sophisticated (at least in their own terms) body of knowledge (Armstrong 1985). Their success in institutionalizing management accounting practices as they became more numerous and more influential provided a protective bubble for their work. In the absence of the detailed operational understanding that had informed its development, management accounting came to be seen as a collection of dangerous and misleading abstractions (Armstrong and Jones 1992). Its focus held on old issues through institutional inertia; it was unclear that management accounting was capable of developing responses to new strategic priorities such as quality, just in time, or zero defects (Johnson and Kaplan 1987).

---

[1] Interestingly, technology was an area in which Johnson and Kaplan (1987: 6) remained optimists: 'The computing revolution of the past two decades has so reduced information collection and processing costs that virtually all technical barriers to design and implemention of effective management accounting systems have been removed.'

In fact, recent decades have seen many developments in management accounting. Dent (1990) in helping to open up the study of strategy and management control noted that responses to Johnson and Kaplan's critique (1987) of the strategic usefulness of management accounting might be analysed in terms of two broad groupings. On the one hand there have been calls to refine the nature of management accounting practice (largely from accountants), and on the other there have been calls for its abandonment (from pretty much every one else)—a basic dichotomy that Hansen et al. (2003) have recently drawn upon in their study of budgeting innovations.

In terms of calls for development, one early response was the specific attempt to draw strategy into the realm of accounting practice (Bromwich 1990).[2] Rather than seeking to establish a new field of accounting practice, others worked within existing accounting paradigms, seeking to bring on board new strategic priorities (e.g. Cheatham and Cheatham 1996). Costing techniques were substantially reworked with the introduction of activity-based costing (ABC) (e.g. Cooper and Kaplan 1992). Still others sought to develop old techniques such as residual income (Bromwich and Walker 1998).

These various innovations have not met with unqualified endorsement. Budgetary control remains subject to widespread and sustained critique (see Hope and Fraser (2003) for a recent and high-profile example). Recent studies that sought to track the development of strategic management accounting practices found little use of the term, and limited application of the techniques, noting some uncertainty as to what exactly strategic management accounting might be (Tomkins and Carr 1996; Guilding et al. 2000; Roslender and Hart 2003). High-profile and active authors such as Goldratt and Cox (1992) argued strongly against the benefits of ABC, and many surveys on the subject report its limited take-up, poor performance, and subsequent abandonment as an organizational practice (Innes et al. 2000). Analysis of the success of economic value–based measures are also mixed (e.g. O'Hanlon and Peasnell 1998; Kleiman 1999). Whilst there might be an emerging consensus that such measures help provide a benchmark for quantifying strategic success, it is often seen to be difficult to link such measures to strategy directly. As such, their potential as systems of strategic control remains open to question.

---

[2] The term strategic management accounting had in fact been coined a decade earlier with the call to introduce more management accounting into marketing work (Simmonds 1981).

Whilst it too has its fair share of detractors, the most explicit and direct contemporary claims to recapture the strategic significance of management control practice are based around the development of the balanced scorecard (BSC) (e.g. Kaplan 2001*a*, *b*), a technique that started as a relatively straightforward call for greater levels of non-financial performance measurement (Kaplan and Norton 1992). Whilst the BSC seems ubiquitous it remains curiously flexible and undefined (see Hansen and Mouritsen, this volume), making it problematic as the conceptual basis for a re-analysis of the relationship between strategy and MCS.

Parallel to these concerns in accounting literature, recent developments in strategy literature are suggestive of new ways of considering the relationship between strategy and MCS. Recent interest in hyper-competitive environments has resulted in a reconceptualization of the strategy-making process from an episodic to a continuous endeavour (e.g. Brown and Eisenhardt 1997). The resource-based view on strategy has been an important development to relate organizational missions with organizational capabilities by introducing the notion of routines to the strategy debate (e.g. Johnson et al. 2003). The idea is that strategic capabilities are grounded in day-to-day organizational action. Despite Mintzberg's much earlier contribution (1987) on this topic the relationship between strategy-making by senior management and the day-to-day activity is only beginning to be systematically explored by strategists (Marginson 2002; Johnson et al. 2003; Whittington 2003; Feldman 2004). The emphasis on the daily routine of strategy-making is suggestive of a very different role for MCS than the previously predominant model of straightforward implementation of strategy (e.g. Simons 1991).

Explicit analysis of the role of MCS in the strategy literature has not stood still during this upheaval in the status of management accounting. Schreyögg and Steinmann (1987) and Lorange et al. (1986) are examples of early attempts to move beyond simple cybernetic models of control (Anthony 1965). More recently still there has been further elaboration. Muralidharan (1997), for example, carefully distinguishes between strategic control and management control, developing a clearer framework of roles. MCS remain strategically passive however. There is a growing tradition of studies in the accounting literature that speaks directly to emerging concerns in strategy literature (e.g. Roberts 1990; Simons 1990; Ahrens 1997; Mouritsen 1999; Briers and Chua 2001; Ahrens and Chapman 2002, 2004; Malmi and Ikaheimo 2003; Preston et al. 1992). The careful consideration of the relationship between ideas on strategy and the details of day-to-day management control activity underpins much of the analysis of more emphatically active and strategically constitutive roles for management control systems contained in the various contributions to this volume.

The chapter by Chenhall begins with a broad overview of the ways in which the issue of strategy has been theorized by strategists. After outlining the distinction between content and process approaches, the chapter goes on to bring out some of the ways in which the study of the relationship between MCS and strategy might benefit from research that synthesizes ideas from both perspectives. A number of these issues are addressed in subsequent chapters. For example, the role of consultants is discussed in Hansen and Mouritsen's chapter; organizational inertia and institutional pressures are seen to undermine attempts at data analysis in Ittner and Larcker's chapter. Chenhall also begins to outline the ways in which MCS may play a role in organizational learning and change, both areas in which they have not traditionally been expected to play a significant role.

Davila systematically develops a framework for understanding the role of MCS in managing innovation and change in organizations. Beginning with a review of the theoretical underpinnings of thinking on the subject, his chapter goes on to make the point that whilst innovation is frequently seen as something external to the organization, the careful use of MCS can play a vital role in developing and shaping innovation. The analysis moves beyond traditional theorizing in exploring the various roles that MCS might play in either a structural or a strategic context, depending on whether the intention is to refine or replace existing strategy.

Langfield-Smith sketches the contours of the empirical literature on the relationship between MCS and strategy, highlighting areas for future research. Through the detailed discussion of selected studies she demonstrates that the extant literature concerning the BSC, and capital budgeting in particular, highlights the difficulties of incorporating strategy into management control activity. Two subsequent chapters in this volume demonstrate through fieldwork the complex ways in which MCS can inform strategy.

Ittner and Larcker, drawing on the results of a range of studies and their own fieldwork, unpack the ways in which strategic data analysis plays a central role in supporting (or, done wrong, undermining) the communication of strategic assumptions, the identification and measurement of strategic value drivers, processes of resource allocation, and target setting. Their analysis has clear implications for situations in which MCS are intended as mechanisms for the implementation of strategy. Along with the other chapters, it demonstrates the ways in which strategic data analysis might play a central role in redefining strategic agendas (both negatively by challenging previously untested assumptions and positively by refining them).

Ahrens and Chapman draw on contemporary developments in social theory around notions of practice. In the light of these they draw out of their study of marketing analysis in a restaurant chain the ways in which MCS simultaneously report on external phenomena as they serve to render them amenable to manipulation according to internal agendas. For example, we see the ways in which 'the customer' is at once analysed in terms of their dining habits, and becomes established as an ideal through financial analysis.

Hansen and Mouritsen, likewise, are concerned with the ways in which MCS, and the BSC in particular, provides organizations with a framework through which they can pursue their pre-existing control and strategic agendas. Through a series of studies of scorecard implementations we see that far more is at stake than the adoption of a simple approach for strategy implementation.

Finally Miller and O'Leary study the ways in which MCS support intra- and interorganizational coordination in the technologically and environmentally uncertain context of Intel. Here again, the detailed study of processes of management control, analysed through the lens of complementarity theory, takes us beyond simple cybernetic models affirming the diversity and subtlety of management control as a means of controlling strategy.

The discussions of management control and strategy in this volume help bring together insights from these various fields, helping to consolidate our understanding of the relationship thus far, as well as helping to map more clearly the areas in which we remain unclear. A consistent theme running through the chapters is that traditional understandings of the relationship between MCS and strategy is at best limited in scope. Traditional models frequently argue against the benefits of MCS in environments and settings in which they nonetheless remain ubiquitous. The chapters that follow develop grounds for understanding why their continued presence may be more than a question of pathological organizational choice. Reviewing what we do know, the chapters that follow more importantly open up new questions at the same time as they suggest new ways of asking old ones. The promise is the development of a far richer understanding of the relationship between MCS and strategy.

References

Ahrens, T. (1997). 'Strategic Interventions of Management Accountants: Everyday Practice of British and German Brewers', *European Accounting Review*, 6: 557–88.

—— and Chapman, C. S. (2002). 'The Structuration of Legitimate Performance Measures and Management: Day-to-Day Contests of Accountability in a U.K. Restaurant Chain', *Management Accounting Research*, 13(2): 1–21.

—— —— (2004). 'Accounting for Flexibility and Efficiency: A Field Study of Management Control Systems in a Restaurant Chain', *Contemporary Accounting Research*, 21(2): 271–301.

Anthony, N. (1965). *Management Control Systems*, 3rd edn. Boston, MA: Harvard Business School Press.

Argyris, C. (1953). 'Human Problems with Budgets', *Harvard Business Review*, 31(1): 97–110.

Armstrong, P. (1985). 'Changing Management Control Strategies: The Role of Competition between Accountancy and other Organisational Professions', *Accounting, Organizations and Society*, 10(2): 129–48.

—— and Jones, C. (1992). 'The Decline of Operational Expertise in the Knowledge-Base of Management Accounting', *Management Accounting Research*, 3: 53–75.

Briers, M. and Chua, W. F. (2001). 'The Role of Actor Networks and Boundary Objects in Management Accounting Change: A Field Study of an Implementation of Activity-Based Costing', *Accounting, Organizations and Society*, 26(3): 237–69.

Bromwich, M. (1990). 'The Case for Strategic Management Accounting: The Role of Accounting Information for Strategy in Competitive Markets', *Accounting, Organizations and Society*, 13(1/2): 27–46.

—— and Walker, S. (1998). 'Residual Income Past and Future', *Management Accounting Research*, 9(4): 391–419.

Brown, S. and Eisenhardt, K. M. (1997). 'The Art of Continuous Change: Linking Complexity Theory and Time-Paced Evolution in Relentlessly Shifting Organizations', *Administrative Science Quarterly*, 42(1): 1–34.

Chapman, C. S. (1997). 'Reflections on a Contingent View of Accounting', *Accounting, Organizations and Society*, 22(2): 189–205.

—— (1998). 'Accountants in Organisational Networks', *Accounting, Organizations and Society*, 23(8): 737–66.

Cheatham, C. and Cheatham, L. (1996). 'Redesigning Cost Systems: Is Standard Costing Obsolete?', *Accounting Horizons*, 10(4): 23–31.

Cooper, R. and Kaplan, R. S. (1992). 'Activity-Based Systems: Measuring the Cost of Resource Usage', *Accounting Horizons* (Sept.): 1–13.

Dent, J. F. (1990). 'Strategy, Organization and Control: Some Possibilities for Accounting Research', *Accounting, Organizations and Society*, 3–26.

Diebold, J. (1965). 'What's Ahead in Information Technology', *Harvard Business Review*, 43(5): 76–82.

Ezzamel, M., Hoskin, K. W., and Macve, R. H. (1990). 'Managing It All by Numbers: A Review of Johnson and Kaplan's *Relevance Lost*', *Accounting and Business Research*, 20(78): 153–66.

Feldman, M. S. (2004). 'Resources in Emerging Structures and Processes of Change', *Organization Science*, 15(3): 295–309.

Goldratt, E. and Cox, J. (1992). *The Goal: A Process of Ongoing Improvement*, 2nd edn. Croton-on-Hudson, NY: North River Press.

Goold, M. and Campbell, A. (1987). *Strategies and Styles : The Role of the Centre in Managing Diversified Corporations*. Oxford: Blackwell.

Guilding, C., Cravens, K. S., and Tayles, M. (2000). 'An International Comparison of Strategic Management Accounting Practices', *Management Accounting Research*, 11(1): 113–35.

Hansen, S., Otley, D., and Van der Stede, W. (2003). 'Practice Developments in Budgeting: An Overview and Research Perspective', *Journal of Management Accounting Research*, 15: 49–70.

Hayes, R. H. and Abernathy, W. (1980). 'Managing Our Way to Economic Decline', *Harvard Business Review*, 58(4): 67–77.

Hope, J. and Fraser, R. (2003). 'Who Needs Budgets?', *Harvard Business Review*, 81(2): 108–16.

Innes, J., Mitchell, F., and Sinclair, D. (2000). 'Activity-Based Costing in the U.K.'s Largest Companies: A Comparison of 1994 and 1999 Survey Results', *Management Accounting Research*, 11(3): 349–62.

Johnson, G., Melin, L., and Whittington, R. (2003). 'Guest Editors' Introduction: Micro Strategy and Strategizing: Towards an Activity-Based View', *Journal of Management Studies*, 40(1): 3–22.

Johnson, H. and Kaplan, R. (1987). *Relevance Lost: The Rise and Fall of Management Accounting*. Boston, MA: Harvard Business School Press.

Kaplan, R. S. (2001*a*). 'Transforming the Balanced Scorecard from Performance Measurement to Strategic Management: Part I', *Accounting Horizons*, 15(1): 87–105.

—— (2001*b*). 'Transforming the Balanced Scorecard from Performance Measurement to Strategic Management: Part II', *Accounting Horizons*, 15(2): 147–60.

—— and Norton, D. P. (1992). 'The Balanced Scorecard—Measures that Drive Performance', *Harvard Business Review* (Jan.–Feb.): 71–9.

Kleiman, R. (1999). 'Some Evidence on EVA Companies', *Journal of Applied Corporate Finance*, 12: 88–91.

Lorange, P., Scott Morton, M. F., and Ghoshal, S. (1986). *Strategic Control Systems*, St. Paul, MN: West Publishing.

Malmi, T. and Ikaheimo, S. (2003). 'Value-Based Management Practices—Some Evidence from the Field', *Management Accounting Research*, 14(3): 235–54.

Marginson, D. (2002). 'Management Control Systems and Their Effects on Strategy Formation at Middle-Management Levels: Evidence from a UK Organization', *Strategic Management Journal*, 23: 1019–31.

Miller, P. (1998). 'The Margins of Accounting', in M. Callon (ed.), *The Laws of the Markets*. Oxford: Blackwell Publishers, 174–93.

Mintzberg, H. (1987). 'Crafting Strategy', *Harvard Business Review*, 65(4): 66–75.

Mouritsen, J. (1999). 'The Flexible Firm: Strategies for a Subcontractor's Management Control', *Accounting, Organizations and Society*, 24(1): 31–56.

Muralidharan, R. (1997). 'Strategic Control for Fast-Moving Markets: Updating the Strategy and Monitoring Performance', *Long Range Planning*, 30(1): 64–73.

Norman, B. (1965). 'Strategic Planning in Conglomerate Companies', *Harvard Business Review*, 43(3): 79–92.

O'Hanlon, J. and Peasnell, K. (1998). 'Wall Street's Contribution to Management Accounting: The Stern Stewart EVA(R) Financial Management System', *Management Accounting Research*, 9(4): 421–44.

Preston, A., Cooper, D., and Coombs, R. (1992). 'Fabricating Budgets: A Study of the Production of Management Budgeting in the National Health Service', *Accounting, Organizations and Society*, 17(6): 561–93.

Ridgway, V. (1956). 'Dysfunctional Consequences of Performance Measurement', *Administrative Science Quarterly*, 1(2): 240–7.

Roberts, J. (1990). 'Strategy and Accounting in a U.K. Conglomerate', *Accounting, Organizations and Society*, 15: 107–26.

Roslender, R. and Hart, S. J. (2003). 'In Search of Strategic Management Accounting: Theoretical and Field Study Perspectives', *Management Accounting Research*, 14(3): 255–79.

Schreyögg, G. and Steinmann, H. (1987). 'Strategic Control: A New Perspective', *Academy of Management Review*, 12(1): 91–103.

Simmonds, K. (1981). 'Strategic Management Accounting', *Management Accounting*, 59(4): 26–9.

Simons, R. (1990). 'The Role of Management Control Systems in Creating Competitive Advantage: New Perspectives', *Accounting, Organizations and Society*, 15(1/2): 127–43.

—— (1991). 'Strategic Orientation and Top Management Attention to Control Systems', *Strategic Management Journal*, 12: 49–62.

—— (1995). *Levers of Control*. Boston, MA: Harvard Business School Press.

Tomkins, C. and Carr, C. (1996). 'Reflections on the Papers in this Issue and a Commentary on the State of Strategic Management Accounting', *Management Accounting Research*, 7(2): 271–80.

Whittington, R. (2003). 'The Work of Strategizing and Organizing: For a Practice Perspective', *Strategic Organization*, 1(1): 117–25.

Content and Process Approaches to Studying Strategy and Management Control Systems

Robert H. Chenhall

This chapter is concerned with developing our understanding of the role of management control systems (MCS) in formulating and implementing strategy. Strategy has become a dominant influence in the study of organizations. Researchers in areas such as economics (Milgrom and Roberts 1992; Seth and Thomas 1994), human resource management (Miller 1991; Kochan and Osterman 1994), information technology (IT) (Grover et al. 1997), and organizational behaviour (Knights and Morgan 1991; Rowe et al. 1994; Rouleau and Seguin 1995) all seek to understand the ways in which their disciplines assist in understanding how managers use strategy to achieve desired outcomes. Management accounting has been informed by these literatures to such an extent that strategic management accounting is seen by many commentators as the key to understanding the effective design and implementation of MCS (Simmonds 1981; Bromwich 1990; Ward 1992).

Costing has developed a strategic focus whereby activity-based cost management (ABCM) has moved from refining the attribution of fixed costs to cost objects to systems that link costs and value drivers to alternate strategies, thereby enabling cost–benefit analysis and an understanding of process requirements to effect strategies (Shank and Govindarajan 1995; Kaplan and Cooper 1998). Performance measurement has evolved from enhancing the usefulness of performance measures by including both financial and non-financial measures to more complex systems based on a balanced suite of measures that provides strategic performance management, including causal maps that show the operational implications for different strategies (McNair et al. 1990; Kaplan and Norton 1992, 1996, 2001). More recently, attention has been focused on how MCS can be used interactively to assist in developing responsiveness throughout the organization to the strategic uncertainties facing the organization (Simons 1995, 2000). These advances are reflected in the emphasis given in most contemporary management accounting textbooks to a strategic orientation to management control.

This chapter draws on the distinction between content and process approaches to help develop understanding of existing strategy-based MCS research and provide a unifying perspective for thinking about a future research agenda. The potential contribution is to clarify the different purposes of content and process approaches, thereby opening debate to reflect on past findings in management control research. Also, a variety of issues concerning both content and process are presented as key areas for future research. First, the difference between content and process approaches is discussed. Second, the ways in which management control has been related to content approaches is examined and the potential for future research in this area explored. Third, process approaches are examined, again with an eye to the extant literature and future directions. Finally, the issue of strategic change is discussed to show how both content and process approaches can help consideration of this research agenda.

Content and process approaches: an overview

A precise definition of strategy is illusive. At one extreme, strategy is defined as the careful articulation of objectives and plans for achieving these objectives (Steiner 1969; Andrews 1980; Ansoff 1987). This suggests a highly rational, systematic approach involving formalized procedures that integrate decision-making throughout the organization to achieve desired outcomes. The strategy function involves articulating 'intended strategies' and formulating deliberate policies to achieve these strategies (Mintzberg 1994: 24). This process results in the formulation of a 'strategic position' (Porter 1980, 1985). On the other hand, strategy can be identified as a pattern of behaviour that evolves over time, based on a perspective or understanding of a way to do things (Jelinek 1979). This definition recognizes that strategy is a process where ideas may emerge in 'unintended' ways involving incremental processes (Quinn 1980; Mintzberg 1994: 25).

The distinction between formal rational approaches and more informal incremental approaches is a useful first step to describe the difference between content and process approaches (Fahey and Christensen 1986; Leong et al. 1990). Strategic content approaches tend to be concerned with the product of the strategy process. They aim to identify what is, or what should be, the strategy to lead to optimal organizational performance. This involves describing the effective competitive positioning of the organization and access to resources within the organization's environment. There is an implicit assumption that individuals behave rationally and particular strategies can be identified as appropriate to specific situations. Strategy is seen to follow a logical, linear process of strategy formulation, analysis, and implementation. Strategy content research tends to provide snapshots of ideal strategies, or optimal combinations of strategies for organizations facing different settings. Strategic change is typically categorized as being either radical or incremental and the aim is to identify ideal guidelines to assist in managing these different types of change (Kanter et al. 1992; Phillips 1992; Kotter 1996).

Process approaches are also concerned with the content of strategies. However, the interest is in how processes influence the content of strategies, and how does the content influence process (Van de Ven 1995). What are the dynamic relationships between strategic position, resources and outcomes? How is, and how should, strategy be formulated? Who is involved in the strategy process and how do individual differences have effects? What causes strategy to be changed and what is involved in this process? Given identification of a desired strategy, what processes occur to affect the strategy? Process approaches focus on the incremental strategic processes that involve a messy interlinking between strategy formulation and implementation, with unintended ideas emerging during implementation. Similarly, process approaches are alert to the possibility that inherent resistance derived from organizational and behavioural impediments may obstruct strategic change.

Finally, both content and process approaches may be applied to understanding strategy at many levels: corporate, business unit, functional, and network. While strategies have effects across levels within the organization, the nature of the issues differs. At the corporate level, strategy involves questions of what is the nature of the business, such as the major industries within which the organization operates. At the business-unit level, strategy involves more precise issues of products and technologies, while at the functional level strategy is concerned with functions such as manufacturing and marketing. Network strategies recognize that many strategies may involve cooperative rather than competitive relationships with other firms and involve strategic alliances and joint ventures.

Content approaches

Content approaches to strategy aim to identify practices that are associated with enhanced performance. Approaches to formulating and implementing strategy may be considered as appropriate at a point in time, or the focus may be on identifying the ideal way to manage change over time. In both cases, content approaches seek to identify fundamental principles for developing strategy or guiding strategic change. It is these principles that form the basis for much of the strategic planning literature. In management control, authors draw on the structured 'planning perspective' and separate the work of doing strategy into distinct steps such as setting objectives; formulating corporate, business, and functional strategic priorities; budgeting; monitoring; control; and determining incentives. These processes are often proposed together with contingency plans or scenario planning to allow for changing circumstances. Such approaches are justified as they provide direction, avoid drift, and enhance commitment; they assist optimal allocation of resources; they aid logical task differentiation, enhance coordination between parts of the organization, and provide an orientation to long-term thinking. Management accountants, who favour a rational calculative approach to management, often use this approach.

Content strategists favouring a formal approach to strategy recognize that managers must formulate strategic priorities that will provide competitive advantage. This means developing strategies that enable the organization to adapt to its contextual setting. Such adaptation involves an outside–in perspective that examines the external environment to identify potential threats and opportunities, or an inside–out perspective that concerns the development of internal resources that provides strengths and identifying weaknesses (de Wit and Meyer 1999). Both these approaches have important implications for management control.

Outside–in perspective

Outside–in perspectives provide insights into the nature of the external environment, its threats and opportunities. In its simplest form, a starting point for formal strategic analysis is to consider desired future outcomes and assess how effective current strategies will be in achieving these outcomes. Any shortfall is examined by way of 'gap analysis' that encourages managers to consider both outside–in and inside–out approaches to help understand how to close the gap (Ansoff 1987). A variety of outside–in approaches may be identified. These include an analysis of the nature of markets and their structures using, for example,

Porter's five forces model and product life cycles; and more recently the implications of globalization, networks, and e-commerce.

Porter (1980, 1985) argues that two factors determine the choice of competitive strategy: the potential of an industry for long-term profitability and determinants of relative profitability within the industry. Firms respond to industrial conditions and also shape the conditions to their favour. In any industry, competition is governed by five forces of competition: entry of new competitors, threats of substitutes, bargaining power of buyers and suppliers, and competition between existing firms. The five forces determine industry profitability as they affect prices, costs, and required returns that reflect underlying industry structure as expressed in economic and technical characteristics. From a strategy formulation view these five forces present an outside–in picture of the business environment and direct the manager's attention to developing strategy to compete effectively within the industry. Porter suggests that to cope with the five forces, firms must develop sustainable competitive strategy by effective strategic positioning within the industry. This is achieved by 'product differentiation' or 'cost leadership' either across a broad range of industry segments or 'focused' within a narrow segment.

Porter (1980, 1985) has been important in directing management control research into strategy as it has provided a solid theoretical basis for linking different types of MCS to the generic strategies of product differentiation and cost leadership. From a content perspective, researchers have sought to show what types of MCS best suit these generic strategies. For example, Govindarajan (1988) showed that product differentiation (cost leadership) was associated with a de-emphasis (emphasis) on budgetary goals for performance evaluation. Govindarajan and Fisher (1990) showed that product differentiation with a high (low) sharing of resources and a reliance on behaviour (output) controls was associated with enhanced effectiveness. Van der Stede (2000) identified that product differentiation was associated with less rigid controls that were, in turn, associated with increased budgetary slack.

Other generic typologies of strategy responses have been developed by organizational theorists to categorize managers' reactions to their external environment. As with product differentiation and cost leadership, the adoption of these strategic responses will position the organization within its environment and as such provides insight into the operational setting. Miles and Snow (1978) focused on the rate of change in products and markets, dividing firms into defenders, prospectors, analysers, and reactors. Shortell and Zajac (1990) provided an examination of Miles and Snow's typology, validating it as an important way of conceiving strategy. Miller and Friesen (1982) identified extent of innovation as a style of strategic response. Managers were either conservative or entrepreneurial. Strategic mission was described in terms of developing market share and/or profitability by Gupta and Govindarajan (1984) as being either build (market share), hold (both market share and profitability), or harvest (profitability).

MCS research has used these dimensions to show the effectiveness of different aspects of MCS. Using Miles and Snow's typology, Abernethy and Brownell (1999) showed that hospitals undergoing strategic change, seen as a more prospector-type strategy, used budgets interactively, focusing on dialogue, communication, and learning. Using Miller and Friesen's (1982) conservative-entrepreneurial taxonomy, Chenhall and Morris (1995) showed that conservative managers of successful organizations used tight control systems, while successful entrepreneurial managers used a combination of tight controls and organic decision processes. Drawing on their concept of strategic mission, Govindarajan and Gupta (1985) found build, compared with harvest strategies and a reliance on long-term and subjective evaluation for managers' bonuses, was associated with enhanced effectiveness, while effectiveness and strategy were not associated with short-term criteria for evaluation. Guilding (1999) found that prospector and build strategies differed from harvest companies in having a stronger orientation to competitor-focused accounting for planning. Competitor-focused accounting involved competitor cost assessment, competitor position monitoring, and appraisal based on published financial statement, strategic costing, and strategic pricing.

Recently, strategy researchers have sought to examine more specific elements of strategic responses. These ideas are focused on the business-unit level and consider issues such as priorities of quality, reliability, flexibility, service, and after-sales service (Miller et al. 1992; Kotha and Vadlamani 1995, Kotha et al. 1995; Campbell-Hunt 2000). Often, these priorities can be seen as elaborations of more generic strategies. Recent management accounting research has focused on these elements of strategy. For example, Bouwens and Abernethy (2000) found that customization (a form of product differentiation) was associated with the level of importance to operational decision-making of more integrated, aggregated, and timely information. Chenhall and Langfield-Smith (1998) drew on the strategic priorities given by Miller et al. (1992) and found that firms clustered around combinations that described product differentiation and low cost price, although elements of both differentiation and low cost were found in all strategic profiles. Different types of management practices and MCS practices were associated with these strategic profiles.

In the main, MCS research has applied fairly simple definitions of the generic constructs of strategy with correspondingly simple measures of these constructs. For example, Govindarajan (1988) assessed the importance of product differentiation and cost leadership by presenting survey respondents with short descriptions of product differentiation and cost leadership strategies and asked them to indicate the percentage of their organizations sales that could be described by each category. Other approaches have asked managers to select one category that best describes their organization's strategy, based on Miles and Snow's (1978) typology of prospectors–analysers–defenders (Abernethy and Brownell 1999). There has been considerable debate on the meaning and validity of these constructs. Several studies have refined the properties of product differentiation and cost leadership (Miller and Dess 1993; Kotha and Vadlamani 1995, Kotha et al. 1995), while other researchers have identified strategic priorities as a key to understanding strategy (Miller et al. 1992). Researchers in MCS should be aware of these assessments of generic strategic typologies and of the alternatives that have elaborated upon the generic forms. As indicated above, recent MCS research has focused on refinements of strategy (Chenhall and Langfield-Smith 1998; Bouwens and Abernethy 2000).

At a functional level, researchers have identified a broad range of strategic priorities associated with ensuring that production processes can deliver on strategies of quality, timeliness, reliability, and service. Total quality management (TQM), continuous improvement, and process reengineering have been proposed as important ways of developing strategically focused operations. MCS have been proposed to provide information to assist in these practices. Particularly, ABCM, target costing, and value chain analysis attempt to identify cost and value drivers to encourage effective strategy development. Also, there is considerable MCS research that has examined the relationships between MCS and strategy-driven manufacturing practices. For example, research has related MCS to TQM (Ittner and Larcker 1995, 1997; Chenhall 1997; Sim and Killough 1998; Lillis 2002), just in time (JIT) (Banker et al. 1993; Young and Selto 1993; Kalagnanam and Lindsay 1999; Mia 2000; Fullerton and McWatters 2002), customer-focused manufacturing strategies (Perera et al. 1997), product-focused firms (Davila 2000), and flexible manufacturing (Abernethy and Lillis 1995). Chenhall and Langfield-Smith (1998) linked performance with combinations of various traditional and contemporary controls and a range of strategies and manufacturing practices.

In recent years, outside–in approaches to research into strategy and management control have recognized the emergence of several important aspects of the external environment that have relevance to the design of MCS. These include product life cycles, globalization, networks, and digitization. Each of these will be considered in turn.

Industry analysis has provided a useful basis for examining the development of appropriate strategies that will enable the organization to adapt to business environments and, possibly, change these circumstances to be more advantageous to the organization. However, industry structure is not static and evolves through time, often shifting industries to a point where obsolescence of endowments takes place (Agarwal and Gort 2002). An awareness of industry evolution can assist in developing an outside–in appreciation of strategy formulation to respond to such hazards. Product life cycle analyses provide a way of understanding how an industry and firms within that industry potentially pass through stages involving the introduction of products, rapid growth in demand, maturity, and then decline (Wasson 1978). While industries and firms do not inevitably pass through all stages of product life cycles, an examination of these cycles does alert strategy-makers to the potential growth opportunities or to the impact of sales decline when markets reach maturity (Anderson and Zeihaml 1984). Responses may require decision-makers to develop innovations to capture opportunities or to reposition their operations to avoid decline. Product life cycles have been identified as particularly important in industries, such as computers, telecommunication, and cameras, that require new innovations or modification to existing products every year or so to maintain their competitive edge. Target costing has been proposed as a technique to ensure that products are developed and processes engineered to ensure that novel products can be realized in timely ways to respond to short product cycles (Ansari et al. 1997). However, it is not clear if target costing has gained widespread appeal in Western economies. The life cycle of firms, also, has become important for studying how small- to medium-sized firms evolve into larger entities. Some work in management control has focused on the implication of life cycles for MCS. A study by Moores and Yuen (2001) showed that firms progressing between different life cycles required different types of MCS to sustain their respective strategies. Developing from birth to growth and maturity to revival created a need for more formal MCS designs, with less formal systems evident in transition from growth to maturity and revival to decline.

In recent years outside–in approaches have had to accommodate the fact that many businesses operate in global environments. For many firms the need to become global has moved from a discretionary to an imperative option (Gupta and Govindarajan 2001). When considering the impact of international operations there are two concerns: first, to what extent does globalization present issues related to a diversity of cultures that influence the potential effectiveness of strategies; and second, to what extent does global convergence occur such that strategies can be worldwide. The diversity perspective asserts that cultural differences are so embedded in different countries that national climates present not only unique opportunities for product development but also challenges to monitoring and controlling strategy in ways contingent on local national culture. There is a strong stream of research in MCS that has sought to identify if MCS developed in one country (typically Western countries) can be applied effectively in firms, or divisions of multinationals, in another country that has distinctively different sets of core cultural norms (typically Asian countries). While the results are somewhat indecisive, the topic is important as many firms continue to develop international operations (Harrison and McKinnon 1999).

The second perspective focuses on the view that improvements in infrastructure and communications are resulting in the development of global markets where growing similarities between countries present opportunities to gain global-scale advantages and economies of scope. In this approach global competition requires firms to coordinate strategy across world markets. This presents challenges for coordination and control, with the possibility of strategy being formulated in centralized locations (Ohmae 1990). There are clear implications for the role of MCS in settings characterized by global convergence with the prospect of more formal, centralized planning and controls. The study of the influence of globalization and national culture has generated much debate as to the meaning of culture, its influence on individuals' behaviour, and how it is to be studied (Bhimani 1999). Interestingly, Bhimani (1999: 426) suggests that dissimilarities may be identified in terms of structural configurations within a culture (echoing a content appreciation); however, their modes of realization may differ depending on particular sociocultural characteristics (a process view).

A significant change has occurred in recent years in the way organizations conduct their transactions with suppliers and customers. Traditionally, organizations operated in a highly independent way to source materials, components, and services from a marketplace of suppliers.

Similarly, products were sold to a variety of customers on the basis of price, quality, and other product features. These transactions were at arm's length, conducted under conditions of competition. Recently, organizations have started to develop more cooperative arrangements with a particular supplier and to develop long-term partnerships with customers (Contractor and Lorange 1988; Kanter 1994). These networks involve exploring ways that the collaborating organizations can develop their transactions to gain mutual strategic advantage. Network arrangements may involve occasional joint venture projects and strategic alliances, or more permanent dealings involving, for example, outsourcing arrangements, preferred suppliers, and customer relationships. Such arrangements can provide an internal capability to gain competitive strategic advantage. The choice to develop strategies based on competition or networks has quite different implications for strategy and MCS systems. For competitive situations, strategy formulation typically follows traditional content approaches. However, these traditional content approaches will likely be inappropriate and need refinement in network situations.

The conventional arm's length approach to transactions is based on ideas of independent self-interest, with organizations attempting to get the best deal and gain the dominant position in the trading relationship. However, networking organizations might develop common strategies that accrue benefits to all parties (Best 1990). At the extreme, this collaboration between organizations can become so pronounced that formal controls are substituted with relational or implicit contracts based on trust and mutual advantage (Baxter and Chua 2003). The role of trust has become an important consideration in management controls when considering interorganizational relationships (Tomkins 2001; Chenhall and Langfield-Smith 2003).

While networking has become a popular area for enquiry there are some who are critical of the effectiveness of close relationships between organizations, such as outsourcing. Pinochot and Pinochot (1993: 178–83) contrast the advantages of outsourcing, stressing trade-offs between economies of scale and economies of intimacy, integration and scope, lower fixed costs and sharing of profits, importing outside knowledge and losing inside trade secrets, flexibility in downsizing and loss of internal competencies, focus on core competencies and capacity to grow new competencies. Also, Hamel et al. (1989) argue that self-interest and competition are still important to collaborating partners, with each trying to maximize their gain and minimize that of their partner. The role of MCS in networking situations is just starting to be understood and researched in accounting. Ittner et al. (1999) reported that performance gains from supplier partnership practices were associated with extensive use of non-price selection criteria, frequent meetings and interactions with suppliers, and supplier certification. These controls were not effective for arm's length supplier relations.

The recent growth of the digital economy has had important implication for strategy and management control (Bhimani 2003). Digitization affects the way interdependencies between organizations and their suppliers and customers are managed. Digitization provides ease of direct access to information that can sustain network linkages by providing for integration across organizational boundaries (Amigoni et al. 2003). There are important challenges to understanding how management control can assist decision-making for managers involved in network linkages and to assess the suitability of alliances and to evaluate their effectiveness.

Digitization can have a significant impact on operations within the firm. Transactions can be conducted without the need for intermediaries such as marketers, purchasers, and distributors. Initial searches can identify potential suppliers and customers and provide the basis for first contact and subsequent transactions. This can increase levels of competition. It can also accelerate the development of virtual organizations as e-systems provide connections between value-adding participants of the virtual organization (Chen 2001; Kauffman and Walden 2001; Saloner and Spence 2001). The implication for adapting MCS to accommodate e-commerce is a rich area for future research (Baxter and Chua 2003).

Inside–out perspective

The inside–out perspective sees competitive advantage being derived from the organization's internal strengths. A resource-based or competencies view of strategy asserts that competitive advantage comes from resources that allow the production of unique goods. To achieve this, the organization's physical, human, and organizational resources have to be rare, inimitable, and without substitutes (Barney 1991). This provides the organization with distinctive competencies (Selznick 1957), a set of core competencies (Prahalad and Hamel 1990) or capabilities to develop strategic advantage (Salk et al. 1992). These unique features can provide a competitive edge over rivals. However, this can lock the organization into its competencies and limit or slow its ability to adapt to different market situations. Teece et al. (1997) use the term 'dynamic capabilities' to describe not only how organizations combine the development of firm-specific capabilities but also how they renew competencies to respond to the shifts in business environments.

Competencies may be provided by tangible assets that have physical substance such as machines and materials or they may be intangible, involving intellectual capital and provide knowledge-based strategic advantage. Intangible assets typically involve employee know-how and predispositions to the organization, reputation, intellectual property, and favourable relationships with external entities of importance to the organization. While assets can be separated into tangible and intangible, optimal advantage is achieved when organizations coordinate tangible capabilities with employees' skills, knowledge, and attitudes (Prahalad and Hamel 1990). This involves the continual upgrading of unique bundles of competencies that can be used to develop innovative products and services to both satisfy and create markets. Sometimes intangible assets can be made more tangible by codifying knowledge in routines or programmes or more formally in contracts and patents.

While the reporting and management of tangible assets is well developed in content approaches to strategy, intangible assets present many novel challenges. Frameworks have delineated intangible assets as human capital, customer relational capital, and organizational structural capital (Edvinsson and Malone 1997; Stewart 1997). All three categories involve developing explicit knowledge that can be observed and readily transferred and, importantly, tacit knowledge that is difficult to define and transfer, as it is subjective, being acquired through practice (Grant 1996). Developing advantage from tacit knowledge requires the integration of this knowledge by using network lines of communication and team-based structures rather than conventional hierarchical communication and coordination. In these situations, MCS should be flexible, informal, organic, and should be used in interactive ways to facilitate communication and the transformation of knowledge into innovative strategies (Merchant 1985; Simons 2000; Chenhall 2003). Notwithstanding the use of flexible MCS to assist communication and integration of tacit knowledge, the measurement of potential advantage from tacit knowledge is challenging, being difficult to evaluate, report, and audit (IFAC Report 1998).

In recent years considerable attention has been given to developing intellectual capital management as a source of advantage to formulating and implementing strategy. (For a broad-ranging discussion of many issues related to intellectual capital accounting, see the special edition of the *European Accounting Review* (2003, 12:4). Management control research has attempted to measure this potential source of advantage by way of balanced scorecard (BSC) type approaches or the intangible asset monitor that links customer, structural, and human capital (Sveiby 1997). This follows a content approach to strategy and while such efforts involve the essence of contemporary ideas on management control reporting, it should be noted that considerable challenges remain in understanding the processes involved in understanding and managing the complexity involved in intellectual capital (Fincham and Roslender 2003).

An important area of enquiry is how strategy is implicated in organizational change. Concern with strategic change is inevitable as the formulation of strategy involves considering what needs to be changed to position the organization within its environment, or what is required in terms of resources to adapt to, or influence, its setting. Most organizations face competitive markets, changing technologies, and shifting social preferences that require them to make repeated changes to maintain competitive advantage. However, to understand strategic change it is necessary to clarify what is to be changed and what is 'strategic' about change. This, again, suggests that the meaning of strategy is somewhat elusive.

Content approaches assist in identifying what aspects of the organization can be changed. For example, Kanter et al. (1992) provide extensive suggestions as to what has to be considered to ensure strategic change. This includes, for example, guidelines on environmental analysis to indicate when to change, changing structures and cultures, reengineering technology, and the roles and tasks of change-makers. Waterman et al. (1980) identified seven areas within which changes can occur: structure, strategy, systems, styles, staff, skills, and superordinate goals. Considerable attention has been given to changing production processes by identifying the essential practices within 'continuous improvement', 'process reengineering', and 'kaizen'. Concerns about characteristics of change at the employee level have been addressed in human resource management (Gamache and Kuhn 1989; Kochan and Osterman 1994). The growth in IT has provided opportunities for identifying what has to be changed within IT systems so that they can assist by assessing the desirability of alternative changes in strategies (Mockler 1991, 1992). Data warehousing and mining have become important topics to provide organization-wide approaches to collecting and using data to assist in generating innovative strategies. Other authors have sought to identify characteristics of successful change including the characteristics of the learning organization (West

1994; Carnall 1995), styles of management (Kanter 1982; Kotter 1996), and external and internal sources of change (Huber et al. 1993).

Content approaches have been used to examine the characteristics of successful MCS change. The dominant stream of research has examined the introduction of ABCM. A variety of studies have identified behavioural and organizational characteristics that are associated with effective implementation of ABCM (Shields and Young 1989; Argyris and Kaplan 1994; Anderson 1995; Shields 1995; Foster and Swenson 1997; McGowan and Klammer 1997; Krumwiede 1998; Anderson and Young 1999; Kennedy and Affleck-Graves 2001; Anderson et al. 2002; Chenhall 2004). These characteristics include top management support, linkages to competitive strategy, adequacy of resources, non-accounting ownership, linkages to performance evaluation and compensation, implementing training, clarity of objectives, and number of purposes for ABCM (Shields 1995; Foster and Swenson 1997; McGowan and Klammer 1997).

Another area of interest to content researchers has been the extent to which changes within the MCS depend on the contextual setting. Libby and Waterhouse (1996) found that the number of management accounting system changes relates to the level of competition, decentralization, size, and capacity to learn. Baines and Langfield-Smith (2003) found that competitive environments resulted in an increased focus on differentiation strategies, which, in turn, changed organizational design, advanced manufacturing technology, and advanced management accounting practices (e.g. ABCM, target costing, benchmarking, customer profitability analysis), all of which lead to changes in the use of non-financial information.

Process approaches

While content approaches to strategy do not ignore the processes that have to take place to formulate and implement strategies they see individuals involved in strategy as following a logical process involving patterns of decisions. Individuals are assumed to consciously go through a process of thinking about strategies, to develop and then formulate these into explicit plans. Realized strategy is derived from intended strategies (Mintzberg 1994). Outside–in analysis identifies opportunities and threats and an examination of inside–out factors reveals strengths and weaknesses. A variety of planning and forecasting tools helps formalize and encourage a rational examination of options and their resource requirements. Strategies are implemented by developing action plans, assigning responsibilities, and undertaking post-completion reviews. Information and control systems provide information on the external situation, help in budgeting what has to be done to effect strategies, and assist in assessing how well strategies are going to plan.

Process approaches acknowledge that the rational, ordered processes assumed in content approaches can be useful but these tend to be appropriate for well-understood routine activities that can be programmed. However, more often the processes involved in strategy formulation involve novelty, with ill-structured ideas emerging from the ongoing operations of the organization (Mintzberg 1987; Quinn 1980). This incrementalist view sees new ideas emerging over time as individuals react to unfolding circumstances by discovering ideas to provide advantage. Ideas that do emerge are often partly conceived and need considerable reflection to develop and become viable. Many of these emergent ideas are abandoned while some form the basis to question the existing direction of the organization and provide the foundation for high levels of innovation and significant advances.

A process approach focuses on how individuals go about decision-making involving strategic issues. Specifically, it recognizes that individuals have cognitive limitations such as limited rationality, they prefer to satisfice rather than optimize, and they have limited information processing capabilities and consequently may not consider all alternatives and may accept a second-best alternative (March and Simon 1958), or take an opportunistic decision to muddle through unplanned situations (Braybrooke and Lindblom 1970). Individuals may be driven to try to find problems to which they can apply their solutions (Cohen et al. 1972).

Formal controls are often de-emphasized in process approaches to strategy. Some commentators stress that they can be an impediment to the process of innovation (Quinn 1980; Mintzberg 1994). Quinn (1980) argues that it is virtually impossible to design formal processes that orchestrate all internal decisions, external environmental events, behavioural and power relationships, technical and informational needs, and actions of rivals so that they come together at any precise time. However, Mintzberg (1987, 1994) identifies how formal controls can assist strategy-making within process approaches. Formal strategic plans can be implicated in the process of crystallizing and affirming consensus and commitment as they occur. However, this may influence the process by forcing premature closure on idea generation. As in content approaches, planning can be part of the process of elaborating formulated strategy by way of action plans and budgets linked to strategy. However, this is likely to be a useful process only when external circumstances are stable, technologies are certain, and the organization operates within a highly mechanistic structure.

In more dynamic situations, such elaboration of plans will lose relevance as the operating situation changes, making the plans irrelevant. This does not equate to the irrelevance of MCS in more dynamic situations however, only to the irrelevance of a mechanistic approach to understanding their role. At a broader level, MCS can be used to examine how realized strategies compare with intended strategies, with a view to understanding how strategy evolves within the organization. Formal performance and reward systems provide information for both individual's performance to be assessed in terms of meeting planned outcomes and as the basis for a more flexible reassessment of those plans. During this process, plans can be used by some individuals to control others within the organization. This process of control may extend outside the organization when supplier or customer relationships are incorporated within planning schedules.

Formal plans can be used to assist communication processes. This may involve communicating intentions down and across the organization and may provide a basis for communicating ideas up the organization. An emerging stream of MCS research supports the role of MCS in communication (e.g. Simons 1990; Chenhall and Morris 1995; Chapman 1998). Malina and Selto (2001) found that an important role of balanced scorecards (BSCs) was to communicate strategy throughout the organization. MCS can provide a mechanism where emerging ideas being considered throughout the organization can be identified. Emerging ideas can form a critical part in maintaining the innovativeness of an organization's strategy.

Simon's (1995) interactive controls position MCS as an important part of the process of encouraging and identifying new ideas that can present ways to address the strategic uncertainties facing the organization. MCS encourage a process of dialogue and debate between senior managers and others throughout the organization. Some MCS research has shown that the interactive use of MCS can assist innovation (Bisbe and Otley 2004) and strategic change (Abernethy and Brownell 1999). A recent study that develops a framework for understanding the potential of MCS to act in these more flexible roles is Ahrens and Chapman (2004).

It was noted above, in discussing content approaches to strategy and MCS, that strategy and organizational change are important issues in management control research and that content approaches assist in articulating planned ways of dealing with change. Process approaches to change have been concerned with describing different ways that change progresses and how individuals are implicated in assisting or resisting change. Van de Ven and Poole (1995) present a taxonomy that distinguishes between more formal content-styled approaches and more process-focused approaches. Content approaches are captured by life cycle and teleological approaches. Both assume a regulated approach of change involving stages that are latent within the organization (life cycles) and purposeful constructions of desired end states and methods of selecting alternatives to achieve these states. These can be contrasted with process approaches that are designated dialectic or evolutionary. Dialectic change concerns the struggle between conflicting interests, with stability occurring as a result of the balance of power between these forces. Evolutionary change is the result of a recurrent, cumulative, and probabilistic progression of variation (random chance), selection (survival), and retention (inertia and persistence). The evolutionary, incremental nature of change has been contrasted with radical or revolutionary change by several authors. For example, Jick (1993) and Huber and Glick (1993) distinguish change as developmental (fine-tuning), transitional (evolutionary), and transformational (revolutionary). Tushman and Naylor (1986) see change as incremental, synthetic, and discontinuous. Clearly, the key theme here is whether change is incremental and continuous, or radical and discontinuous.

There is extensive debate as to whether incremental (continuous) or radical (discontinuous) processes are best to explain successful change. In practice, organizations will face different circumstances when one or the other approach will be appropriate. Incremental change involves a gradual process of continuously adapting, improving, and changing. Managers are sensitive to continually acquiring new information, of sharing this across the organization, and of storing valuable explicit knowledge in organizational memory. The 'learning organization' is receptive to the need to unlearn and change the accepted way of doing things. This type of change involves a continual quest for innovation and is best served by structures and decision processes that are flexible and provide opportunities for creativity and acceptance of the uncertainty and complexity generated by the quest for new ideas.

Evidence from content-styled MCS research indicates that a culture of continuous innovation can be encouraged by combinations of formal budgets and organic decision processes (Chenhall and Morris 1995; Chapman 1998) and the interactive use of MCS (Simons 1995; Abernethy and Brownell 1999; Bisbe and Otley 2004). Approaches following more process approaches have demonstrated that MCS can assist or hinder in the process of change. For example, Dent (1991) found that MCS helped move a railway company's culture from engineering to managerialist. Cost control was identified as a mechanism to encourage a move to a more competitive focus (Knight and Willmott 1993). Simon's (1995) research shows how interactive controls can be used to rejuvenate organizations and sustain change. Miller and O'Leary (1997) showed how the processes involved in using capital budgeting that treated assets as diverse but mutually reinforcing 'investment bundles', assisted in the transition from mass production to modern flexible manufacturing at Caterpillar Inc. In a study of strategy based on flexibility with customers, subcontractors, and innovation, Mouritsen (1999) contrasted the way different managers within a firm perceived control as requiring either a formal content, planning style to manage a 'virtual organization', or a more process-oriented human resource management approach that involves a 'political organization'. A formal content style approach (interactions managed by MCS for planning and monitored) aimed at reducing the uncertainties associated with flexibility, while a more hands-on and labour-focused approach (interactions managed by improvisation based on insight) sought to draw attention to how people and politics managed the processes to achieve flexibility. Both approaches were important as they described alternate but coexisting 'means of management'. There are considerable challenges for future research in understanding how attempts to apply content prescriptions based on rationality combine with processes that result as a consequence of political and behavioural influences. For example, to what extent are processes influenced by formal content, or is formal content established as a consequence of processes?

There are arguments and evidence that formal systems can be an impediment to change. Quinn (1985) argues that any formal resource allocation system is an impediment to change. Process approaches in MCS research have shown how resistance to change can occur as a result of MCS focusing attention on existing activities (Archer and Otley 1991) and structures (Scapens and Roberts 1993; Malmi 1997; Vaivio 1999; Granlund 2001). Roberts (1990) found that formal MCS resulted in an emphasis on the individual, conformity, and distorted communications. Chenhall and Langfield-Smith (2003) found that a gainsharing system and associated formal performance measures were incompatible with efforts to sustain continuous change by implementing self-managed teams.

Combining content and process approaches

In this chapter a distinction between content and process approaches has been made to discuss strategy and management control research. While these distinctions can be helpful in clarifying different approaches, there are many areas of interest that require researchers to contemplate the way both content and process combine to effect outcomes. The chapter concludes by exploring, briefly, several areas of research that can readily be informed by considering both content and process. These are developing learning organizations, organizational inertia, and fads and fashions.

Both content and process approaches have assisted researchers in understanding the continuous change that is an integral part of learning organizations (Stenge 1990; Antal et al. 1994), knowledge organizations (Nonaka 1991; Birkett 1995; Grant 1996), and intelligent organizations (Quinn 1992; Pinochot and Pinochot 1993). The thrust of these approaches is that developing organizational knowledge and intelligence involves more than the application of specific techniques such as reengineering, downsizing, TQM, flat structures, empowerment, benchmarking, and profit sharing (Abrahamson 1996). Rather it is how these techniques are used intelligently by managers and others in ways that involve continuous learning, innovation, and sensitivity to the organization's situation (Kanter et al. 1992: 3–19; Rimmer et al. 1996; Donaldson and Hilmer 1998). Understanding both the evolving design of the content of MCS and the processes involved in their use involves a holistic approach that presents many challenges for future research.

In some instances organizations cannot move in an ordered way to adapt to their situations. Unexpected forces for change may occur; there may be dramatic dislocation in the environment, or there may be significant resistance from within the organization. However, notwithstanding these shocks, some argue that organizations have a tendency towards stability, with internal institutional forces reinforcing the status quo (Dermer 1990: 71). Thus organizational belief systems, formal structures and systems, operating procedures, ways of doing things, and the distribution of power will lead to stability. This may be beneficial to efficient operations supporting existing strategies but can lead to inertia and lack of ability to respond to unpredictable shocks. When change is needed it will have to be radical and comprehensive and involve more revolutionary processes. However, once this pressure is removed, the organization reverts to a period of stability. There are challenges to understanding the role of MCS as organizations adapt by way of these processes. There has been some interest in examining the growth in dynamic networks as a structural response to revolutionary strategies that have moved firms away from diversified conglomerates to less diversified, focused operations with close linkages between organizations (Davis et al. 1994). It will be important to study the role of MCS as organizations move from these revolutionary changes to periods of more stability within the network organizational form.

Finally, an important aspect of MCS research is the proposition that MCS are adopted not as a rational approach, either incrementally or as a radical response to shocks; rather managers are coerced to adopt the systems, or they mimic developments in MCS that occur elsewhere. Moreover, new MCS are taken up and discarded in the same way as other managerial fads. Institutional theory has been used by some accounting researchers to show the adoption of MCS for coercive or mimetic reasons (Ansari and Euske 1987; Malmi 1999; Granlund 2001; Modell 2001). Several studies have shown that MCS have been adopted to appear rational to external parties (Ansari and Euske 1987; Gupta et al. 1994; Geiger and Ittner 1996). Malmi (1999) showed that the adoption of the innovation of ABC was in the first instance explained by efficient choice, then take-off was influenced by fashion and further diffusion was explained by both mimetic and efficient choice. Several studies have shown that MCS are adopted as a consequence of both institutional forces together with more content-styled approaches that consider rational, technical, and contingent relationships (Ansari and Euske 1987; Geiger and Ittner 1996; Mignon 2003). Mignon (2003) used a process approach employing institutional theory to show how government departments adopted formal public management planning and control techniques. She then used predictions from a content-based contingency framework to show how these formal practices that did not suit context were not used. Rather, informal controls that suited context were used to achieve desired planning and control. Other studies have combined institutional ideas with other process issues such as power relationships that can influence the source of institutional pressure (see Covaleski et al. 1996 for a review). Finally, the role of consultants is also important in instigating and diffusing MCS. Many MCS have been targeted at providing strategic information. Notably, practices such as ABCM and BSCs have been enthusiastically publicized and promoted by their proponents (Kaplan and Norton 1992, 1996, 2001; Kaplan and Cooper 1998) often working with professional accounting and business consulting forms. These approaches, along with many other management and IT practices, often require organizations to embrace extensive and revolutionary changes to the structures, systems, and ways of doing business. Attention to the subtleties of the processes of change may assist in understanding why many of these content-based innovations have not provided promised benefits.

References

Abernethy, M. A. and Brownell, P. (1999). 'The Role of Budgets in Organizations Facing Strategic Change: An Exploratory Study', *Accounting, Organizations and Society*, 24(3): 189–204.

Abernethy, M. A. and Lillis, A. (1995). 'The Impact of Manufacturing Flexibility on Management Control System Design', *Accounting, Organizations and Society*, 20(4): 241–58.

Abrahamson, E. (1996). 'Management Fashion', *Academy of Management Review*, 21: 254–85.

Agarwal, R. and Gort, M. (2002). 'Firm and Product Life Cycles and Firm Survival', *American Economic Review*, 92(2): 184–90.

Ahrens, T. and Chapman, C. S. (2004). 'Accounting for Flexibility and Efficiency: A Field Study of Management Control Systems in a Restaurant Chain', *Contemporary Accounting Research*, 21(2): 271–301.

Amigoni, F., Caglio, A., and Ditillo, A. (2003). 'Disintegration through Integration: The Emergence of Accounting Information Networks', in A. Bhimani (ed.), *Management Accounting in the Digital Economy*. Oxford: Oxford University Press, 15–35.

Anderson, C. R. and Zeihaml, C. P. (1984). 'Stage of the Product Life Cycle, Business Strategy and Business Performance', *Academy of Management Review*, 27(1): 5–24.

Anderson, S. W. (1995). 'A Framework for Assessing Cost Management System Changes: The Case of Activity Based Costing Implementation at General Motors', *Journal of Management Accounting Research*, 7: 1–51.

—— and Young, M. S. (1999). 'The Impact of Contextual and Process Factors on the Evaluation of Activity-Based Costing Systems', *Accounting, Organizations and Society*, 24(7): 525–59.

——, Hesford, J. W., and Young, S. M. (2002). 'Factors Influencing the Performance of Activity Based Costing Teams: A Field Study of ABC Model Development Time in the Automobile Industry', *Accounting, Organizations and Society*, 27: 195–211.

Andrews, K. R. (1980). *The Concept of Corporate Strategy*. Homewood, IL: Irwin.

Ansari, S. Bell, J. E., and Cam-I Target Cost Core Group. (1997). *Target Costing: The Next Frontier in Strategic Cost Management*. Chicago: Irwin.

—— and Euske, K. (1997). 'Rational, Rationalizing and Reifying Uses of Accounting Data in Organizations', *Accounting, Organizations and Society*, 12(6): 549–70.

Ansoff, H. I. (1987). *The Concept of Corporate Strategy*, Homewood, IL: Irwin.

Antal, A. B., Dierkes, M., and Hahner, K. (1994). Business in Society: Perceptions and Principals in Organizational Learning, *Journal of General Management*, 20: 55–77.

Archer, S. and Otley D. T. (1991). 'Strategy, Structure, Planning and Control System and Performance Evaluation—Rumenco Ltd', *Management Accounting Research*, 263–303.

Argyris, C. and Kaplan, R. (1994). 'Implementing New Knowledge: The Case of Activity Based Costing', *Accounting Horizons* (Sept.): 83–105.

Baines, A. and Langfield-Smith, K. (2003). 'Antecedents to Management Accounting Change: A Structural Equation Approach', *Accounting, Organizations and Society*, 28(7/8): 675–98.

Banker, R. D., Potter, G., and Schroeder, R. G. (1993). 'Reporting Manufacturing Performance Measures to Workers: An Empirical Investigation', *Journal of Management Accounting Research*, 3: 34–55.

Barney, J. B. (1991). 'Firm Resources and Sustained Competitive Advantage', *Journal of Management*, 17(1): 99–120.

Baxter, J. and Chua, W. F. (2003). 'Alternative Management Accounting—Whence and Whither', *Accounting, Organizations and Society*, 28(2/3): 97–126.

Best, M. H. (1990). *The New Competition: Institutions of Industrial Restructuring*. Cambridge: Polity Press.

Bhimani, A. (1999). 'Mapping Methodological Frontiers in Cross-National Management Control Research', *Accounting, Organizations and Society*, 24(5/6): 413–40.

—— (2003). *Management Accounting in the Digital Economy*. Oxford: Oxford University Press.

Birkett, W. P. (1995). 'Management Accounting and Knowledge Management', *Management Accounting* (Nov.): 44–8.

Bisbe, J. and Otley, D. (2004). 'The Effects of the Interactive Use of MCS on Product Innovation', *Accounting, Organizations and Society*, 29: 709–37.

Bouwens, J. and Abernethy M. A. (2000). 'The Consequences of Customisation on Management Accounting System Design', *Accounting, Organizations and Society*, 25(3): 221–59.

Braybrooke, D. and Lindblom, C. E. (1970). *A Strategy of Decision*. New York: Free Press.

Bromwich, (1990). 'The Case for Strategic Management Accounting: The Role of Accounting Information for Strategy in Competitive Markets', *Accounting, Organizations and Society*, 15(1/2): 27–46.

Campbell-Hunt, C. (2000). 'What have We Learned about Generic Competitive Strategy? A Meta-Analysis', *Strategic Management Journal*, 21: 127–54.

Carnall, C. (1995). '*Managing Change in Organizations*'. 2nd edn. London: Prentice-Hall.

Chapman, C. S. (1998). 'Accountants in Organizational Networks', *Accounting, Organizations and Society*, 23(8): 737–66.

Chen, S. (2001). *Strategic Management of E-Business*. New York: John Wiley.

Chenhall, R. H. (1997). 'Reliance on Manufacturing Performance Measures, Total Quality Management and Organizational Performance', *Management Accounting Research*, 8: 187–206.

—— (2003). 'MCS Design within Its Organizational Context: Findings from Contingency-Based Research and Directions for the Future', *Accounting, Organizations and Society*, 28: 127–68.

—— (2004). 'The Role of Cognitive and Affective Conflict in the Early Implementation of Activity-Based Cost Management', *Behavioral Research in Accounting*, 16: 19–44.

—— and Langfield-Smith, K. (1998). 'The Relationship between Strategic Priorities, Management Techniques and Management Accounting: An Empirical Investigation Using a Systems Approach', *Accounting, Organizations and Society*, 23(3): 243–64.

—— —— (1998). 'Factors Influencing the Role of Management Accounting Development of Performance Measures within Organizational Change Programs', *Management Accounting Research*, 9: 361–86.

—— —— (2003). 'The Role of Employee Pay in Sustaining Organisational Change', *Journal of Management Accounting Research*, 15: 117–43.

—— and Morris, D. (1995). 'Organic Decision and Communication Processes and Management Accounting Systems in Entrepreneurial and Conservative Business Organizations, Omega', *International Journal of Management Science*, 23(5): 485–97.

Cohen, M. D., March, J. G., and Olsen, J. P. (1972). 'A Garbage Can Model of Organizational Choice', *Administrative Science Quarterly*, 17: 1–25.

Contractor, F. J. and Lorange, P. (1988). *Cooperative Strategies in International Business*. Lexington, MA: Lexington Books.

Covaleski, M. A., Dirsmith, M. W., and Samuel, S. (1996). Managerial Accounting Research: The Contributions of Organizational and Sociological Theories, *Journal of Management Accounting Research*, 6: 1–35.

Davila, T. (2000). 'An Empirical Study of the Drivers of MCS Design in New Product Development', *Accounting, Organizations and Society*, 25: 383–409.

Davis, F. G., Doekmann, K. A., and Tinsley, C. H. (1994). 'The Decline and Fall of the Conglomerate Firm in the 1980s: The Deinstitutionalization of an Organizational Form', *American Sociological Review*, 59(Aug.): 547–70.

Dent, J. F. (1991). 'Accounting and Organizational Cultures: A Field Study of the Emergence of a New Organizational Reality', *Accounting, Organizations and Society*, 16: 705–32.

Dermer, J. (1990). 'The Strategic Agenda: Accounting for Issues and Support', *Accounting, Organizations and Society*, 15(1/2): 67–76.

de Wit, B. and Meyer, R. (1999). *Strategy Synthesis*. London: Thompson.

Donaldson, L. and Hilmer, F. G. (1998). Management Redeemed: The Case against Fads that Harm Management, *Organizational Dynamics*, 26(4): 6–20.

Edvinsson, L. and Malone, M. (1997). *Intellectual Capital: Realizing your Company's True Value by Finding Its Hidden Brainpower*. New York: HarperCollins.

Fahey, L. and Christensen, H. K. (1986). 'Evaluating the Research of Strategy Content', *Journal of Management*, 12: 167–83.

Fincham, R. and Roslender, R. (2003). 'Intellectual Capital Accounting as Management Fashion: A Review and Critique', *European Accounting Review*, 12(4): 781–95.

Foster, G. and Swenson, D. W. (1997). 'Measuring the Success of Activity-Based Cost Management and Its Determinants', *Journal of Management Accounting Research*, 9: 109–41.

Fullerton, R. R. and McWatters, C. S. (2002). 'The Role of Performance Measures and Incentive Systems in Relation to the Degree of JIT Implementation', *Accounting, Organizations and Society*, 27(8): 711–35.

Gamache, R. D. and Kuhn, R. L. (1989). *The Creativity Infusion—How Managers Can Start and Sustain Creativity and Innovation*. New York: Harper & Row.

Geiger, D. and Ittner, C. (1996). 'The Influence of Funding Source and Legislative Requirements on Government Cost Accounting Practices', *Accounting, Organizations and Society*, 21(6): 549–67.

Govindarajan, V. (1988). 'A Contingency Approach to Strategy Implementation at the Business-Unit Level: Integrating Administrative Mechanisms with Strategy', *Academy of Management Journal*, 31: 828–53.

—— and Fisher, J. (1990). 'Strategy, Control System and Resource Sharing: Effects on Business-Unit Performance', *Academy of Management Journal*, 33: 259–85.

—— and Gupta, A. K. (1985). 'Linking Control Systems to Business Unit Strategy: Impact on Performance', *Accounting, Organizations and Society*, 51–66.

Granlund, M. (2001). 'Towards Explaining Stability in and around Management Accounting Systems', *Management Accounting Research*, 12(2): 141–66.

Grant, R. M. (1996). 'Towards a Knowledge-Based Theory of the Firm', *Strategic Management Journal*, 17 (Winter Special Issue).

Grover, V., Fielder, K. D., and Teng, J. T. C. (1997). 'Corporate Strategy and IT Investment', *Business and Economic Review*, 43(3): 17–22.

Guilding, C. (1999). 'Competitor-Focused Accounting: An Exploratory Note', *Accounting, Organizations and Society*, 24(7): 583–95.

Gupta, A. K. and Govindarajan, V. (1984). 'Business Unit Strategy, Managerial Characteristics, and Business Unit Effectiveness at Strategy Implementation', *Academy of Management Journal*, 27: 695–714.

—— —— (2001). 'Managing Global Expansion: A Conceptual Framework', in Criskota, M. and Ronkainen, I. (eds.), *Best Practice in International Business*. Fort Worth, TX: Harcourt College Publishers, 123–41.

——, Dirsmith, M., and Fogarty, T. (1994). 'Coordination and Control in a Government Agency: Contingency and Institutional Perspectives on GAO Audits', *Administrative Science Quarterly*, 39: 264–84.

Hamel, G., Doz, Y. L., and Prahalad, C. K. (1989). 'Collaborate with Your Competitors and Win', *Harvard Business Review* (Jan./Feb.): 133–9.

Harrison, G. L. and McKinnon, J. (1999). 'Cross Cultural Research in Management Accounting Systems Design: A Review of the Current State', *Accounting, Organizations and Society*, 24(5/6): 483–506.

Huber, G. P. and Glick W. H. (1993). *Organizational Change and Redesign: Ideas and Insights for Improving Performance*. New York: Oxford University Press.

——, Sutcliffe, K. M., Miller, C. C., and Glick, W. H. (1993). 'Organizational Change and Redesign: Ideas and Insights for Improving Performance', *Understanding and Predicting Organizational Change*. New York: Oxford University Press.

IFAC Report. (1998). *The Measurement and Management of Intellectual Capital: An Introduction*. New York: International Federation of Accountants, 7 (Oct.).

Ittner, C. D. and Larcker, D. F. (1995). 'Total Quality Management and the Choice of Information and Reward Systems', *Journal of Accounting Research*, 33(Supp.): 1–34.

—— and Larcker, D. F. (1997). 'Quality Strategy, Strategic Control Systems, and Organizational Performance', *Accounting, Organizations and Society*, 22(3/4): 295–314.

—— Larcker, D. F., Nagar, V., and Rajan, M. V. (1999). 'Supplier Selection, Monitoring Practices and Firm Performance', *Journal of Accounting and Public Policy*, 18(3): 253–81.

Jelinek, M. (1979). *Institutionalizing Innovation*. New York: Praeger.

Jick, T. D. (1993). *Managing Change, Cases and Concepts*. Boston, MA: Irwin/McGraw-Hill.

Kalagnanam, S. S. and Lindsay, R. M. (1999). 'The Use of Organic Models of Control in JIT Firms: Generalizing Woodward's Findings to Modern Manufacturing Practices', *Accounting, Organizations and Society*, 24(1): 1–30.

Kanter, R. M. (1982). 'The Middle Manager as Innovator,' *Harvard Business Review* (Jul./Aug.): 95–105.

—— (1994). 'Collaborative Advantage: The Art of Alliances', *Harvard Business Review*, (Jul./Aug.): 96–108.

——, Stein, B. A., and Jick, T. D. (1992). *The Challenge of Organizational Change: How Companies Experience It and Leaders Guide It*. New York: Free Press.

Kaplan, R. S. and Cooper, R. (1998). *Cost and Effect: Using Cost Systems to Drive Profitability and Performance*. Boston, MA: Harvard University Press.

—— and Norton, D. P. (1992). 'The Balanced Scorecard: Measures that Drive Performance', *Harvard Business Review* (Jan./Feb.): 71–9.

—— and Norton, D. P. (1996). *The Balanced Scorecard: Translating Strategy into Action*. Boston, MA: Harvard Business School Press.

—— and Norton, D. P. (2001). 'Transforming the Balanced Scorecard from Performance Measurement to Strategic Management', *Accounting Horizons*, Part I (Mar.): 87–104; Part II (June): 147–60.

Kauffman, R. and Walden, E. (2001). 'Economics and E-Commerce', *International Journal of E-Commerce*, (Summer).

Kennedy, T. and Affleck-Graves, J. (2001). 'The Impact of Activity-Based Costing Techniques on Firm Performance', *Journal of Management Accounting Research*, 13: 19–45.

Knight, D. and Willmott, H. (1993). 'It's a Very Foreign Discipline: The Genesis of Expenses Control in a Mutual Life Insurance Company', *British Journal of Management*, 1–18.

Knights, D. and Morgan, G. (1991). 'Corporate Strategy, Organizations, and the Subject: A Critique', *Organization Studies*, 12(2): 251–73.

Kochan, T. A. and Osterman, P. (1994). *The Mutual Gains Enterprise*. Boston, MA: Harvard Business School Press.

Kotha, S. and Vadlamani, B. L. (1995). 'Assessing Generic Strategies: An Empirical Investigation of Two Competing Typologies in Discrete Manufacturing Industries', *Strategic Management Journal*, 16, 75–83.

—— , Dunbar, R. L. M., and Bird, A. (1995). 'Strategic Action Generation: A Comparison of Emphasis Placed on Generic Competitive Methods by US and Japanese Managers', *Strategic Management Journal*, 16: 195–220.

Kotter, J. P. (1996). *Leading Change*. Boston, MA: Harvard Business School Press.

Krumwiede, K. R. (1998). 'The Implementation Stages of Activity Based Costing and the Impact of Contextual and Organizational Factors', *Journal of Management Accounting Research*, 10: 239–77.

Leong, G. K., Snyder, D. L., and Ward, P. T. (1990). 'Research in the Process and Content of Manufacturing Strategy', *Omega: International Journal of Management Science*, 18(2): 109–22.

Libby, T. and Waterhouse, J. H. (1996). 'Predicting Change in Management Accounting Systems', *Journal of Management Accounting Research*, 8: 125–50.

Lillis, A. M. (2002). 'Managing Multiple Dimensions of Manufacturing Performance—An Exploratory Study', *Accounting, Organizations and Society*, 27: 497–529.

McGowan, A. S., and Klammer, T. P. (1997). 'Satisfaction with Activity-Based Cost Management Implementation', *Journal of Management Accounting Research*, 9: 217–37.

McNair, C. J., Lynch, R. L., and Cross, K. F. (1990). 'Do Financial and Nonfinancial Performance Measures Have to Agree?', *Management Accounting*, (Nov.): 28–36.

Malina, M. A. and Selto, F. H. (2001). 'Communicating and Controlling Strategy: An Empirical Study of the Effectiveness of the Balanced Scorecard', *Journal of Management Accounting Research*, 13: 47–90.

Malmi, T. (1997). 'Towards Explaining Activity-Based Costing Failure: Accounting and Control in a Decentralized Organization', *Management Accounting Research*, 8: 71–90.

—— (1999). 'Activity-Based Costing Diffusion Across Organizations: An Exploratory Empirical Analysis of Finnish Firms', *Accounting, Organizations and Society*, 24(8): 649–72.

March, J. G. and Simon, H. A. (1958). *Organisations*. New York: John Wiley.

Merchant, K. (1985). *Control in Business Organisations*. Boston, MA: Pitman.

Mia, L. (2000). 'Just-in-time Manufacturing, Management Accounting Systems and Profitability', *Accounting and Business Research*, 30(2): 137–51.

Mignon, H. (2003). 'Impact of Output Management within MCS on Performance in Victorian Government Departments'. Ph.D. Thesis, Clayton, Victoria: Monash University.

Miles, R. W. and Snow, C. C. (1978). *Organizational Strategy, Structure and Process*. New York: McGraw-Hill.

Milgrom, P. and Roberts, J. (1992). *Economics, Organization & Management*. Englewood Cliffs, NJ: Prentice-Hall.

Miller, A. and Dess, G. G. (1993). 'Assessing Porter's (1980) Model in Terms of Its Generalizability, Accuracy and Simplicity', *Journal of Management Studies*, 30(4): 553–85.

Miller, D. and Friesen, P. H. (1982). 'Innovation in Conservative and Entrepreneurial Firms: Two Models of Strategic Momentum', *Strategic Management Journal*, 1–25.

Miller, J. M., DeMeyer, A., and Nakane, J. (1992). *Benchmarking Global Competition: Understanding International Suppliers, Customers and Competitors*. Homewood, IL: Irwin.

Miller, P. (1991). 'Strategic Human Resource Management: An Assessment of Progress', *Human Resource Management Journal*, 1(4): 23–39.

—— and O'Leary, T. (1997). 'Capital Budgeting Practices and Complementarity Relations in the Transition to Modern Manufacturing: A Field-Based Analysis', *Journal of Accounting Research*, 35(2): 257–71.

Mintzberg, H. (1978). 'Patterns in Strategy Formation', *Management Science*, XXIV: 934–48.

—— (1987). Crafting Strategy, *Harvard Business Review*, 65(4): 66–75.

—— (1994). *The Rise and Fall of Strategic Planning*. New York: Free Press.

Mockler, R. J. (1991). *Computing Software to Support Strategy Formulation Decision-Making.* Columbus, OH: Merrill.

—— (1992). *Developing Knowledge-Based Systems: A Managerial Decision-Making Approach.* Columbus, OH: Merrill.

Modell, S. (2001). 'Performance Measurement and Institutional Processes: A Study of Managerial Responses to Public Sector Reform', *Management Accounting Research,* 12(4): 437–64.

Moores, K. and Yuen, S. (2001). 'Management Accounting Systems and Organizational Configuration: A Life-Cycle Perspective', *Accounting, Organizations and Society,* 26: 351–89.

Mouritsen, J. (1999). 'The Flexible Firm: Strategies for a Subcontractor's Management Control', *Accounting, Organizations and Society,* 24(1) 26: 31–55.

Nonaka, I. (1991). 'The Knowledge-Creating Company', *Harvard Business Review* (November/December): 96–104.

Ohmae, K. (1990). *The Borderless World: Power and Structure in the Interlinked Economy.* London: Fontana.

Perera, S., Harrison, G., and Poole, M. (1997). 'Customer Focused Manufacturing Strategy and the Use of Operations Based Non-financial Performance Measures: A Research Note', *Accounting, Organizations and Society,* 22(6): 557–72.

Phillips, D. (1992). *Lincoln on Leadership: Executive Strategies for Tough Times.* New York: Warner Books.

Pinochot, G. and Pinochot, E. (1993). *The End of Bureaucracy and the Rise of the Intelligent Organization.* San Francisco: Berrett-Koehler Publishers.

Porter, M. E. (1980). *Competitive Strategy: Techniques of Analyzing Industries and Competitors.* New York: Free Press.

—— (1985). *Competitive Advantage: Creating and Sustaining Superior Performance.* New York: Free Press.

Prahalad, C. K. and Hamel, G. (1990). 'The Core Competence of the Corporation', *Harvard Business Review,* 68(3): 79–91.

Quinn, J. B. (1980). *Strategies for Change: Logical Incrementalism.* Homewood, IL: Irwin.

—— (1985). 'Managing Innovation: Controlling Chaos', *Harvard Business Review, (May/June):* 73–84.

—— (1992). *Intelligent Enterprise: A Knowledge and Service Based Paradigm for Industry.* New York: Free Press.

Rimmer, M. J., Macneil, R., Chenhall, K., Langfield-Smith, K., and Watts, L. (1996). *Reinventing Competitiveness: Achieving Best Practice in Australia.* South Melbourne, Australia: Pitman Publishing.

Roberts, J. (1990). 'Strategy and Accounting in a U.K. Conglomerate', *Accounting, Organizations and Society,* 15(1/2): 107–26.

Rouleau, L. and Seguin, F. (1995). 'Strategy and Organization Theories: Common Forms of Discourse', *Journal of Management Studies,* 32(1): 101–17.

Rowe, A. J., Mason, R. O., Dickel, K. E., Mann, R. B., and Mockler, R. J. (1994). *Strategic Management: A Methodological Approach.* Reading, MA: Addison-Wesley.

Salk, G., Evans, P., and Schulman, L. E. (1992). 'Competing on Capabilities: The New Rules of Corporate Strategy,' *Harvard Business Review* (Mar./Apr.): 57–69.

Saloner, G. and Spence, A. M. (2001). *Creating and Capturing Value.* New York: John Wiley.

Scapens, R. and Roberts, J. (1993). 'Accounting and Control: A Case Study of Resistance to Accounting Change', *Management Accounting Research,* 5: 301–21.

Selznick, P. (1957). *Leadership in Administration: A Sociological Interpretation.* New York: Harper & Row.

Seth, A. and Thomas H. (1994). 'Theories of the Firm: Implications for Strategy Research', *Journal of Management Studies,* 31(2): 165–91.

Shank, J. W. and Govindarajan, V. (1995). *Strategic Cost Management: The New Tool for Competitive Advantage*. New York: Free Press.

Shields, M. D. (1995). 'An Empirical Analysis of Firms' Implementation Experiences with Activity-Based Costing', *Journal of Management Accounting Research*, 7: 148–66.

—— and Young, S. M. (1989). 'A Behavioral Model for Implementing Cost Management Systems', *Journal of Cost Management* (Winter): 17–27.

Shortell, S. M. and Zajac, E. J. (1990). 'Perceptual and Archival Measures of Miles and Snow's Strategic Types: A Comprehensive Assessment of Reliability and Validity', *Academy of Management Journal*, 33(4): 817–32.

Sim, K. L. and Killough, L. N. (1998). 'The Performance Effects of Complementarities between Manufacturing Practices and Management Accounting Systems', *Journal of Management Accounting Research*, 10: 325–46.

Simmonds, K. (1981). *The Fundamentals of Strategic Management Accounting*. ICMA Occasional Paper Series. London: ICMA.

Simons, R. (1990). 'The Role of Management Control Systems in Creating Competitive Advantage: New Perspectives', *Accounting, Organizations and Society*, 15(1/2): 127–43.

—— (1995). *Levers of Control*. Boston, MA: Harvard University Press.

—— (2000). *Performance Measurement & Control Systems for Implementing Strategy*. Upper Saddle River, NJ: Prentice-Hall.

Steiner, G. (1969). *Top Management Planning*. New York: Macmillan.

Stenge, P. D. (1990). 'The Leader's New Work: Building Learning Organizations', *Sloan Management Review* (Fall): 7–23.

Stewart, T. A. (1997). *Intellectual Capital: The New Wealth of Nations*. New York: Doubleday Dell Publishing.

Sveiby, K. E. (1997). 'The Intangible Assets Monitor', *Journal of Human Resource Costing and Accounting*, 2(1): 73–97.

Teece, D. J., Pisano, G., and Shuen, A. (1997). 'Dynamic Capabilities and Strategic Management', *Strategic Management Journal*, 18(7): 509–33.

Tomkins, C. (2001). 'Interdependence, Trust and Information in Relationships, Alliances and Networks', *Accounting, Organizations and Society*, 26: 161–91.

Tushman, M. and Naylor D. (1986). 'Organizing for Innovation', *California Management Review* (Spring): 74–92.

Vaivio, J. (1999). 'Exploring a "Non-financial" Management Accounting Change', *Management Accounting Research*, 10: 409–37.

Van der Stede, W. A. (2000). 'The Relationship between Two Consequences of Budgetary Controls: Budgetary Slack Creation and Managerial Short-term Orientation', *Accounting, Organizations and Society*, 25(6): 609–22.

Van de Ven, A. H. and Poole, M. S. (1995). 'Explaining Development and Change in Organizations', *Academy of Management Review*, 20(3): 510–40.

Ward, K. (1992). *Strategic Management Accounting*. Oxford: Butterworth Heinemann.

Wasson, C. R. (1978). *Dynamic Competitive Strategy and Product Life Cycles*. Austin, TX: Austin Press.

Waterman, R. H., Peters, T. J., and Phillips, J. R. (1980). 'Structure Is Not Organization', *Business Horizons* (June): 14–26.

West, P. (1994). 'The Concept of the Learning Organization', *Journal of European Industrial Training*, 18: 15–21.

Young, S. M. and Selto, F. H. (1993). 'Explaining Cross-Sectional Workgroup Performance Differences in a JIT Facility: A Critical Appraisal of a Field-Based Study', *Journal of Management Accounting Research* (Fall): 300–26.

The Promise of Management Control Systems for Innovation and Strategic Change

Tony Davila

This chapter proposes a framework for analysing the different roles that formal management control systems (MCS) may play in managing various types of innovation, and, the effect that these innovations have on changes in business strategy. Traditionally, MCS have been associated with mechanistic organizations (Burns and Stalker 1961), where their purpose was to reduce variety and implement standardization as portrayed in the cybernetic model (Ashby 1960; Anthony 1965). Accordingly, they were frequently perceived as a hindrance to any innovation and change effort in the organization. For example, Ouchi (1979) used an innovation-intensive activity, an R&D department, to illustrate clan control—a control approach that rejects formal MCS and instead relies on social norms. Tushman and O'Reilly (1997: 108) summarize this view: 'With work requirements becoming more complex, uncertain, and changing, control systems cannot be static and formal. Rather, control must come in the form of social control systems that allow directed autonomy and rely on the judgment of employees informed by clarity about vision and objectives of the business.'

Recent theory and empirical studies have questioned these commonly held assumptions about the negative effect of MCS on innovation and laid the foundations for this topic to develop. They highlight instead the positive effect that MCS may have on innovation and develop alternative interpretations to the command-and-control view. Rather than a rigid mould that rejects the unexpected, MCS may be flexible and dynamic, adapting and evolving to the unpredictable needs of innovation, but stable enough to frame cognitive models, communication patterns, and actions. This new way of looking at MCS is consistent with innovation being not a random exogenous event that certain organizations happen to experience, but rather an organizational process susceptible to management that explains why certain organizations are more successful than others.

This emerging line of research identifies how MCS enhance the learning, communication, and experimentation required for innovation in strategy formation. However, it has not yet considered different types of innovation, different ways in which innovation emerges, and how innovation gets embedded in the strategy of the firm. Without a model that frames MCS within this context, the advancement of our knowledge about these systems is likely to remain unstructured, with anecdotal pieces of evidence unrelated to each other and relying on diverse concepts that are not specifically designed for this task.

The strategic management field has also made important progress to better understand the impact of innovation on strategy. Researchers in this field have argued for specific approaches that bring innovation into the formulation and implementation of strategic change. They propose new 'mental models' (Markides 1997; Christensen and Raynor 2003) for strategy formulation. These models redefine an organization's self-image (Boulding 1956) and help managers break away from static views and create new strategies for the future. These researchers also examine the implementation of innovation as a key aspect of strategic change from a strategic process perspective: how to design organizational structures that are more innovative (Chesbrough 2000), how to design supportive cultures (Tushman and O'Reilly 1997), and how innovation 'happens' (Van de Ven et al. 1999; Burgelman 2002). These advances offer a fertile ground to extend the relationship between strategic process and MCS (Langfield-Smith 1997, 2005) and recognize the importance of MCS to strategic change.

This chapter provides the background and develops a typology of MCS based on current knowledge on innovation and strategic change. It examines strategy as a process, leaving aside its content aspect (Chenhall 2005). Strategic process literature (Mintzberg 1978; Barnett and Burgelman 1996; Burgelman 2002) focuses on how strategy happens within organizations: that is, how organizational forces shape the formulation, implementation, and the interplay of these two components of strategy, sometimes through incremental improvements and at other times through significant redefinitions. As such, it offers the concepts to ground the proposed model.

The chapter is organized as follows. The first part of the chapter gives an overview of recent developments within MCS literature. These developments have moved the field beyond their traditional role as implementation tools in stable environments towards a facilitating role to formulate and implement strategy in dynamic environments. Next, the chapter develops the strategic process framework that is used in developing the model of MCS. The final part presents the model. MCS are argued to be relevant to the implementation and the evolution in the formulation of current strategy as well as to nurturing radical innovation that fundamentally redefines the future strategy of an organization.

The promise of MCS for innovation

Our understanding of MCS has evolved very significantly over the last decade: from systems that imposed standardization and rejected innovation both at the operational and at the strategic level, to systems that support organizations in their effort to respond and adapt to changing environments. This section summarizes this evolution and describes how recent theory and evidence identifies MCS as a key aspect of innovation.

The purpose of early formulations of MCS was to guide the organization through the implementation of its explicit goals, which were decided at the strategic planning level (Anthony 1965). A further elaboration of this formulation became known as the cybernetic model (Ashby 1960), where implementation happened through mechanisms that minimized deviations from expected performance. The functioning of a thermostat, where a control mechanism intervenes when the temperature deviates from the preset standard, has been a frequent metaphor for this model. This characterization describes an important role of MCS and, as such, it is commonly integrated in current formulations—for instance as diagnostic systems (Simons 1995).

Because the purpose of the cybernetic model is to minimize deviations from pre-established objectives, it limits the use of MCS to mechanistic organizations (Burns and Stalker 1961) where standardized routines are repeatedly performed with few if any changes. MCS also reinforce the extrinsic, command and control, contractual relationships of hierarchical organizations. Therefore, their use in formulating and implementing innovation strategies—where uncertainty, experimentation, flexibility, intrinsic motivation, and freedom are paramount—is limited to minor improvements. They are purposefully designed to block innovation for the sake of efficiency and make sure that processes deliver the value they are intended to generate. Learning is anticipatory and accrues from planning ahead of time, from examining the different alternatives before the organization dives into execution, and from outlining a path. Empirical studies confirmed these predictions

(Chapman 1997; Chenhall 2005, Langfield-Smith 2005). For instance, Abernethy and Brownell (1999) report higher reliance on personnel control in R&D departments. Rockness and Shields (1988) echo these conclusions.

Given the characteristics of the cybernetic model, it is not surprising that MCS were perceived as stifling innovation and change (Ouchi 1979; Amabile et al. 1996; Tushman and O'Reilly 1997). Accordingly, researchers relied on informal processes such as culture (Tushman and O'Reilly 1997), communication patterns (Allen 1977), team composition (Dougherty 1992), and leadership (Clark and Fujimoto 1991) to manage innovation. Uniformity and predictability—the hallmarks of the cybernetic model—are at odds with the need for the rich informational environment with intense communication to create the abrasiveness (Leonard-Barton 1992) required for ideas to spark, intense communication inside the organization and with outside parties to nurture ideas (Dougherty 1992), a supportive organization that rewards experimentation (Tushman and O'Reilly 1997), and a strong leader with the authority to execute the vision (Clark and Fujimoto 1991). Walton (1985) argues for a human resource model of coordination and control based on shared values that substitute 'rules and procedures'. In support of these ideas, Damanpour's meta-analysis (1991) of empirical work on organizational determinants of innovation reveals a negative association between innovation and formalization.

However, recent empirical evidence questions the validity of this interpretation. Formalization is positively related to satisfaction in a variety of settings (Jackson and Schuler 1985; Stevens et al. 1992). Environmental uncertainty has repeatedly been associated with intense MCS (Khandwalla 1972; Chenhall and Morris 1986, 1995; Simons 1987). Directly investigating the role of accounting in highly uncertain conditions, Chapman (1998: 738) used four case studies and concluded: '[T]he results of this exploratory study strongly support the idea that accounting does have a beneficial role in highly uncertain conditions.' Howard-Grenville (2003) used an ethnographic approach in one high-technology company to document the relevance of organizational routines to confront uncertain and complex situations. Abernethy and Brownell (1997) use Simons' model to examine the use of budgets 'as a dialogue, learning, and idea creation machine' during episodes of strategic change. The learning aspect associated with budgets (Lukka 1988) and participative budgeting (Shields and Shields 1998) also breaks from the command-and-control view to suggest a different view, less rigid and more open to innovation. Ahrens and Chapman (2002, 2004) in their detailed field study of a restaurant chain identified MCS as not only a traditional tool for standardizing strategy implementation but also an effective tool for supporting flexible adaptation to unexpected contingencies. Mouritsen's *BusinessPrint* case study (1999) also reflects the tension between an efficiency-focused control strategy relying on a 'paper' version of management control and an innovation-focused control strategy relying on a 'hands-on' version of management control. Similar observations have been made in product development studies (Zirger and Maidique 1990; Cooper 1995; McGrath 1995; Brown and Eisenhardt 1997; Nixon 1998; Davila 2000; Cardinal 2001).

Conceptual work proposes new approaches to explain these empirical observations. The capability of an organization to innovate depends on its ability to accumulate, assimilate, and exploit knowledge (Fiol 1996). This ability depends not only on its informal processes, but also on the mechanisms that support them. The concept of enabling bureaucracy (Adler and Borys 1996: 68) is designed to 'enhance the users' capabilities and to leverage their skills and intelligence' as opposed to 'a fool-proofing and deskilling rationale' typical of a cybernetic model. Organizations exploit the knowledge through flexible, transparent, user-friendly routines that facilitate learning associated with the innovation process. Formal systems need not be coercive controls that suppress variation; rather they may support the learning that derives from exploring this variation. In this way, enabling bureaucracies constantly improve organizational processes through constant interaction between the formalized process and its users; as such, they are able to bring innovation into the learning routines of the organization. Simons' interactive systems (1995) have similar learning properties. They provide the information-based infrastructure to engage organizational members in the communication pattern required to address strategic uncertainties. A key feature of these systems is that they allow top management to influence the exploration associated with innovation and strategic change.

Another line of research offers additional arguments through the concept of adaptive routines. Weick et al. (1999) describe routines as resilient because of their capacity to adapt to unexpected events. This concept portrays routines as flexible to absorb novelty rather than rigid to suppress it. They also offer organizational members a stable framework to interpret and communicate when facing unexpected events. They 'usefully constrain the direction of subsequent experiential search' (Gavetti and Levinthal 2000: 113). These authors argue that a learning model where companies jointly rely on planning and learning-by-doing performs better in uncertain environments. Feldman and Rafaeli (2002) extend this argument to include routines as drivers of key patterns of communication among organizational members. Miner et al. (2001) describe the constant interaction between routine activities and improvization in new product development.

These studies highlight the positive role that MCS may play on innovation. They develop alternatives to the command-and-control view of the cybernetic model. Rather than being viewed as a rigid mould that rejects the unexpected, MCS are theorized as flexible and dynamic frames adapting and evolving to the unpredictable bends of innovation, but stable enough to frame cognitive models, communication patterns, and actions.

Evolving views on the process of innovation and strategic change

The organizational process associated with innovation at operational and strategic levels (both inextricably intertwined) includes the organizational forces that identify, nurture, and translate the seed of an idea into value. Rather than a random exogenous event that certain organizations happen to experience, innovation can be an organizational process susceptible to management that explains why certain organizations are more successful than others. Grounded in strategic process literature, this section identifies four processes that capture the effect of different types of innovation on strategic change: from innovations that modify the current strategy but keep the organization within its current strategy trajectory to innovations that radically redefine the future strategy of the organization. Table 1 summarizes the four types described in

Table 1 Strategic concepts for MCS

	Type of innovation defining strategic change	
	Incremental	Radical
Locus of innovation		
Top management formulation	Deliberate strategy	Strategic innovation
Day-to-day actions	Emergent strategy / intended strategic actions	Emergent strategy / autonomous strategic actions

the section along two dimensions. The first one is the locus of innovation—whether it happens at the top management level or throughout the organization. The second dimension is the type of innovation—whether it incrementally modifies the current strategy (incremental innovation) or it radically redefines the future strategy (radical innovation).

The initial concept of strategy described the process as linear, with formulation being followed by implementation (Andrews 1971). Changes to strategy were designed at the top of the organization as part of the formulation stage, with MCS having no role and coming in only at the implementation stage. Over time, the concept of strategy evolved to include different aspects (Hoskisson et al. 1999; Chenhall 2005). One of these aspects examines strategy as an internal evolutionary process where formulation and implementation happen simultaneously. Because both stages happen together, strategic change is not an isolated event at the beginning of the process; rather it is embedded throughout the process. Mintzberg (1978) identified strategy as having a *deliberate* component that comes from top management's formulation and implementation efforts and an *emergent* component that happens through day-to-day decisions. Innovation is shaped from the top but also as organizational members interpret and adapt the deliberate strategy to execute their task. *Realized* strategy is the strategy that ends up happening and it is a combination of deliberate and emergent strategies. In the absence of an emergent strategy, this model becomes the traditional Andrews' model; but the presence of this new component—emergent strategy—reflects the impact on strategy of innovations that happen throughout the organization to adapt to unexpected events. Within this formulation, MCS' role is still limited to implementing the deliberate strategy—much as in Andrews' two-stage model, with little if any effect on the emergent strategy. It is only with Simons' concepts (1995) of interactive and boundary systems that MCS become relevant in managing emergent strategy.

Burgelman (1983), building on Bower's resource allocation model (1970), further advanced the evolutionary perspective. He identifies innovation in strategy as not only happening within the current business model (incremental innovation) but also as being able to redefine it (radical innovation). This is an important distinction that is absent from the idea of emergent strategy.

Innovation that incrementally changes the current strategy of the organization builds upon competencies already present in the organization or those that are relatively easy to develop or acquire. Because it moves within an existing technology trajectory or business model, the organization can readily identify its effect and it entails fewer organizational and industry changes; it also involves lower risks and the associated lower expected returns (Ettlie et al. 1984; Green et al. 1995; Damanpour 1996). In contrast, innovation that radically redefines the future strategy is high-risk and high expected return; it significantly upsets organizations—shifting the power structure (Damanpour 1991), redefining the relevance of core competencies, and requiring a redesign of the competitive strategy—and changes dramatically the industry structure.

The concept of *induced strategic actions* incorporates the idea that top management can only guide actions (Burgelman 1983). Top management does not formulate a deliberate strategy that is randomly mixed with the emergent strategy. Rather, top management knows that the deliberate strategy will never be implemented and instead of trying to force it, top management focuses on defining the guidelines that shape the emergent strategy. Induced strategic actions are 'oriented toward gaining and maintaining leadership in the company's core businesses' (Burgelman 2002: 11). They embed the objectives that top managers have defined as the strategy of the organization rather than prescribe what the organization should do. Day-to-day actions within the guidelines end up defining the realization of strategy. In this sense, these actions incorporate emergent strategy. Because they move the organization forward within the frame of the existing business model, these actions tend to be incremental refinements that push the performance frontier (Quinn 1980). Strategy evolves through incremental innovations—embedded in the evolution of objectives and in day-to-day actions. These innovations are low risk; do not upset the existing image of strategy, organizational processes, structures, and systems; and do not significantly change the parameters of industry competition. Even if incremental, these innovations are not necessarily cheap—incremental improvements in existing technologies may be expensive propositions and incremental changes to a business model can require significant investments in enabling technologies. Moreover, if these innovations are well executed they may cumulate over long enough periods of time into significant competitive advantage.

Induced strategic actions are managed through the *structural context* of the organization—which includes structures, MCS, and culture—that top managers design to coordinate the actions so that they are consistent with the business strategy (Burgelman 2002). MCS as part of the structural context, are designed to encourage employees' actions to happen within the strategy that top management has defined. However, they do not dictate actions; rather they provide the framework that people within the organization refer to when acting. Because MCS provide the framework for action, day-to-day actions can embrace incremental innovations that end up defining the realized strategy.

Burgelman's model identifies an additional strategic process that may lead to significant redefinitions of the strategy. *Autonomous strategic actions* are outside the current strategy of the firm and they emerge throughout the organization from individuals or small groups. In contrast to an emergent strategy embedded within intended strategic actions, autonomous strategies are emergent but outside the current strategy. An example of a successful autonomous action is Intel's transition from a memory strategy to a microprocessor strategy (Burgelman 2002). The shift into microprocessors did not start at the top of the organization; rather by accepting and rejecting certain orders, developing the manufacturing technology, and designing the products, middle management shifted Intel's strategy towards microprocessors without much top management awareness. By the time top management decided to shift Intel's deliberate strategy, these products were already a substantial percentage of company sales.

Autonomous strategic actions are based on radical innovations—innovations grounded on significantly different technologies, organizational capabilities, and departing from the current strategic trajectory of the firm. Because they may happen throughout the organization and do not fit within the current strategy, the structural context does not provide adequate tools to support radical innovation. Structural context redefines actions to make them coherent with the current strategy. To do so, it reduces variation to bring about consistency. Autonomous strategies require a context that encourages variation—where variation increases the likelihood of an autonomous strategic action to happen, where selection disregards the coherence of actions with the current strategy, and where the retention process encourages the translation of action into a new business strategy. This *strategic context* 'serves to evaluate and select autonomous strategic actions outside the regular structural context' (Burgelman 2002: 14). Research on the strategic context (Noda and Bower 1996) has adopted a variation–selection–retention model of cultural evolutionary theory (Weick 1979), examining how various organizational forces affect this process.

Autonomous strategic actions happen anywhere in the organization without top management being aware of such initiatives shaping up—given the low likelihood of success, most radical innovation efforts are invalidated before they even attract top management's attention. However, radical innovations are not limited to independent efforts at the bottom of the organization, rather top management itself can be an important innovator (Rotemberg and Saloner 2000). In the same way that top management shapes the current strategy through its definition of the deliberate strategy, it may choose to fully redefine the strategy of the organization and then it becomes the source of radical innovations. The concept of *strategic innovation* captures the idea of radical innovation happening at the top of the organization. Strategic innovation is 'a fundamental re-conceptualization of what the business is about, which in turn leads to a dramatically different way of playing the game in the industry' (Markides 2000: 19). The strategic context of the top management team—different from the strategic context that they define for the rest of the organization—leads these managers to significantly change the strategy currently being pursued. Strategic innovation captures how strategy can be radically modified through the strategy formulation process that happens at the top of organizations. Top management's role in formulation is not limited to strategic incrementalism (Quinn 1980), which has been a frequent criticism and is blamed on static mental models (Mintzberg 1994). New models of strategy formulation have been proposed to provide perspectives that contemplate opportunities for radical innovations (Hamel and Prahalad 1994; Markides 2000; Christensen and Raynor 2003; Prahalad and Ramaswamy 2004). From a strategic process perspective, the strategic context of top management becomes another critical design variable to facilitate strategic innovation, a design variable where MCS are likely to play a relevant role (Lorange et al. 1986).

Incremental changes to the current strategy that originate at the top of the organization are reflected in deliberate strategy. Radical changes championed at the top lead to strategic innovation. When the innovation happens throughout the organization, it translates into emergent strategy through induced strategic actions when it is within the current strategy and through autonomous strategic actions when it is outside the current strategy.

A model of MCS design for innovation

Empirical evidence and theory reviewed earlier in the chapter point to a relevant role of MCS in innovation processes. However, they do not yet describe the effect of different types of innovation, different ways in which innovation emerges, and how innovation gets embedded in the strategy of the firm. Without a model that frames MCS within this context, the advancement of our knowledge about these systems is likely to remain unstructured. This section develops a typology of MCS based on current knowledge of the impact of different types of innovation (incremental and radical) and of the impact of the strategic process on strategic change: it is illustrated in Table 2.

MCS as structural context: executing deliberate strategy

The role of MCS to implement strategy has long been accepted (Anthony 1965). As part of the structural context, they support the translation of deliberate strategy into actions. Their relevance comes from their ability to execute efficiently and with speed—an important aspect when competitive advantage depends on timely delivery. They simplify the application of knowledge and leverage resources. Their strength—and, at the same time, their weakness—is their effectiveness in translating deliberate strategies into action plans, monitoring their execution, and

Table 2 A model of MCS for innovation strategy

Components of strategy	Organizational context	MCS role
Current strategy		
Deliberate strategy	Structural context	Support the execution of the deliberate strategy and translate it into value
Induced strategic actions	Structural context	Provide the framework for incremental innovations that refine the current strategy throughout the organization
Future strategy		
Autonomous strategic actions	Strategic context	Provide the context for the creation and growth of radical innovations that fundamentally redefine the strategy
Strategic innovation	Strategic context	Support the building of new competencies that radically redefine the strategy

identifying deviations for correction. In the process of enhancing effi-ciency, they potentially sacrifice the organization's ability to innovate.

In certain environments innovation is unwanted and MCS that focus on delivering value do not give up much by forgoing flexibility. At the extreme, they specify every action in every contingent state. These stand-ard operating procedures are required in high-risk environments—such as day-to-day operations of power generating plants where these systems integrate vast amount of knowledge and small deviations may have devastating consequences. Chip fabrication plants and their procedures are copied to the smallest detail from one site to another because the science is so complex that even small changes in the design may have large effects on productivity. MCS deliver the consistency and reliability to avoid costly mistakes. They specify how to execute procedures, how to identify significant deviations, and how to react to them.

Detailed standard operating procedures are at one extreme of the efficiency criterion—where innovation is ruled out in favour of safety. Efficiency also plays an important part in action controls (Merchant 1985)—systems that influence organizational actors by prescribing the actions they should take. These systems limit the action space and code certain behaviours with the objective of reducing risk (and the associated experimentation) and waste. Certain boundary systems—statements that define and communicate specific risks to be avoided, mostly business conduct boundaries—also block innovation in certain directions to reduce risk exposure (Simons 1995).

MCS also assist efficiency by facilitating delegation. They are the foundation of management by exception. Supervisors delegate execu-tion to subordinates knowing that MCS will monitor and capture any deviation from expectations. These systems leverage resources because they permit supervisors to reduce the attention that they devote to activities managed by exception. Anthony's original formulation best describes these systems: systems for strategy implementation first translate strategic plans into operational targets, then monitor whether these targets are achieved, and finally take actions to correct deviations from targets. Diagnostic systems, a 'primary tool for management-by-exception' (Simons 1995: 49), capture this concept.

Another aspect of MCS that rely on preset goals to deliver value is accountability. Goals have a motivational rather than a monitoring purpose and managers are held accountable to these goals. In contrast to standard operating procedures, here innovation is not such a block as it is disregarded. Managers can be innovative in achieving their goals, but these systems do not capture these innovations. They only create the motivational setting for managers to deliver performance. Diagnostic systems can also play this role to 'motivate, monitor, and reward achievement of specified goals' (Simons 1995: 5). Sales targets exemplify this argument; these targets are intended to motivate salespeople to deliver regardless of how they do it (other than conduct boundaries), thus ignoring any learning that may accrue to the individual salespeople. Budgets, the most common MCS to implement strategy, also use targets against which performance is compared. They do not specify actions but focus on the financial consequences of these actions. Because these systems typically track process outcomes, they have also been defined as results controls—systems that influence organizational actors by measuring the result of their actions.

The purpose of these MCS is to transform the current strategy into a set of actions that deliver the expected value. Accordingly, these systems are valued in terms of efficiency (ability to leverage existing resources) and speed (ability to quickly execute; at the expense of innovation and experiential learning). Because they forgo the latter two aspects, they are only effective in stable, mechanistic environments where the thermostat metaphor is most robust. Relying exclusively on these systems when these rather unique environmental conditions do not hold leads to coercive systems—systems that impose work procedures when granting voice (repair capability), context (transparency), and decision rights (flexibility) to the user are more appropriate (Adler and Borys 1996). The unsuitability of MCS to innovation, discussed in previous sections, comes from limiting these systems to their role in executing the deliberate strategy. When only this role is contemplated and innovation is needed (as most environments require), MCS become coercive and dysfunctional, sacrificing the long term for the sake of short-term performance. But when the organization has MCS to guide the emergent strategy, to craft radically new strategies, and to build strategic innovations, the role discussed in this section—executing the current strategy—is crucial to translate innovation into value.

MCS as structural context: guiding induced strategic actions

MCS can be designed to capture the learning that happens as processes are periodically enacted. Most environments are dynamic, with new situations emerging that require innovative solutions outside the existing codified knowledge. Systems to execute the current strategy ignore these solutions as noise to the process. In contrast, systems that guide induced strategic actions capture and code these experiences to improve execution. Learning here is not as much anticipatory as experiential. The interaction between day-to-day actions and deliberate strategy leads to knowledge creation and a better understanding of how to refine the current strategy; MCS can be designed to capture these incremental innovations to the current strategy.

Different interpretations of product development manuals in two companies exemplify this distinction. Both companies were in the medical devices industry. A first look at their product development process would suggest that both had good processes in place, with stages and gates, clear procedures intended to liberate development teams' attention from routine activities, and checklists to coordinate the support activities of all departments. However, when talking with the managers of the process two distinct realities emerged. In the first company, the manager saw her job as disciplining the project teams to follow the routine. She made sure that all the documents were in place, that every gate was properly documented, that every step in the process was carefully followed. Her objective was to maintain the routines—no change and strict adherence to it, which she saw as a blueprint to be closely followed. She perceived deviations from the manual as exceptions that required corrective action. Her interpretation of the manual was a system to facilitate efficient and speedy product development, not a system to capture and code new knowledge. Project managers saw her role as controlling them. In contrast, the manager in the second company saw her role very differently. She saw the routine as an evolving adaptive tool. She sat down with project teams to tailor the process to the project's needs, to make sure that the routine provided value to the teams. Not only was the routine adaptive, most importantly, the manager reviewed each finished project with the project team to update the product development manual and make it even more helpful the next time. Deviations from expectations were opportunities to bring about improvements to the current processes. The manual was alive, constantly evolving and incorporating learning. The product development manager saw MCS as not only helping execution but also capturing learning, which in the former company was lost.

In contrast to systems to deliver value where the knowledge is explicit, coded in the systems that govern the innovation process, systems for incremental innovation are intended to structure the interactions involved, support any search required, and translate the tacit knowledge—in the heads of the people but not being systematically accessed—generated every time a process is transformed into explicit knowledge (Nonaka 1994).

Innovation is a pivotal aspect of these types of MCS. By stimulating innovation, these systems refine existing organizational processes. Quality circles, a tool within the total quality management movement (Cole 1998), provide an illustration of these systems. Teams involved in quality circles have the sole purpose of improving existing processes. The organization funds them to gain competitive advantage through constant incremental innovations to current processes. They may do so by providing the infrastructure to periodically interact with external constituencies. Product development systems offer another illustration of systems with the objective of refining current processes. Systems within product development can be designed to establish constant feedback mechanisms with potential customers through market research, product concept development, and prototyping (Hippel 2001). These formalized, information-based procedures bring knowledge inside the company to stimulate innovation and translate it into a product. Because of the nature of customer knowledge, these innovations are typically incremental. Here, MCS are part of the enabling bureaucracy, maintaining a constant conversation between the current knowledge base and the current experiences of organizational members. MCS are not imposed regardless of the particular events facing employees; rather they support work by clarifying the context, giving voice and decision rights to adapt to employee needs. Moreover, they capture the knowledge developed and code it to enhance the ability of supporting organizational tasks. This knowledge, which advances existing processes, is associated with incremental innovation.

Finally, these MCS are part of the structural context and as such they have an effect on the strategic process. As part of the structural context of the firm, they are in charge of moving the current strategy forward. Because of the dynamism of the strategic process, top management needs to stimulate the relentless advancement of the current business model through incremental innovations in technology, products, processes, and strategies. These systems purposefully engage the organization in search activities, typically bounded by the framework that strategy defines, thus leading in most cases to incremental innovation. They provide clear goals, with the freedom and resources needed for innovation, the setting to exchange information and search for new solutions, and consistent information to gauge progress over time.

Because the information captured through these MCS is associated with the current strategy of the firm, the discussion tends to stay close to the current deliberate strategy and seldom leads to radical innovations in the business model. Planning mechanisms, such as strategic planning and budgeting, inasmuch as they facilitate exchange of information that stimulates organizational members to explore alternatives previously not considered—through budgetary participation or what-if analyses, they advance the current business model and code this progress into expectations.

Interactive systems—that top managers use to involve themselves regularly and personally in the decision activities of subordinates—stimulate discussion around the strategic uncertainties of the current business model (Simons 1995). The fact that interactive systems are defined at the top management level positions them as more adequate for incremental innovation, with the objective of making the strategy more robust to these uncertainties. The discussion around information deemed critical to the current business model that is stimulated by interactive systems frames the innovation such that current strategy is consolidated rather than totally redefined. In contrast to enabling bureaucracies that embed learning at the operational level, interactive systems capture incremental innovation associated with the formulation of the current strategy of the firm.

MCS as strategic context: crafting autonomous strategic actions

Autonomous strategic actions, which radically change the future strategy of a company, are more unpredictable than incremental innovation. They may happen anywhere in the organization, at any point in time. The process from ideation to value creation is much less structured, with periods when the path forward—technology, complementary assets, business assumptions, or interface with the organization—is unclear. Because radical innovation is outside the current strategy, it is managed through the strategic context rather than the structural context.

Autonomous strategic actions can be interpreted as a variation, selection, and retention process (Weick 1979). Because of the low odds associated with radical innovation, an organization that wants to follow an aggressive innovation strategy needs to create the appropriate setting to generate variation, put in place the context to select among very different alternatives, and design the organization to create a new business (Barnett and Burgelman 1996). An important piece of this soil is culture and, not surprisingly, it has received significant attention (Amabile et al. 1996; Tushman and O'Reilly 1997). However, the importance of culture does not imply that formal systems are unsuited and case studies suggest the need to examine them also (Van de Ven et al. 1999). For instance, organizations need to think how to organize, motivate, and evaluate people; how to allocate resources; how to monitor and when to intervene; and how to capture learning in a setting much more uncertain and alien than the current business model (Sathe 2003).

Because of their association with predictability, routines, and the structural context, MCS have received scant attention in this setting (Christiansen 2000). However, their presence has an effect on radical innovation and they can be used proactively to define the strategic context. Moreover, the fact that their characteristics in this role are almost opposite to those of traditional systems makes them an interesting research setting. They encourage experimentation, discovery, exceptions; the goals associated with these systems are broad and the path to them unknown; they support local efforts and nurture their way up the organization; they provide information for decision-making in a highly uncertain setting; and they contemplate value creation alternatives seldom used in routine processes.

Motivating organizational members to explore, experiment, and question encourages variation. Strategic intent (the gap between current resources and corporate aspirations: Hamel et al. 1994), stretch goals (Dess et al. 1998), or belief systems (Simons 1995) are potential approaches to create the motivation to experiment beyond the current strategy. The existence of stable goals that people can relate to has been found to enhance creativity (Amabile et al. 1996). However, strategy is about choosing, and strategic boundary systems (Simons 1995) impose a certain structure upon exploration and experimentation. Variation also gains from exposure to learning opportunities. Internal processes, such as interest groups, that bring together people with different training and experiences (Dougherty and Hardy 1996), and external collaborations that allow organizational members to explore alternative views may lead to the creative abrasion (Leonard-Barton 1995) needed for radical innovation. Access to resources, through slack that permits initial experimentation and funding that facilitates the growth of the project, is another aspect of the variation stage. Finally, variation requires the existence of systems to facilitate information exchange so that promising ideas are identified and supported. The roles of 'scouts' and 'coaches' (Kanter 1989) or the concept of an 'innovation hub' (Leifer et al. 2000) where ideas receive attention are examples of solutions through formal systems to the radical innovation management.

The resource allocation process also relies on MCS. However, the descriptions available about these systems (Van de Ven et al. 1999; Christiansen 2000) suggest a very different design. The requirements are sufficiently different from those within the structural context to suggest separating both types of funding processes, with resources being committed prior to examining the investment opportunities (Christensen and Raynor 2003). Because of their higher level of technological, market, and organizational risks, and longer time horizons, radical innovations appear as less attractive than incremental innovations using criteria—usually financial criteria—applied to the latter type of innovations. Radical innovations require a funding process that relies to a larger extent upon the qualitative appreciation of different types of experts, generates commitment from various organizational players to provide specific resources, and has frequently been compared to venture capital investments (Chesbrough 2000). In addition to the resource allocation process, the selection stage—when the innovation moves from the seed stage to a business proposition—requires MCS beyond resources to monitor and intervene in the project if required, to balance the tension between having access to organizational resources and protecting the innovation from the structural context that is designed to eliminate significant deviations, and to develop the complementary assets that the innovation requires.

The retention stage—when the innovation becomes part of the corporate strategy and is integrated into the structural context of the organization—has been identified as a key stage in the process (Van de Ven et al. 1999; Leifer et al. 2000; Burgelman 2002). The outcomes available are not limited to incorporating the innovation within the current organization—as it would happen with incremental innovation. In addition, the innovation may redefine the entire organization, become a separate business unit or a separate company as a spin-off, be sold as intellectual capital to another firm that has the complementary assets, or be included in a joint venture (Chesbrough 2000). Moreover, the transition has to be carefully managed, especially if it becomes part of the existing organization, and MCS help structuring this integration through planning, incentives, and training.

MCS as strategic context: building strategic innovation

Probably because of the mystique associated with a change down in the organization being able to redefine an industry or because of the management challenge of identifying, protecting, nurturing, and helping an idea succeed against the odds, autonomous strategic actions have received the most attention (Van de Ven et al. 1999; Hamel 2000; Burgelman 2002). However, top management is often the origin of radical innovations. Sometimes, these managers are the entrepreneurs that create the organization out of their idea; in other cases, they identify the need for a radical change and formulate the strategy that will respond to this need. Strategic innovation, the process of formulating a strategy at the top management level that radically changes the current strategy, also requires a well-managed strategic context. In the same way that structural context has two dimensions relevant to MCS—a dimension that delivers the value from the current strategy and another one that stimulates incremental innovation through induced strategic actions—strategic context has two dimensions. One dimension, presented in the previous section, stimulates the creation and nurturing of radical innovations throughout the organization. The other dimension, examined in this section, supports top management in evaluating the need for radical changes and the opportunities to formulate strategies that build upon radical innovations. In both cases, a successful radical innovation will be incorporated as part of the corporate strategy and the structural context will be redesigned to implement and refine this new strategy.

MCS that support incremental innovation may be a relevant part of the strategic context. These systems examine ways in which the current strategy can be improved and, accordingly, they supply information on strategic uncertainties. Most of the time, this information leads to refinements; but careful analysis may in some cases suggest radical changes. For instance, measurement systems such as balanced scorecards rely on maps of the current strategy (Kaplan and Norton 1996); the information that they provide may be used not only as a monitoring system to track how the organization implements the strategy, but also as interactive systems (Simons 1995) that highlight opportunities for incremental improvements, and for radical changes in strategy that respond to risks that threaten the current strategy. A similar analysis is applicable to any other system used to monitor the current strategy, such as strategic planning systems, budgets, or profitability reports.

Creating a certain level of uneasiness with the status quo, through stretch goals, demanding objectives help stimulate search. Having adequate systems to capture and move these ideas up to top management, traditional systems such as budgets or strategic planning systems may fulfil this role, as may alternatives such as second-generation suggestion systems (Robinson and Stern 1997). Once the initial idea is formulated, experimentation and exploration of the idea benefits from progress reports, analysis of external developments, and open questions to the future of the innovation.

Finally, strategic innovation benefits from MCS that carefully monitor the environment (Lorange et al. 1986). From business opportunities associated with changes in regulation, trends in customer needs, potential acquisitions, opening of new markets, or new technologies, top management relies on a strategic context that will keep it informed about these developments—through not only informal networks but also MCS that extend top management information network beyond a limited set of informants. Moreover, discovery events require further analysis involving local experiments, where MCS play a significant role in leveraging the learning associated with them, and building economic models that rely on control systems such as scenario planning.

Managing learning in strategic innovation also contrasts with learning in the structural context. While incremental innovation relies to a large extent on plans that work as a reference point to gauge learning, the explicit knowledge that frames these plans is not there for radical innovation. Instead, MCS help proactively manage the learning process. The planning involved does not outline specific reference points; rather it lays out the motivation for developing new competencies, deploys the resources to developing competencies, and puts together the measurement systems to adapt the new business model as learning evolves. MCS also structure a constant back-and-forth between vision and action through periodic meetings and deadlines to review progress. In contrast to incremental innovation, where systems to deliver value compare plans with progress to make sure that the project is on track, systems to build competencies use these periodic deadlines to pace the organization and to bring together different players to exchange information and crystallize knowledge. These meetings are comparable to board meetings in start-ups. Board meetings pace the organization, force management to leave tactics and look at the strategy, and bring together people with different backgrounds to give the company a fresh new look.

Conclusions

The aim of this chapter is to highlight an important link between strategy and MCS, namely the role of these systems in bringing innovation to strategy. This idea, grounded on the strategic process literatures' concepts of structural and strategic contexts, forms the basis of the model proposed. Traditional MCS research has focused on the role they play as tools to implement the deliberate strategy of the organization. More recently, their role within the learning process associated with incremental innovations to the current strategy—where they provide the infrastructure for this learning to happen—has been researched. While the attention to these two aspects of MCS as a critical part of the structural context of organizations is granted, our current understanding of how these systems affect the strategic context is much less developed. Descriptions of radical innovations to strategy challenge the unproven assumption that MCS are unsuited for these types of innovation. However, these descriptions do not directly deal with the role of MCS and their evidence is incomplete and lacks the theoretical background required to structure this question. The model presented in the chapter proposes two different aspects of MCS within the strategic context of the firm. The first one supports radical innovation efforts throughout the organization. The second one deploys the infrastructure that top management needs to recognize potential risks to their current strategy and identifies opportunities that grant a redefinition of the strategy.

Certain MCS are more attuned to the particular demands of each of these four roles, but they should not be seen as mutually exclusive categories. For example, the execution of a particular project—governed through systems to implement deliberate strategy—may raise some questions that lead to a radical idea. Similarly, systems to refine the current strategy may uncover a potential risk that leads to strategic innovation. Moreover, strategic process and MCS, as an important part of the organizational context, are dynamic. In particular, the role of MCS will change as the strategy changes. Young strategies may require that organizations put more emphasis on systems for incremental innovation to accelerate the learning process associated with refining a new strategy. As strategies mature, the weight on these incremental learning mechanisms is expected to decay in favour of systems to implement strategy. Similarly, the emphasis on the strategic context may vary with the success of the current strategy, with the location of relevant knowledge, or with the dynamism of the environment.

References

Abernethy, M. A. and Brownell, P. (1997). 'Management Control Systems in Research and Development Organizations: The Role of Accounting, Behavior and Personnel Controls', *Accounting, Organizations and Society*, 22: 233–49.

—— —— (1999). 'The Role of Budgets in Organizations Facing Strategic Change: An Exploratory Study', *Accounting, Organizations and Society*, 24(3): 189–204.

Adler, P. S. and Borys, B. (1996). 'Two Types of Bureaucracy: Enabling and Coercive', *Administrative Science Quarterly*, 41(1): 61–89.

Ahrens, T. and Chapman, C. (2002). 'The Structuration of Legitimate Performance Measures and Management: Day-to-Day Contests of Accountability in a U.K. Restaurant Chain', *Management Accounting Research*, 13(2): 1–21.

—— —— (2004). 'Accounting for Flexibility and Efficiency: A Field Study of Management Control Systems in a Restaurant Chain', *Contemporary Accounting Research*, 21(2): 271–301.

Allen, T. J. (1977). 'Communications, Technology Transfer, and the Role of Technical Gatekeeper', *R&D Management*, 14–21.

Amabile, T. M., Conti, R., Coon, H., Lazenby, J., and Herron, M. (1996). 'Assessing the Work Environment for Creativity', *Academy of Management Journal*, 39: 1154–84.

Andrews, K. R. (1971). *The Concept of Corporate Strategy*. Homewood, IL: Irwin.

Ansoff, H. I. (1977). 'The State of Practice in Planning Systems', *Sloan Management Review* (Winter): 1–24.

Anthony, R. N. (1965). *The Management Control Function*. Boston, MA: Harvard Business School Press.

Ashby, W. R. (1960). *Design for a Brain: The Origin of Adaptive Behavior*. New York: John Wiley.

Barnett, W. P. and Burgelman, R. A. (1996). 'Evolutionary Perspectives on Strategy', *Strategic Management Journal*, 17: 5–19.

Boulding, K. E. (1956). *The Image: Knowledge in Life and Society*. Ann Arbor, MI: University of Michigan Press.

Bower, J. L. (1970). *Managing the Resource Allocation Process*. Boston, MA: Graduate School of Business Administration, Harvard University.

Brown, S. L. and Eisenhardt, K. M. (1997). 'The Art of Continuous Change: Linking Complexity Theory and Time-Paced Evolution in Relentlessly Shifting Organizations', *Administrative Science Quarterly*, 42: 1–34.

Burgelman, R. A. (1983). 'A Model of the Interaction of Strategic Behavior, Corporate Context, and the Concept of Strategy', *Academy of Management Review*, 8: 61–70.

—— (2002). *Strategy is Destiny: How Strategy-Making Shapes a Company's Future*. New York: Free Press.

Burns, T. and Stalker, G. M. (1961). *The Management of Innovation*. London: Tavistock.

Cardinal, L. 2001. 'Technological Innovation in the Pharmaceutical Industry: The Use of Organizational Control in Managing Research and Development', *Organization Science*, 12(1): 19–36.

Chapman, C. S. (1997). 'Reflections on a Contingent View of Accounting', *Accounting, Organizations and Society*, 22(2): 189–205.

—— (1998). 'Accountants in Organisational Networks', *Accounting, Organizations and Society*, 23(8): 737–66.

Chenhall, R. (2005). 'Content and Process Approaches to Studying Strategy and Management Control', in C. Chapman (ed.), *Controlling Strategy: Management, Accounting and Performance*. Oxford: Oxford University Press.

—— and Morris, D. (1986). 'The Impact of Structure, Environment, and Interdependence on the Perceived Usefulness of Management Accounting Systems', *Accounting Review*, 61(1): 16–35.

—— —— (1995). 'Organic Decision and Communication Processes and Management Accounting Systems in Entrepreneurial and Conservative Business Organizations', *Omega, International Journal of Management Science*, 23(5): 485–97.

Chesbrough, H. (2000). 'Designing Corporate Ventures in the Shadow of Private Venture Capital', *California Management Review*, 42(3): 31–49.

Christensen, C. M. and Raynor, M. E. (2003). *Innovator's Solution: Creating and Sustaining Successful Growth*. Boston, MA: Harvard Business School Press.

Christiansen, J. A. (2000). *Building the Innovative Organization: Management Systems that Encourage Innovation*. New York: St. Martin's Press.

Clark, K. and Fujimoto, T. (1991). *Product Development Performance*. Boston, MA: Harvard Business School Press.

Cole, R. E. (1998). 'Learning from the Quality Movement: What Did and Didn't Happen and Why?', *California Management Review*, 41(1): 43–74.

Cooper, R. G. (1995). 'Developing New Products on Time, in Time', *Research Technology Management*, 49–57.

Damanpour, F. (1991). 'Organizational Innovation: A Meta-Analysis of Effects of Determinants and Moderators', *Academy of Management Journal*, 34(3): 555–90.

—— (1996). 'Organizational Complexity and Innovation: Developing and Testing Contingency Models', *Management Science*, 42(5): 693–701.

Davila, T. (2000). 'An Empirical Study on the Drivers of Management Control Systems' Design in New Product Development', *Accounting, Organizations and Society*, 25(4/5): 383–409.

Dess, G. G., Picken, J. C., and Lyon, D. W. (1998). 'Transformational Leadership: Lessons from U. S. Experience', *Long Range Planning*, 31(5): 722–32.

Dougherty, D. (1992). 'Interpretive Barriers to Successful Product Innovation in Large Firms', *Organization Science*, 3: 179–202.

—— and Hardy, C. (1996). 'Sustained Product Innovation in Large, Mature Organizations: Overcoming Innovation-to-Organization Problems', *Academy of Management Journal*, 39: 1120–53.

Ettlie, J., Bridges, W., and O'Keefe, R. (1984). 'Organization Strategy and Structural Differences for Radical Versus Incremental Innovation', *Management Science*, 30: 682–95.

Feldman, M. S. and Rafaeli, A. (2002). 'Organizational Routines as Sources of Connections and Understandings', *Journal of Management Studies*, 39: 309–32.

Fiol, C. M. (1996). 'Squeezing Harder Doesn't Always Work: Continuing the Search for Consistency in Innovation Research', *Academy of Management Review*, 21(4): 1012–21.

Gavetti, G. and Levinthal, D. (2000). 'Looking Forward and Looking Backward: Cognitive and Experiential Search', *Administrative Science Quarterly*, 45: 113–37.

Green, S., Garvin, M., and Smith, L. (1995). 'Assessing a Multidimensional Measure of Radical Innovation', *IEEE Transactions Engineering Management*, 42(3): 203–14.

Hamel, G. (2000). *Leading the Revolution*. Boston, MA: Harvard Business School Press.

—— and Prahalad, C. K. (1994). *Competing for the Future*. Boston, MA: Harvard Business School Press.

Hippel, E. V. (2001). 'Innovation by User Communities: Learning from Open-Source Software', *Sloan Management Review*, 42(4): 82–7.

Hoskisson, R. E., Hitt, M. A., Wan, W. P., and Yiu, D. (1999). 'Theory and Research in Strategic Management: Swings of a Pendulum', *Journal of Management*, 25(3): 417–56.

Howard-Grenville, J. A. (2003). ' "Making It Work": The Resilience of Organizational Routines', Working paper, Boston University.

Jackson, S. E. and Schuler, R. S. (1985). 'A Meta-Analysis and Conceptual Critique of Research on Role Ambiguity and Role Conflict in Work Settings', *Organizational Behavior and Human Decision Process*, 36: 17–78.

Kanter, R. M. (1989). *When Giants Learn to Dance*. New York: Simon & Schuster.

Kaplan, R. S. and Norton, D. P. (1996). 'Using the Balanced Scorecard as a Strategic Management System', *Harvard Business Review*, 74(1): 75–86.

Khandwalla, P. N. (1972). 'The Effect of Different Types of Competition on the Use of Management Controls', *Journal of Accounting Research*: 275–85.

Langfield-Smith, K. (1997). 'Management Control Systems and Strategy: a Critical Review', *Accounting, Organizations and Society*, 22: 207–32.

—— (2005). 'New Directions and Achievements in Management Control Systems and Strategy', In C. Chapman (ed.), *Controlling Strategy: Management, Accounting and Performance*. Oxford: Oxford University Press.

Leifer, R., McDermott, C. M., Colarelli O'Connor, G., Peters, L. S., Rice, M., and Veryzer, R. W. (2000). *Radical Innovation: How Mature Companies Can Outsmart Upstarts*. Boston, MA: Harvard Business School Press.

Leonard-Barton, D. (1992). 'Core Capabilities and Core Rigidities: A Paradox in Managing New Product Development', *Strategic Management Journal*, 13: 111–25.

—— (1995). *Wellsprings of Knowledge: Building and Sustaining the Sources of Innovation*. Boston, MA: Harvard Business School Press.

Lorange, P., Scott-Morton, M. F., and Goshal, S. (1986). *Strategic Control*. St Paul, MN: West Publishing.

Lukka, K. (1988). 'Budgetary Biasing in Organizations: Theoretical Framework and Empirical Evidence', *Accounting, Organizations and Society*, 13(3): 281–301.

McGrath, M. D. (1995). *Product Strategy for High-Technology Companies*. New York: Irwin.

Markides, C. (1997). 'Strategic Innovation', *Sloan Management Review*, 9–23.

—— (2000). *All the Right Moves: A Guide to Crafting Breakthrough Strategy*. Boston, MA: Harvard Business School Press.

Merchant, K. A. (1985). *Control in Business Organizations*. Boston, MA: Pitman.

Miner, A. S., Bassoff, P., and Moorman, C. (2001). 'Organizational Improvisation and Learning: A Field Study', *Administrative Science Quarterly*, 46: 304–37.

Mintzberg, H. (1978). 'Patterns in Strategy Formation', *Management Science*, 24: 934–48.

—— (1994). 'The Fall and Rise of Strategic Planning', *Harvard Business Review*, 74(3): 75–84.

Mouritsen. (1999). 'The Flexible Firm: Strategies for a Subcontractor's Management Control', *Accounting, Organizations and Society*, 24(1): 31–56.

Nixon, B. (1998). 'Research and Development Performance Measurement: A Case Study', *Management Accounting Research*, 9: 329–55.

Noda, T. and Bower, J. L. (1996). 'Strategy Making as Iterated Process of Resource Allocation', *Strategic Management Journal*, 17(7): 159–93.

Nonaka, I. (1994). 'A Dynamic Theory of Organizational Knowledge Creation', *Organization Science*, 5(1): 14–38.

Ouchi, W. (1979). 'A Conceptual Framework for the Design of Organizational Control Mechanisms', *Management Science*, 25: 833–48.

Prahalad, C. K. and Ramaswamy, V. (2004). *The Future of Competition: Co-creating Unique Value with Customers*. Boston, MA: Harvard Business School Press.

Quinn, J. B. (1980). *Strategies for Change: Logical Incrementalism*. Homewood, IL: Irwin.

Robinson, A. G. and Stern, S. (1997). *Corporate Creativity: How Innovation and Improvement Happen*. San Francisco, CA: Berrett-Koehler.

Rockness, H. O. and Shields, M. D. (1988). 'Organizational Control Systems in Research and Development', *Accounting, Organizations and Society*, 9: 165–77.

Rotemberg J. J. and Saloner, G. (2000). 'Visionaries, Managers, and Strategic Direction', *RAND Journal of Economics*, 31: 693–716.

Sathe, V. (2003). *Corporate Entrepreneurship: Top Managers and New Business Creation.* Cambridge, UK: Cambridge University Press.

Shields, J. F. and Shields, M. D. (1998). 'Antecedents of Participative Budgeting', *Accounting, Organizations and Society*, 23: 49–76.

Simons, R. (1987). 'Accounting Control Systems and Business Strategy: An Empirical Analysis', *Accounting, Organizations and Society*, 12(4): 357–75.

—— (1995). *Levers of Control: How Managers Use Innovative Control Systems to Drive Strategic Renewal.* Boston, MA: Harvard Business School Press.

Stevens, F., Philipsen, H., and Diedriks, J. (1992). 'Organizational and Professional Predictors of Physician Satisfaction', *Organization Studies*, 13(1): 35–50.

Tushman, M. L. and O'Reilly, III, C. A. (1997). *Winning through Innovation: A Practical Guide to Leading Organizational Change and Renewal.* Boston, MA: Harvard Business School Press.

Van de Ven, A. H., Polley, D. E., Garud, R., and Venkataraman, S. (1999). *The Innovation Journey.* New York: Oxford University Press.

Walton, R. E. (1985). 'Toward a Strategy of Eliciting Employee Commitment Based on Policies of Mutuality', in R. E. Walton and P. R. Lawrence (eds.), *HRM Trends and Challenges.* Boston, MA: Harvard Business School Press.

Weick, K. E. (1979). *The Social Psychology of Organizing* (1st edn., 1969). Reading, MA: Addison-Wesley.

—— Sutcliffe, K. M., and Obstfeld, D. (1999). 'Organizing for High Reliability: Processes of Collective Mindfulness', in R. I. Sutton and B. M. Staw (eds.), *Research in Organizational Behavior.* Stanford, CA: JAI Press.

Zirger, B. J. and Maidique, M. A. (1990). 'A Model of New Product Development: An Empirical test', *Management Science*, 36(7): 867–84.

What Do We Know about Management Control Systems and Strategy?

Kim Langfield-Smith

Over the past decade, there has been a massive growth in published research that investigates the interrelationship between management control systems (MCS) and strategy. It is a popular theme and much of the research has important practical implications for the design of MCS and the formulation and implementation of strategy in a range of organizations. The previous two chapters set out a broad range of theoretical perspectives that have emerged to help us understand the ways in which MCS both direct strategic thinking and influence behaviours towards the attainment of strategic goals. This chapter focuses on some key areas of empirical research that investigate strategy and MCS.

The purpose of the chapter is to summarize and explain what we know about this relationship, and what we need to investigate in the future. The objective is not to provide a comprehensive review of all papers that have been written in the area, but to explore this relationship through examining a series of issues that have emerged as central in this literature. These are the relationships between performance measures and reward systems including the balanced scorecard (BSC) and business strategy; capital investment processes and the initiation of strategic investment projects; interactive controls and strategic change; operational strategies and control systems; the design and operation of MCS in interfirm relationships, such as joint ventures and outsourcing; and the strategic style of corporate headquarters (HQ) and the MCS of business units.

Each of these themed areas is appraised, to assess what we can conclude in terms of the practical implications of the research. The chapter concludes with a discussion of some of the areas where we are still developing our knowledge. Some of these topics will be explored in detail in subsequent chapters.

Early research

Despite the intense interest in business strategy in the academic and professional literatures, up to the mid-1990s there were relatively few empirical papers published in the area of strategy and MCS. This was emphasized by Langfield-Smith (1997), who provided a review and critique of empirical research in the area and highlighted a range of deficiencies and areas for future research.[1] This review concluded that research published up to that time was fragmentary, and the approach taken and research findings were sometimes conflicting.

Up to the mid-1990s, much of the research that studied strategy and MCS adopted a contingency perspective, where the focus was on the fit between business strategy, some aspects of MCS, other contextual variables, and sometimes organizational effectiveness. Business strategy was characterized using various typologies: prospector/defender, differentiation/cost leadership, and build/harvest. It has been argued that when common characteristics of these strategy classifications are considered, particularly the degree of environmental uncertainty, prospector/differentiation/build strategies are at one end of a continuum, and defender/cost leadership/harvest are at the other end (Shank and Govindarajan 1992; Langfield-Smith 1997). This apparent equivalence makes it easier to compare and integrate the results of various studies.

The research of the 1980s and 1990s was dominated by studies that utilized surveys, which took a snapshot of the status of the business strategy and various aspects of MCS at a point in time. Many of these studies adopted a content approach, while only a few used case study approaches to focus more on process. However, the Langfield-Smith (1997) review took place at an early stage in the 'life cycle' of MCS/strategy research, and it is timely to revisit the area to review achievements and new directions.

In the following sections, recent research that addresses MCS and strategy is discussed by major theme.

Performance measures and reward systems and business strategy

A significant area of research in this area is the fit between strategy and performance and reward systems. Relative to other published studies in strategy/MCS, this is one area where there is a critical mass (Langfield-Smith 1997). When the 'equivalence' of various strategic typologies used

---

[1] Langfield-Smith (1997) provided a review of survey research up to 1992 and case study research up to 1995.

in these studies is taken into account, the findings are consistent. More recent work has focused on the BSC and its capacity to direct strategic thinking and behaviours.

Simons (1987), Govindarajan (1988), Gupta (1987), Porter (1980), and Govindarajan and Gupta (1985) provide consistent evidence that objective performance evaluation and reward systems support defender strategies, whereas for prospector strategies more subjective performance evaluation is appropriate. One aspect that may be driving this consistency is the level of environmental uncertainty associated with prospector-type strategies and defender-type strategies. Prospector-type strategies are usually associated with high levels of environmental uncertainty, where it may be difficult to set targets accurately and to measure objectively managerial performance. Many studies have found a positive relationship between high environmental uncertainty and subjective performance evaluation (see Briers and Hirst (1990) for a review). In these situations, critical success factors include new product development, innovation, and R&D. These goals tend to be long term and difficult to quantify, and so may be better served by subjective measures. Defender-like strategies are associated with low environmental uncertainty and a focus on stability and internal efficiency implies there is a high knowledge of input-output relationships. Thus, it is easier to develop objective performance measures and targets.

In Langfield-Smith (1997), areas for future research were identified: the mix of salary and non-salary components of rewards, the potential for linking managerial performance to both business unit and corporate performance, the frequency of performance measures and reward payments, and performance and rewards systems of employees other than middle and senior managers. Chenhall and Langfield-Smith (2003) address the last of these future research areas. They provide a detailed case study of how a performance measurement and gainsharing reward system was used to achieve strategic change over a fifteen-year period. The gainsharing system applied to employees and managers at all levels, and was introduced to encourage increased productivity, at a time when the competitive market was stable and predictable. Targets were based on material and labour productivity and the strategic orientation of the business was towards productivity, efficiency, and profitability. In its early years, the gainsharing scheme was successful in overcoming hostility and low morale within the workforce, and it was successful in encouraging the cooperation of employees to work towards the successful implementation of strategic initiatives. Gainsharing is a mechanistic form of control system, and hence it was supportive of the high level of certainty and stability in the external and internal environment and of managers' attempts to encourage organizational trust.

Over time, the company found itself competing in an increasingly competitive marketplace as global competitors began to enter local markets, and as customers increased their demands for high-quality products and prompt delivery. The company came to focus on cost reduction, cycle time, quality, and flexibility. The measures within the gainsharing scheme were adjusted to reflect increased needs for productivity improvements. However, the company found it necessary to develop more creative and innovative ways of competing, to boost overall competitiveness and performance to higher levels. A series of management initiatives were introduced, such as total quality management (TQM) and value-added management, and eventually self-managed work teams were formed. During these developments, the gainsharing scheme remained, but was not as effective as in the early days. The firm introduced team-based structures to enhance employee enthusiasm to work towards sustaining strategic change. However, this did not result in significant performance improvements. This result was attributed, in part, to the continued role of the gainsharing scheme, a mechanistic control, which inhibited the development of the personal trust that was needed to encourage employees to adopt creative and flexible approaches to management and to work effectively in team structures.

Since the early 1990s, BSC has emerged as a popular framework for combining financial and non-financial performance measures. It has been well documented and praised in a range of professional journals. By providing explicit links between strategy, goals, performance measures, and outcomes the BSC is presented as the key to achieving high-level performance (Kaplan and Norton 1992, 1996). The BSC is said to provide a powerful tool for communicating strategic intent and motivating performance towards strategic goals (Ittner and Larcker 1998). However, despite the high profile and apparent high levels of acceptance of BSC in practice, there has been only limited research attention given to testing the claims or outcomes of the BSC and the processes involved in using the BSC for its intended purposes (Ittner and Larcker 1998; Ittner et al. 2003b; Malina and Selto 2001; Bisbe and Otley 2004).

Hoque and James (2000) was one of the first papers to address empirically the BSC and strategy linkage. Taking a contingency approach, they hypothesized that organizational performance is dependent on the usage of BSC, which was influenced by three contextual variables: organizational size, stage of product life cycle, and strength of market position. BSC usage was measured by asking managers the extent to which they used twenty performance measures to assess the organization's performance. These measures covered the four dimensions of the Kaplan and Norton (1992) BSC. This study found that larger organizations were more likely to make use of a mix of measures. One reason suggested was that larger firms can more easily afford to support a more sophisticated system of performance measures. It was also suggested that firms that had a higher proportion of new products also made greater use of the BSC. However, there was no relationship found between market position and the use of BSC measures. An important feature of the BSC that was not investigated in this study was the 'fit' between the design of the BSC and the strategy of the firm. The measure that was used to assess usage of BSC did not assess the cause-and-effect linkages between the measures within and between the different perspectives, nor did it assess the alignment of these measures with the competitive strategy of the firm. This is critical, as the BSC is not just a collection of financial and non-financial measures; it is an integrated set of measures based on the firm's business model (Kaplan and Norton 1996). Even so, it has been argued that even when measures are selected to reflect a business model, major shifts in the environment can cast doubt on whether 'balance' has or will continue to be achieved (Ittner and Larcker 1998).

Ittner et al. (2003a) studied how different types of performance measures were used in a subjective BSC bonus plan, in a financial services firm. Using a BSC to reward managers has the potential to counter many of the criticisms of short-term accounting-based reward systems. However, Ittner et al. (2003a) found that the varying subjective weighting given by managers to performance measures allowed supervisors to ignore many of the performance measures when undertaking evaluations and awarding bonuses, even when some of those measures were leading indicators of the bank's strategic objectives of financial performance and customer growth. In addition, a large proportion of the bonuses awarded were not a 'legitimate' part of the system, as they were based on criteria not included in the BSC. The weightings used in the reward system were regarded with uncertainty and criticized by managers as being based on favoritism. The BSC and the reward system were abandoned.

What is of interest in this case study is how an apparently 'balanced' scorecard of measures was used in a way that was inconsistent with the original 'good intentions'. The focus of the measures used to award bonuses was more on achieving financial outcomes. It seems that in some situations the technical design of a reward system or BSC may be less important that the implementation issues. This issue is expanded in Hansen and Mouritsen (2005). Ittner et al. (2003a) argued that psychology-based explanations can be more relevant in explaining the success of a compensation scheme than economic-based explanations. Further support for the importance of implementation of the BSC is provided by Banker et al. (2004) in their experimental study of the judgment effects of performance measures and strategy. They found that the evaluations of business unit managers were influenced more by measures linked to strategy than those not linked to strategy, but only when managers are familiar with details of the business unit strategies.

One innovative study of the BSC is Malina and Selto (2001), which is a case study that focuses on the effectiveness of the BSC as a management control to communicate strategy. The BSC is designed to aid in communication by specifying the causal linkages between various performance measures and strategic outcomes, and hence provides an understanding of the decisions and activities that must be followed to achieve high financial performance (Kaplan and Norton 1996). Malina and Selto (2001: 54) summarized the characteristics of an effective management control device that can lead to the achievement of targeted outcomes as having the following control attributes:

First, attain strategic alignment:

- A *comprehensive* but parsimonious set of measures of critical performance variables, linked with strategy;
- Critical performance measures *causally linked* to valued organizational outcomes;
- *Effective*—accurate, objective, and verifiable—performance measures, which appear to be related to effective communication.

Second, to further promote positive motivation, an effective management control device should have the attributes of:

- Performance measures that reflect managers' *controllable actions* and/or *influenceable actions*,
- Performance targets or *appropriate benchmarks* that are challenging but attainable,
- Performance measures that are related to *meaningful rewards*.
(Italics from original reference).

Malina and Selto (2001) stated that adherence to these attributes within the BSC should lead to strategic alignment and positive performance outcomes for the organization. The case study provided evidence that the BSC may provide *opportunities* for the development and communication of strategy. In their case study, managers reorganized their resources and activities to achieve the required performance targets, which they perceived as improving the overall performance of the company. However, like all performance measurement systems there were difficulties experienced in the design and implementation of the BSC, which influenced the perceived credibility of the BSC and resulted in conflict and tension that led to the inability of the BSC to meet its stated outcomes. Difficulties included the development of inaccurate or subjective measures, top–down rather than participatory communication process, and the use of inappropriate benchmarks for performance evaluation. There should be little surprise at these shortcomings, as these types of difficulties are common to performance measurement systems in general (see Merchant 1989; Simons 2000). In particular, Ittner et al. (2003b) found that subjectivity in the design of the performance measures and reward system in the BSC of a financial services firm led to uncertainty and complaints among managers, and the abandonment of the BSC. We might expect that the BSC will share some design issues with that of other 'non-balanced' performance measurement systems.

Capital investment processes and initiation of strategic investments

There has been only limited research on controls over capital investment decisions and business strategy. This is despite the significant implications that many capital investment decisions have for the strategic direction and the long-term success of a business.

Some of the literature of the 1980s and early 1990s took a contingency approach to considering the form of capital expenditure evaluation process that should be used under various organizational and strategy situations (Larcker 1981; Haka 1987; Shank and Govindarajan 1992). For example, Haka (1987) focused on the fit between the use of DCF techniques for capital expenditure evaluation and specific contingencies of business strategy, external environment, information systems characteristics, reward systems structure, and degree of decentralization. Another stream of research highlights the limitations of the use of accounting-based methods to evaluate capital investments, arising from the difficulty of incorporating measures of strategic issues that go to the heart of a firm's competitiveness (Kaplan 1986; Samson et al. 1991). An outcome of this research stream is the development of decision rules for tailoring capital investment decision models to a given strategy. However, these static decision models do not provide insights into how control systems can encourage the initiation of capital investment proposals that support a specific strategy and the long-term performance of a firm (Slagmulder 1997). While Haka (1987) states that the firm's strategy influences the search process for attractive capital investments, encouraging managers to direct their attention to certain forms of projects, there is only limited research that has examined the MCS processes that can be used to provide incentives to direct attention towards such strategic searches. These are even more important in large complex organizations, where there is high reliance on indirect ways of controlling behaviour and decisions. O'Leary and Miller (2005) provide a case study of capital investment decisions.

Slagmulder (1997) takes a grounded theory approach to study the control systems associated with the evaluation of multiple investment projects across six companies. Rather than aligning specific forms of controls with specific forms of strategy, she focuses on how the MCS for strategic investment decisions (SIDs) adapt as a response to strategic change. She proposes that the primary role for the control systems used in SIDs is to achieve alignment between the firm's investment stream and its strategy. Specifically, as the external environment of the firm changes, the MCS used to control SIDs must also be modified to maintain strategic alignment in the selection and evaluation of strategic investment projects.

Strategic misalignment can be caused by vertical or horizontal information asymmetry about the strategy of the organization, a lack of understanding about the strategic implications of an investment, and a lack of goal congruence among managers at different levels. Such strategic misalignment can be apparent in four ways. First, there may be poor strategic fit that can lead to valuable projects never being proposed or overlooked in the evaluation process, or inappropriate projects being approved. Second, there may be low responsiveness in the MCS where the procedures are poorly structured and inefficient, delaying decision-making. Third, an inefficient MCS can be in place involving too many managers and excessive managerial time. Finally, there may be inefficient use of capital though approval of investments with low returns or of duplicate investments in different parts of the firm.

Slagmulder (1997) proposed four ways for changing controls in the face of a changing environment and strategy: introducing new control mechanisms for SIDs, changing the tightness of controls, changing the degree of formalization of controls, and changing the locus of decision-making. For example, a change in strategy may cause the attractiveness of certain projects to decline, and the guidelines over the mix of projects that senior management advises may be submitted for approval may change. In addition, the availability of a new technology in the market-place may lead to a shift in strategy and to a loosening of controls over the level of investment hurdles for those technology-type projects, or to a shift in responsibility away from middle managers to more senior managers who can speedily make decisions to invest in the right technology. For the alignment process to work, the information that flows up and down the organization must be effective.

This study provides a perspective of how the processes for encouraging the initiation and the evaluation of various capital investment proposals may be adapted to accommodate and support changes in business strategy. So rather than matching the type of strategy to the attributes of MCS, the focus is on continually adapting MCS to provide incentives and encouragement for managers to submit capital investment proposals that support an evolving strategy. The drive to achieve strategic alignment underlies the process.

Miller and O'Leary (1997) also focus on the processes of aligning capital investment decisions with strategy. They provide a case study of changes that were made to controls over capital budgeting practices at Caterpillar in 1997 to accommodate a change in focus from a mass production technology to flexible manufacturing systems. Like many organizations, Caterpillar evaluated capital investment proposals as discrete projects, and this was thought appropriate in managing investments in the company's mass production technologies. Post-audits of some investments were undertaken to assess whether outcomes for asset functionality and net present value (NPV) matched forecasts. However, this system failed to recognize the complementarity between some investment projects.

A new control system was developed based on defining and managing 'investment bundles', which were capital investment proposals consisting of diverse and mutually reinforcing assets needed to manufacture a set of core product modules. Investment bundles were formed to improve the functionality, cost, and competitiveness of key product assemblies. Plant managers were given the task of replacing low-velocity functional plant layouts with high-velocity, core-product production modules, with integrated technologies to reverse the company's severe cost disadvantage relative to competitors, and to increase to production responsiveness to shifts in demand.

The evaluation of a proposed investment bundles took place through a 'concept review', which aimed to ensure that the proposal supported the firm-level vision of modern manufacturing. Managers needed to provide a 'convincing demonstration' that the proposal would improve the competitiveness of manufacturing processes. This process was described by some managers as 'tense, difficult and painful'. Senior head office (HO) managers examined the concept at a high level of detail and plant managers were encouraged to learn from other plants' experiences.

The implementation of capital investments was managed through 'bundle monitors', where each investment bundle was regarded as a responsibility centre. These performance reports were given high status within the company and became one of the three major measurement systems for cost management at the plant level. Results for each investment bundle were compared with internal and external benchmarks to monitor the impact of the implementation on competitiveness. Process capability targets were developed for a specific investment bundle and were particularly important in measuring the performance of competitive design and development, and the internal rate of return (IRR) needed to be traced to improvements in product and process competitiveness. Bundle monitors were used intensely by senior managers to facilitate the implementation of investment bundles that were underperforming.

This case provides an example of how control systems can reinforce the new strategy at the proposal, evaluation, and monitoring stages of capital investments. Intense involvement in the process by senior managers through consultation, meetings, and reports was important in emphasizing the critical strategic issues and in encouraging managers to orient their thinking towards the new strategy. This process of *interactive use* of control systems (see the following section) and the heavy emphasis on assessing the strategic impact of the expenditure is a stark contrast to 'traditional' capital investment expenditure and evaluation controls that emphasize individual projects and their impact on NPV.

Interactive controls and strategic change

Simons (1990, 1995) presented a framework that highlights how MCS can be used by senior management to direct attention to areas of strategic uncertainties and thus effect strategic change. When senior managers select controls to be used interactively, they pay frequent and regular attention to monitoring these controls. This sends signals to all organizational members to collect relevant information, and to engage in face-to face dialogue and debate, which leads to a focus on strategic uncertainties. This process may lead to strategic change, through the formation of emergent strategies. In contrast, when controls are used in a diagnostic manner, they are used on an exception basis to monitor and reward the achievement of goals. Controls will support key success factors and the current strategy. Thus, in contrast to the content-focused studies in the 1980s and 1990s, Simons' framework does not examine which controls are used to support certain strategies; it considers the style of use of formal controls by senior management.

Abernethy and Brownell (1999) studied how budgets can be used interactively in a hospital setting, to moderate the relationship between business strategy and organizational performance. They found that organizational performance would be enhanced if budgeting was used interactively in an organization to reduce the disruptive effect associated with strategic change. The interactive mode was characterized as an ongoing dialogue between organizational members as to why budget variances occur, how systems and behaviours could be adapted to minimize variances, and the actions that should be taken. This facilitates organizational learning. Survey data were collected from sixty-three public hospitals. The aspect of strategic change that was studied was the move to a more market-oriented stance, which was common across the hospital sector.

Bisbe and Otley (2004) provide a comprehensive study of the effect of the interactive use of control systems on product innovation. They conducted a survey of 120 medium-sized mature Spanish manufacturing firms, and tested whether the interactive use of controls leads companies to develop and launch new products, and whether it contributes to the impact of the new innovative products on organizational performance. The control systems that were studied were the budgeting system, the BSC system, and the project management system. Their results indicated that in low innovating firms, the use of an interactive control system may lead to greater innovation, by providing guidance for the search, triggering, and stimulus of initiatives and through providing legitimacy for autonomous initiatives. However, in high innovating firms, interactive use of controls seemed to reduce innovation. This was thought to be caused by the filtering out of initiatives that result from the sharing and exposure of ideas. Another finding was that the interactive use of controls moderated the impact of innovation on organizational performance. This was though to be a result of the direction, integration, and fine-tuning those interactive control systems provide. Overall, support was found for the positive impact of formal MCS on innovation and long-term performance.

Operational strategies and control systems

The focus of most studies up to the mid-1990s was on relating the design of MCS to business strategies, which were identified in generic terms: differentiation versus cost leadership, prospector versus defender. However, in recent years, a range of studies have emerged that focus on specific aspects of differentiation, such as strategies based on quality, timeliness, reliability, and customer service. These aspects of strategies form the focus of operational strategies. Various management innovations such as TQM, just in time (JIT), business process engineering, and continuous improvement have developed to support such strategies, and there are consequent implications for the development of MCS. These MCS include 'strategically focused' MCS that have only emerged in recent times, such as activity-based cost management (ABCM) and target costing. They also include more traditional forms of MCS, such as performance measurement systems and budgeting systems, which may be tailored to provide specific support for the operational strategy. The following section provides a review of studies that have focused on the design of MCS to support quality strategies, product-related strategies, and manufacturing flexibility strategies.

Quality strategies

The earliest studies that focused on quality strategies and MCS were Daniel and Reitsperger (1991, 1992). In two more recent related studies, Daniel and Reitsperger (1994) and Daniel et al. (1995) focused on the relationships between MCS and quality strategies in US and Japanese firms. They distinguished between two forms of quality strategies: zero-defect strategy and economic conformance level (ECL) strategies.[2]

---

[2] The ECL model of quality control assumes that 'quality is costly' and proposes that a cost-minimizing quality level can be achieved by balancing prevention and appraisal costs against internal and external failure costs. The optimal ECL is the points at which costs are minimized—where the marginal prevention and appraisal costs equal marginal failure costs. Under this model the ECL would never occur at the zero-defect level. A zero-defect strategy focuses on continuous improvement to achieve perfect quality performance.

While the literature suggests that Japanese managers follow a zero-defect quality strategy and US managers an ECL strategy (e.g. Hayes 1981; Schonberger 1982), Daniel and Reitsperger (1994) found that most of the Japanese and US managers in their sample adhered to a zero-defect quality strategy, with significantly more followers in the USA than in Japan. The aspect of MCS that was studied in both Daniel and Reitsperger (1994) and Daniel et al. (1995) was the provision of goal setting and feedback information about quality performance.

Daniel and Reitsperger (1994) found that while US manufacturing managers adhered to zero-defect strategies more than Japanese managers, fewer US managers received MCS information to support their zero-defect strategies. Japanese managers were found to receive MCS regardless of which of the two quality strategies they followed. Interestingly Daniel et al. (1995) found that in US companies, as managers moved up the corporate hierarchy they viewed quality as a high strategic priority and were provided with more quality goals and more feedback on quality performance. Quality strategies and feedback in US companies were linked, but quality as a goal setting was not associated with a quality strategy. In the Japanese companies no association was found between quality strategies and the quality goals setting or feedback.

In a survey of automotive and computer companies across four countries, Ittner and Larcker (1997) found that organizations following a quality-oriented strategy made greater use of strategic control practices that were consistent with the quality orientation. The strategic control practices were oriented towards specifically supporting a quality strategy, and focused on strategic implementation practices (action plans, project controls, and management rewards), internal monitoring practices (feedback mechanisms, meetings, and board reviews) and external monitoring practices (benchmarking, market research, and strategic audits of products and processes). However, the extent of the relationship between strategy and control practices varied by country. The results indicated that in US and German organizations there was a very strong relation, while in Japan extensive use was made of quality-related control systems, regardless of the strategic orientation. Interestingly, the alignment of quality strategies and strategic control practices was not always associated with high organizational performance, and this varied by industry. For some control practices there was a negative performance effect, suggesting that formal control systems might reduce performance.

Product-related strategies

Product-related strategies may be considered an aspect of not only business strategy but also operational strategy, as their success may be affected directly at the manufacturing, marketing, or product design levels.

Davila (2000) studied MCS in new product development projects and became aware of the role of MCS in reducing uncertainty. MCS were a source of information used to close the gap between information required to perform a task and information already on hand (Tushman and Nadler 1978). He argued that as well as strategy and structure influencing the design of MCS in the new product development area, three forms of information gap (uncertainty) shape the design of MCS. These are market-related uncertainty, technology-related uncertainty, and project scope. Using both case studies and a survey, Davila (2000) included both financial and non-financial information in his definition of MCS. He found that cost and design information had a positive effect on performance, but time-related information hinders performance. He also found that cost information was related to a low-cost strategy and time-related information to a time-to-market strategy. However, there was no significant relationship between customer information and customer strategy. Davila (2000) found that MCS were not the only source of information used to reduce uncertainty and that when technology is the main source of uncertainty, prototyping may substitute for MCS. However, when uncertainty comes from project scope or from the market, MCS are more suited to reducing that uncertainty.

Abernethy et al. (2001) presented five case studies that focused on product diversity and the design of the product costing system. While costing systems are not always considered an aspect of MCS, in this case the orientation was the use of costing systems to facilitate decision-making and control. The study questioned the accepted premise that sophisticated costing systems are associated with high levels of product diversity and high levels of investment in advanced manufacturing technology (AMT) and the associated increase in overhead cost. They found that higher the product diversity, the more sophisticated is the costing system, while low product diversity is associated with a simple costing system. They found that if there was little or no investment in AMT, an increase in product diversity would create a demand for a sophisticated costing system. If there was a larger investment in AMT, the costing system may not be as sophisticated.

Manufacturing flexibility and customer-focused strategies

Abernethy and Lillis (1995) interviewed managers of forty-two manufacturing businesses to study the impact of a manufacturing flexibility strategy, as a form of customer-responsive strategy, on the design of MCS. From their interviews they extracted a series of constructs. Flexibility was defined as having three dimensions: technological difficulty in making product changes, strategic commitment to flexibility, and turnaround time to meet customer demands. MCS were defined in terms of integrative liaison devices—teams, task forces, meetings, and spontaneous contacts—and efficiency-based performance measures. As predicted, they found a positive relation between a flexibility strategy and the use of integrative liaison devices, supporting the role of such devices to manage functional interdependencies needed in the pursuit of flexibility. However, for both flexible and non-flexible firms there was a positive relation between the use of integrative liaison devices and firm performance. There was a negative relation between the use of efficiency-based performance measures for the evaluation of manufacturing performance and the commitment to flexibility, and only in firms that were 'not flexible' did the use of efficiency-based performance measures correlate with higher firm performance.

Perera et al. (1997) extended Abernethy and Lillis (1995) by using a survey method to examine customer-focused manufacturing strategies that included cost, quality, flexibility, and dependability. They set out to research an unanswered question from Abernethy and Lillis—whether firms that follow a customer-focused strategy emphasize non-financial manufacturing measures, and whether that is associated with enhanced performance. Support was found for the association between a customer-focused strategy and an emphasis on non-financial measures. However, there was no link to performance. One explanation provided for this result is that the role of the operational measurement system is to direct attention and to motivate managers to focus attention towards those aspects of operations that are of strategic importance, so relevant outcomes may be increased job satisfaction and motivation rather than firm-level performance outcomes. As with many studies of this nature that seek to relate the use of various practices and systems with improved firm performance, there are always questions about the nature of the lag between behavioural outcomes and firm-level performance, or more broadly how or if this linkage works in the light of so many other factors that may mitigate such relationships.

MCS and strategy in interfirm relationships

In recent years, the design and operation of MCS in interfirm relation-ships has sparked the interest of several researchers. MCS is said to play a role in the management of interdependencies between organizations, in situations of outsourcing, joint ventures, and other strategic alliances. Most studies have taken a process approach to examining the issues, and various frameworks have been used to interpret the findings. For example, Mouritsen et al. (2001) used actor-network theory, and van der Meer-Kooistra and Vosselman (2000) and Langfield-Smith and Smith (2003) use a modified transaction cost economics approach. However, to date there are few studies that have focused on strategy and MCS in interfirm relationships.

Mouritsen et al. (2001) provide two case studies of outsourcing that highlight the interdependencies between strategy and control systems of both partners. It is widely believed among many researchers and practitioners that an important determinant of success in interorgani-zational relationship is a supportive cooperative relationship based on trust. Thus, careful consideration is needed in designing the control system to manage the relationship. In both case studies, outsourcing was regarded as part of the strategy of the firms, and was considered critical for maintaining competitiveness. In both companies the advent of outsourcing left a gap in the control system and new controls were introduced to reinstall control and to retain a sense of involvement in the outsourced activities.

The strategy of NewTech was focused on rapid technological devel-opment. Technological innovation was considered key to maintaining competitiveness, and in the light of this, some would say that such a critical function should not have been outsourced. Functional analysis, a part of target costing, was introduced to regain control over the product development function and became a way to improve the sup-pliers' understanding of the technology, strategy, and organization and to direct the suppliers' development activities. NewTech became a tech-nology coordinator and manager through these changes, and gained a new identity.

Lean Tech found that, as customer demands changed, the strategy of flexibility towards individual customers gave way to productivity. This led not only to the outsourcing of production, but also to a lack of control over those outsourced processes. Open book accounting was introduced to provide logistics management with access to time and cost information about production processes, which assisted the company to coordinate supplier activities and improved production flexibility. However, open book accounting also led to a new conception of competitive strategy and a reinterpretation of what technological edge and customization meant for the firm.

In both these case studies, the new controls that were introduced to gain control over the outsourced activities led to changes in company perception of what were the core competencies of the two firms and new conceptualizations of the nature of their strategy and competitive edge.

Strategic style of corporate HQ and the MCS of business units

The spread of multinational organizations and the increasing complexity of many business structures and arrangements have highlighted the difficulty of managing at a distance, and the importance of achieving control and strategic objectives. Some of the earliest research into management control addressed the issue of decentralization, and specified appropriate control mechanisms. Bruns and Waterhouse (1975) found that larger organizations tend to be more decentralized and place greater reliance on formal administrative controls, such as budgets (see Chenhall (2003) for a review of the literature). Distance seems to make control more difficult, as there is less visibility of operations.

There are two interrelated perspectives that may be taken into account when researching this issue: the control systems that are used by the parent to control business units, and the control systems that are used within business units. Chenhall (2005) distinguishes between the 'outside–in' and 'inside–out' perspectives in considering the relationships between strategy and MCS. However, the design of MCS within business units can be influenced by a variety of factors, including the will of the head office (HO) or parent company. Such MCS may be imposed by mandate on divisions or subsidiaries to satisfy desires for uniformity across a wider organization. Parental control can also extend to actions and activities that exert control through various socialization experiences and HRM interventions. From an HO perspective, one of the challenges in controlling, particularly far-flung divisions, is communicating and coordinating decision-making, behaviours, activities, and operations.

There are several ways of conceptualizing the form of control exercised by a parent. Yan and Gray (2001) distinguish between strategic control (exercised by the parent company or HO), operational control (exercised by the business unit/divisional management), and structural control (where procedures and routines are imposed on the business unit by the parent). Nilsson (2000) and Chung et al. (2000) both used the classification of financial control, strategic planning, and strategic control. Ahrens and Chapman (2004) adopted an enabling and coercive classification to describe the control style of the HO.

Nilsson (2000) found a relationship between the parenting style and the MCS in four company groups, as well as a relationship between the business strategy pursued and the MCS. The Goold et al. (1994) classification of parenting style of financial control, strategic planning, and strategic control were used. A parenting style of financial control implies a high degree of decentralization, where strategic planning is carried out by the business units and those business units operate in stable mature industries where there are opportunities to generate strong profit and cash flows. In these situations a cost leadership strategy is appropriate and the parent exercises controls through financial targets and reporting. A strategic planning style involves a high degree of synergy between the business units and the parent, and parental involvement in planning and decision-making. This is thought to suit situations where there is a turbulent competitive environment and where a long-term perspective is relevant. A differentiation strategy is often followed by the business unit. Control is exercised by parents through their involvement in the decision-making process and an emphasis on informal planning and follow-up and non-financial information.

Chung et al. (2000) investigated how the strategic management (parental) style employed by corporate HO to manage a diverse range of subsidiaries affected the type of controls used. Again, the three forms of strategic management style were strategic planning, strategic control, and financial control (Goold and Campbell 1987). For those HOs using a financial control style, emphasis was on output controls, namely setting and monitoring financial targets. The development of business strategy was delegated to the business units. The strategic planning style entails the HO participating with and influencing the business strategy of the business unit, and close interaction with the business unit is required. A heavy focus was on behaviour controls. HOs that had a strategic control style are strongly committed to decentralization, so they will not directly impose business strategies or interfere in major decisions. Rather, they will look for ways of socializing managers of subsidiaries into the philosophy of the HO. While results did not support their hypotheses for the strategic planning and strategic control style, they found that a strategic control style was the most prevalent. They also found a strong emphasis on socialization controls across all subsidiaries.

Ahrens and Chapman (2004) used a framework of coercive and enabling (Adler and Borys 1996) uses of MCS to view the relationship between HO and operational units within a restaurant chain. Coercive use is a top–down approach that emphasizes centralization, pre-planning, and detailed specification of organizational rules. An enabling use aims to design a formal system that capitalizes on the intelligence of managers by helping operational managers to deal more effectively with contingencies, rather than tightly constraining them. The usability of formal systems can be assessed in terms of repair, internal transparency, global transparency, and flexibility. Repair provides the capability for users to fix breakdowns in control processes. Internal transparency is an understanding of the workings of local control processes whereas global transparency is an understanding of where and how these local processes fit into the control systems of the organization as a whole. Flexibility is the employees' discretion over the use of control systems, even to the point of turning these controls off. In their case study, Ahrens and Chapman (2004) found that the HO used a mixture of coercive and enabling controls. While this chapter does not deal explicitly with strategy, it is argued that enabling control systems can provide operational managers with the capability to deal with emerging contingencies in a way that will further the local and organization-wide goals. In the case of their restaurant chain case study, customer satisfaction was a driver of sustained financial success. This was a broader concept than producing high-quality meals and attentive service; it captured the restaurant 'experience'. Thus, rigidly specified rules would not necessarily provide the answer to achieving this strategic goal. Restaurant managers needed to be able to respond to local circumstances, but without violating strict efficiency parameters.

Summary and directions for future research

This chapter presented some research studies in the area of MCS and strategy, following several themes. These are the relationship between performance measures and reward systems (including BSC) and business strategy; capital investment processes and the initiation of strategic investment projects; interactive controls and strategic change; operational strategies and control systems; the design and operation of MCS in interfirm relationships, such as joint ventures and outsourcing; and the strategic style of corporate HQ and the MCS of business units. Various different approaches have been taken in these studies, which have added to our understanding of the complexity of the MCS–strategy relationship. However, there is still so much that we need to understand, which could form the focus for future research.

One promising direction for future research is in the area of performance measurement, reward systems, and BSC. Ittner et al. (2003b) emphasized the need to go beyond the search for alignment of performance measures with strategy, to investigate more fully specific value drivers of strategic success. 'Traditional' approaches to the study of performance measures and strategy have focused on the use and benefits of, or emphasis on, performance measures (Abernethy and Lillis 1995; Chenhall and Langfield-Smith 1998; Baines and Langfield-Smith 2003) and this is also true for empirical studies that have focused on BSC and strategy (see Hoque and James 2000). However, other studies have highlighted the critical nature of implementation issues, including behavioural issues, in influencing whether or not these frameworks achieve their intended outcomes. In pursuing this issue in more detail, Ittner et al. (2003a) highlight the various interpretations that companies may give to operationalizing the BSC concept, so that many firms do not fully adopt the original Kaplan and Norton prescription. Many of the future research directions in the area of performance measures and strategy highlighted in Langfield-Smith (1997) remain unanswered, but perhaps we have now moved on to focus on more important and challenging areas.

Several studies have highlighted the many functions that control systems may play within an organization, in influencing strategic change, strategic thinking, and performance. Performance targets may direct employee efforts towards improving key success criteria of the firm (Chenhall and Langfield-Smith 2003). MCS may direct managerial thinking towards initiating capital expenditure proposals that consider the impact of the project on competitiveness (Miller and O'Leary 1997; Slagmulder 1997). MCS can also influence managers' conceptions of the purpose and strategic direction of the firm (Mouritsen et al. 2001), and lead to the building up of strategic knowledge among managers and employees. Simons' framework focuses attention on how managers can select certain controls to use interactively to guide and direct attention towards strategic uncertainties and strategic change.

As organizations expand globally and operations move beyond their traditional boundaries, there is a need to understand how MCS can be designed and used to control these decentralized operations, and outsourced or joint venture activities, to promote strategic thinking, strategic behaviour, and sustained performance. It is only in the last few years that these areas have emerged and they represent large unexplored opportunities for future studies.

Control systems seem to be designed to meet several purposes. However, can control systems that focus on influencing strategic thinking also motivate employees to perform, as well as provide accountability and control? Further research is needed to enhance our understanding of the multiple objectives of control systems and whether a control system that is designed to effect change or to influence thinking can be used for other purposes.

This chapter has highlighted several areas for future research, which are developed in other chapters of this book. These include developing an understanding of how multiple objectives of control systems can be achieved (Hansen and Mouritsen 2005); how strategic capital investment practices and processes can be developed to encourage strategic thinking; the design of controls systems in interorganizational relationships (Miller and O'Leary 2005); and how MCS can be designed and used to promote improved strategic performance and control through the creation of strategic knowledge and strategic thinking (Ittner and Larcker 2005). These topics will be explored in more detail in subsequent chapters.

References

Abernethy, M. A. and Brownell, P. (1999). 'The Role of Budgets in Organizations Facing Strategic Change: An Exploratory Study', *Accounting, Organizations and Society,* 24: 189–204.

—— and Lillis, A. M. (1995). 'The Impact of Manufacturing Flexibility on Management Control System Design', *Accounting, Organizations and Society,* 20(4): 241–58.

—— ——, Brownell, P., and Carter, P. (2001). 'Product Diversity and Costing System Design Choice: Field Study Evidence', *Management Accounting Research,* 12: 261–79.

Adler, P. and Borys, B. (1996). 'Two Types of Bureaucracy: Enabling and Coercive', *Administrative Science Quarterly,* 41(1): 61–90.

Ahrens, T. and Chapman, C. S. (2002). 'The Structuration of Legitimate Performance Measures and Management: Day-to-Day Contests of Accountability in a U.K. Restaurant Chain', *Management Accounting Research,* 13(2): 151–71.

—— —— (2004). 'Accounting for Flexibility and Efficiency: A Field Study of Management Control Systems in a Restaurant Chain', *Contemporary Accounting Research,* 21(2): 271–301.

Baines, A. and Langfield-Smith, K. (2003). 'Antecedents to Management Accounting Change: A Structural Equation Approach', *Accounting, Organizations and Society*, 28(7/8): 675–98.

Banker, R. D., Chang, H., and Pizzini, M. J. (2004). 'The Balanced Scorecard: Judgmental Effects of Performance Measures Linked to Strategy', *The Accounting Review*, 79(1): 1–23.

Bisbe, J. and Otley, D. (2004). 'The Effects of the Interactive Use of Management Control Systems on Product Innovation', *Accounting, Organizations and Society*, 29: 709–37.

Briers, M. and Hirst, M. (1990). 'The Role of Budgetary Information in Performance Evaluation', *Accounting, Organizations and Society*, 15: 373–98.

Bruns, W. J. Jr. and Waterhouse, J. H. (1975). 'Budgetary Control and Organizational Structure', *Journal of Accounting Research* (Autumn): 177–203.

Chenhall, R. H. (2003). 'Management Control Systems Design Within Its Organizational Context: Findings from Contingency-Based Research and Directions for the Future', *Accounting Organizations and Society*, 28(2/3): 127–68.

—— (2005). 'Content and Process Approaches to Studying Strategy and Management Control Systems', in C. S. Chapman (ed.), *Controlling Strategy: Management, Accounting and Performance Measurement*. Oxford: Oxford University Press.

—— and Langfield-Smith, K. (1998). 'The Relationship between Strategic Priorities, Management Techniques and Management Accounting: An Empirical Investigation Using a Systems Approach', *Accounting, Organizations and Society*, 23(3): 243–64.

—— —— (2003). 'Performance Measurement and Reward Systems, Trust and Strategic Change', *Journal of Management Accounting Research*, 15: 117–44.

Chung, L. H., Gibbons, P. T., and Schoch, H. P. (2000). 'The Influence of Subsidiary Context and Head Office Strategic Management Style on Control in MNCs: The Experience in Australia', *Accounting, Auditing and Accountability Journal*, 13(5): 647–66.

Daniel, S. J. and Reitsperger, W. D. (1991). 'Linking Quality Strategy with Management Control Systems: Empirical Evidence from Japanese Industry', *Accounting, Organizations and Society*, 16: 601–18.

—— —— (1992). 'Management Control Systems for Quality: An Empirical Comparison of the US and Japanese Electronic Industries', *Journal of Management Accounting Research*, 4: 64–78.

—— —— (1994). 'Strategic Control Systems for Quality: An Empirical Comparison of the Japanese and U.S. Electronics Industries', *Journal of International Business Studies*, 25: 275–94.

—— ——, and Gregson, T. (1995). 'Quality Consciousness in Japanese and U.S. Electronics Manufacturers: An Examination of the Impact of Quality Strategy and Management Control Systems on Perceptions of the Importance of Quality to Expected Management Rewards', *Management Accounting Research*, 6: 367–82.

Davila, T. (2000). 'An Empirical Study on the Drivers of Management Control Systems' Design in New Product Development', *Accounting, Organizations and Society*, 25: 383–409.

Govindarajan, V. (1988). 'A Contingency Approach to Strategy Implementation at the Business-Unit Level: Integrating Administrative Mechanisms with Strategy', *Academy of Management Journal*, 31(4): 828–53.

Govindarajan, V. and Gupta, A. K. (1985). 'Linking Control Systems to Business Unit Strategy: Impact on Performance', *Accounting, Organizations and Society*, 20: 51–66.

Goold, M. and Campbell, A. (1987). 'Managing Diversity: Strategy and Control in Diversified British Companies', *Long Range Planning*, 20(5): 42–52.

—— ——, and Alexander, M. (1994). *Corporate Level Strategy: Creating Value in the Multibusiness Company*. New York: John Wiley.

Gupta, A. K. (1987). 'SBU Strategies, Corporate-SBU, and SBU Effectiveness in Strategy Implementation', *Academy of Management Journal*, 30(3): 477–500.

Haka, S. F. (1987). 'Capital Budgeting Techniques and Firm Specific Contingencies: A Correlational Analysis', *Accounting, Organizations and Society*, 12(1): 31–48.

Hansen, A. and Mouritsen, J. (2005). 'Strategies and Organisational Problems: Constructing Corporate Value and Coherence in Balanced Scorecard Processes', in C. S. Chapman (ed.), *Controlling Strategy: Management, Accounting and Performance Measurement*. Oxford: Oxford University Press.

Hayes, R. H. (1981). 'Why Japanese Factories Work', *Harvard Business Review* (July/Aug.) 56–66.

Hoque, Z. and James, W. (2000). 'Linking Balanced Scorecard Measures to Size and Market Factors: Impact on Organizational Performance', *Journal of Management Accounting Research*, 12: 1–17.

Ittner, C. and Larcker, D. (1997). 'Quality Strategy, Strategic Control Systems, and Organizational Performance', *Accounting, Organizations and Society*, 22(3/4): 293–314.

—— —— (1998). 'Innovations in Performance Measurement: Trends and Research Implications', *Journal of Management Accounting Research*, 10: 205–38.

—— —— (2005). 'Moving from Strategic Measurement to Strategic Data Analysis', in C. S. Chapman (ed.), *Controlling Strategy: Management, Accounting and Performance Measurement*. Oxford: Oxford University Press.

—— ——, and Meyer, M. W. (2003a). 'Subjectivity and the Weighting of Performance Measures: Evidence from a Balanced Scorecard', *The Accounting Review*, 78(3): 725–58.

—— ——, and Randall, T. (2003b). 'Performance Implications of Strategic Performance Measurement in Financial Services Firms', *Accounting, Organizations and Society*, 28: 715–41.

Kaplan, R. S. (1986). 'The Role for Empirical Research in Management Accounting', *Accounting, Organizations and Society*, 11: 429–52.

—— and Norton, D. P. (1992). 'The Balanced Scorecard—Measures that Drive Performance', *Harvard Business Review* (Jan./Feb.): 71–79.

—— —— (1996). 'Using the Balanced Scorecard as a Strategic Management System', *Harvard Business Review* (Jan./Feb.): 75–85.

Langfield-Smith, K. (1997). 'Management Control Systems and Strategy: A Critical Review', *Accounting, Organizations and Society*, 22: 207–32.

—— and Smith D. (2003). 'Management Control and Trust in Outsourcing Relationships', *Management Accounting Research*, 14(3): 281–307.

Larcker, D. F. (1981). 'The Perceived Importance of Selected Information Characteristics for Strategic Capital Budgeting Decisions', *Accounting Review*, 56: 519–38.

Malina, M. A. and Selto, F. H. (2001). 'Communicating and Controlling Strategy: An Empirical Study of the Effectiveness of the Balanced Scorecard', *Journal of Management Accounting Research*, 13: 47–90.

Merchant, K. A. (1989). *Rewarding Results: Motivating Profit Center Managers*. Boston, MA: Harvard Business School Press.

Miller, P. and O'Leary, T. (1997). 'Capital Budgeting Practices and Complementarity Relations in the Transition to Modern Manufacturing: A Field-Based Analysis', *Journal of Accounting Research*, 35(2): 257–71.

—— —— (2005). 'Capital Budgeting, Coordination and Strategy: A Field Study of Inter-firm and Intra-firm Mechanisms', in C. S. Chapman (ed.), *Controlling Strategy: Management, Accounting and Performance Measurement*. Oxford: Oxford University Press.

Mouritsen, J., Hansen, A., and Hansen C. O. (2001). 'Inter-organization Controls and Organizational Competencies: Episodes around Target Cost Management/Functional Analysis and Open Book Accounting', *Management Accounting Research*, 12: 221–44.

Nilsson, F. (2000). 'Parenting Styles and Value Creation: A Management Control Approach', *Management Accounting Research*, 11: 89–112.

Perera, S., Harrison, G., and Poole, M. (1997). 'Customer-Focused Manufacturing Strategy and the Use of Operations-Based Non-Financial Performance Measures: A Research Note', *Accounting, Organizations and Society*, 22: 557–72.

Porter, M. E. (1980). *Competitive Strategy.* New York: Free Press.

Samson, D. A., Langfield-Smith, K., and McBride, P. (1991). 'The Alignment of Management Accounting with Manufacturing Priorities—a Strategic Perspective', *Australian Accounting Review*, 1(1): 29–40.

Schonberger, R. J. (1982). *Japanese Manufacturing Techniques: Nine Hidden Lessons in Simplicity.* New York: Free Press.

Shank, J. K. and Govindarajan, V. (1992). 'Strategic Cost Analysis of Technological Investments', *Sloan Management Review* (Fall): 39–51.

Simons, R. (1987). 'Accounting Control Systems and Business Strategy: An Empirical Analysis', *Accounting, Organizations and Society*, 12: 357–74.

—— (1990). 'The Role of Management Control Systems in Creating Competitive Advantage: New Perspectives', *Accounting, Organizations and Society*, 15: 127–43.

—— (1995). *Levers of Control.* Cambridge, MA: Harvard Business School Press.

—— (2000). *Performance measurement and control systems for implementing strategy.* Upper Saddle River, NJ: Prentice-Hall.

Slagmulder, R. (1997). 'Using Management Control Systems to Achieve Alignment between Strategic Investment Decisions and Strategy', *Management Accounting Research*, 8: 103–39.

Tushman, M. and Nadler, D. (1978). 'Information Processing as an Integrating Concept in Organizational Design', *Academy of Management Review*, 3: 613–24.

van der Meer-Kooistra, J. and Vosselman, E. (2000). 'Management Control of Inter-firm Transactional Relationships: The Case of Industrial Renovation and Maintenance', *Accounting, Organizations and Society*, 25(1): 51–77.

Yan, A. and Gray, B. (2001). 'Antecedents and Effects of Parent Control in International Joint Ventures', *Journal of Management Studies*, 38(3): 393–416.

Moving from Strategic Measurement to Strategic Data Analysis

Christopher D. Ittner and David F. Larcker

Management control theories argue that the key goals of strategic control systems are communicating strategic direction and priorities, developing mechanisms for determining whether the chosen strategy is achieving its objectives, and providing information that can be used to modify actions in order to achieve desired goals. As discussed in other chapters, the initial development of strategic control systems requires the firm to determine the system's primary objectives (Hansen and Mouritsen 2005), allocate resources to achieve these objectives (Miller and O'Leary 2005), and develop formal and informal control systems for guiding and evaluating routines and practices for consistency with strategic goals (Ahrens and Chapman 2005). While choices regarding system objectives, resource allocation methods, and specific performance measures are all critical issues in strategic control system implementation and success, an equally important issue is establishing the organizational mechanisms needed to promote ongoing analysis of strategic success and encourage strategic learning. Although management control literature argues that such 'feedback loops', 'double-loop learning', and 'strategic data analyses' are critical components of strategic control systems (e.g. Schreyogg and Steinmann 1987; Kaplan and Norton 1996; Julian and Scifres 2002), relatively little is known about *how* these strategic analysis mechanisms influence strategic control system design and effectiveness. Moreover, despite growing evidence that greater use of these mechanisms is associated with higher perceived measurement system success and improved financial performance (Sandt et al. 2001; Ittner and Larcker 2003; Marr 2004), surveys indicate that most companies with strategic performance measurement systems *do not* perform these analyses (Gates 1999; Ittner and Larcker 2003; Ittner et al. 2003), raising important questions about the factors that promote or hinder their use and effectiveness.

Over the past decade, we have investigated these issues in a variety of contexts, ranging from the measurement of quality improvement initiatives and customer satisfaction programmes to the development of balanced scorecards (BSC) and executive dashboards. In this chapter, we synthesize our findings on the potential benefits from accompanying strategic performance measurement systems with ongoing strategic data analysis, and discuss some of the technical and organizational factors hindering the development of effective strategic data analysis mechanisms.

The roles of data analysis in strategic control systems

Simon's classic study of the controllership function (Simon et al. 1954) identified three roles for accounting information: attention directing, scorekeeping, and problem solving. Similarly, the strategic measurement and control literature describes three analogous roles for these systems: (*a*) communicating strategic direction and priorities, (*b*) determining whether the strategy is being implemented as planned and the results produced by the strategy are those intended, and (*c*) providing information that can be used to promote organizational learning, to identify avenues for improving strategic performance, and to adapt the strategy to emerging conditions.

According to this literature, data acquisition and analysis are critical elements in strategic measurement and control system effectiveness. A representative strategic data analysis process, developed by one of our research sites, is illustrated in Figure 1. Lorange et al. (1986) contend that 'strategic controllers' should undertake such a process in order to better understand the underlying drivers of strategic results. Julian and Scifres (2002) argue that data analysis and interpretation are essential in facilitating the identification of factors that trigger the need for strategic change. Schreyogg and Steinmann (1987) point out that the very premises underlying the strategy being communicated to the organization are based on assumptions that must be verified through data analysis. In a similar vein, Kaplan and Norton (1996) emphasize that the 'strategy maps' communicating how improvements in chosen BSC performance measures are expected to produce strategic results are merely hypotheses that need to be tested.

Assessment of implementation and strategic success, in turn, requires the development of valid and reliable measures for the hypothesized key success factors (e.g. what *specific* measures and measurement methodologies actually tell us whether we are achieving our implementation goals or strategic objectives?), the weighting of different types of measures (e.g. how do we 'balance' short-term goals against longer-term

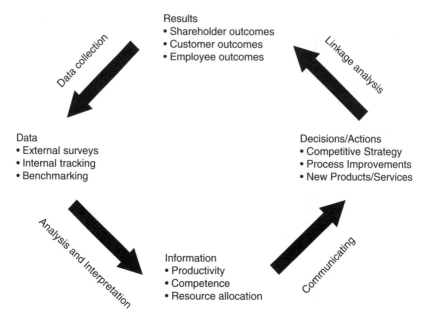

Figure 1 Strategic data analysis process

strategic objectives?), and the identification of performance standards for the hypothesized success factors (e.g. do we want to maximize performance on every dimension, i.e. every customer or employee is 100 per cent satisfied or loyal, or is some other performance standard more appropriate?). These assessments require analysis of available data, or the gathering and interpretation of new data when the existing system does not provide the information needed to examine these issues (Muralidharan 1997; Ittner and Larcker 2003).

Finally, the use of strategic measurement systems for decision-making and learning purposes requires organizations to undertake increasingly detailed data analyses to uncover the underlying drivers or root causes of strategic success, the potential benefits from specific strategic investments, and the reasons behind deviations from strategic targets (e.g. Argyris 1982; Hayes et al. 1988; Kaplan and Norton 1996; Julian and Scifres 2002).

To examine these potential uses and benefits in greater detail, we conducted extensive field research in more than sixty companies, and supplemented this field research with survey-based studies in a broad spectrum of public-and private-sector organizations. Our research identified three primary benefits from strategic data analysis, including

enhanced communication of strategic assumptions, better identification and measurement of strategic value drivers, and improved resource
allocation and target setting. The following examples illustrate the role
of strategic data analysis in achieving these benefits.

Strategic marketing metrics in a convenience store chain

Although most companies make some effort to tie their performance
measures to the organization's strategy, these links are often based on
management intuition or organizational folklore about these relations
rather than rigorous analysis. A study of strategic performance measurement systems by the Conference Board (Gates 1999), for example,
found that 69 per cent of companies attempt to determine the associations between their performance measures and the organization's
strategy when choosing performance measures, but only 22 per cent
assess these links in a rigorous manner.

One important reason for the intuitive approach to choosing performance measures is the absence of any formal attempt to understand how
the company's various financial and non-financial measures are
expected to fit together or produce desired strategic results. Many proponents of strategic performance measures argue that companies
should develop causal 'business models' or 'value driver maps' that
articulate the cause-and-effect relations among performance measures,
and show how improvements in these measures are expected to improve long-term strategic and economic performance. However, less
than 30 per cent of the companies we surveyed have developed these
strategic 'business models' or 'value driver maps', and even fewer actually test whether the *specific* performance measures they have chosen
are associated with expected results. In fact, only 21 per cent of the
companies we surveyed even attempt to demonstrate that improvements in their strategic performance measures actually influence future
financial results.

Typical is a large retailer in the US. The company owns and operates
hundreds of convenience stores that sell gasoline along with various food
and convenience items. A number of unarticulated assumptions under-
pinned its strategic plan and performance measures, with little or no
attempt to determine the validity of these assumptions. One of the most
firmly held assumptions was that gasoline sales and food sales were
unrelated. Rather than seeing these as complementary product lines

that offered cross-selling opportunities, the company saw their joint sale as an opportunity to increase the utilization of fixed resources. When we questioned a wide variety of managers at different organizational levels about this assumption, each asserted that no one had ever found a relationship between gasoline sales and food sales. However, when pushed, no one could tell us where this analysis was or who had done it.

Based on the assumption that gasoline and food sales were unconnected, each product line was set-up as a separate profit centre. Marketing decisions across the two profit centres were not coordinated, and the performance measures reported to one profit centre manager were not reported to the other. When we subsequently analysed the company's data, we found no support for this key strategic assumption. As shown in Figure 2, gasoline sales were highly correlated with food sales. Given the higher profit margins on food sales, these results suggested the potential to reduce gasoline prices (and increase gallons sold) in order to increase profits through food sales. For example, by reducing gasoline prices below those of nearby competitors, the stores could attract more gasoline buyers, who were then likely to buy high-margin food products during the visit. The net effect would be an overall increase in store profitability. In contrast, under the existing strategic assumption that gasoline and food sales were independent, prices on low-margin gasoline would never be reduced below that of competitors unless the resulting increase in volume had a *direct* effect on gasoline profits, with no consideration given to spillover effects on other products.

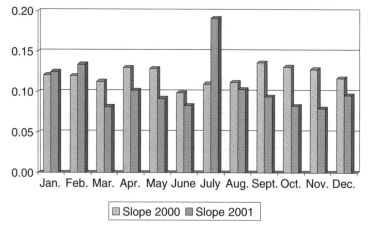

Figure 2 Estimated elasticities from cross-sectional regressions of convenience store food sales ($US) on gasoline sales (gallons)

Additional analysis also found that the elasticity between food and gasoline sales varied with factors such as store size, location, and time of year, providing information that allowed the company to tailor its strategic pricing policy. For example, in settings where gasoline and food sales were highly interdependent, it made economic sense to reduce gasoline prices (and therefore gasoline profitability) in order to increase higher-margin food sales and overall store profits. The expected return from each one penny drop in prices could be calculated based on the estimated increase in food sales and profits for each store, providing information on the optimal trade-off between gasoline profitability reductions and increased food profitability. Conversely, in settings where gasoline and food sales were unrelated, the existing practice of pricing the two product lines independently could be retained.

The results from these analyses prompted the company to explicitly articulate and analyse some of its other implicit strategic assumptions. These included the belief that the only factors explaining food profitability were store location and the sales of beer and cigarettes. To assess the attractiveness of a given store location, the company used a scoring model developed by a consulting firm that weighted factors such as income level, traffic patterns, and competition into an overall index of location desirability. Employee measures were not considered important to store profits, and were not reported to the gasoline and food profit centre managers.

Analysis of this broader strategic model of food profitability provided only partial support for the company's beliefs. Consistent with their expectations, the resulting statistical model (shown in Figure 3) indicated that food profitability was positively related to beer and cigarette sales. That is, stores that sold more beer and cigarettes as a percentage of total food sales had higher food profitability due to the higher margins on these two product lines. However, gasoline sales continued to predict food sales profitability, as did employee measures such as turnover and workforce injuries, which were believed to have no effect on store performance. Higher employee turnover had an indirect effect on food profitability through its negative impact on customer satisfaction (as measured using 'mystery shopper' results). The number of workplace injuries, on the other hand, exhibited a direct negative effect on food profits, reflecting the impact of poor working conditions on employee safety and morale. In contrast, the store location index had no ability to differentiate food (or store) profitability, even though the company used this index for assessing new store locations and closing existing stores. While some of the individual location factors, such as the

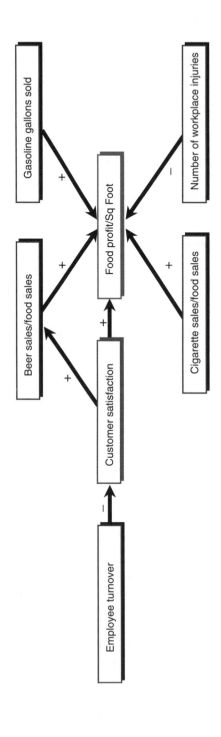

Notation: +/– refers to a strong statistical positive/negative link;
insignificant links are not reported
(precise numbers are not reported at company request)

Figure 3 Analysis of the drivers of food sales profitability in convenience stores

number of parking spaces and market demographics, later proved to have an influence on profitability, the aggregated index used for decision-making lacked any predictive ability.

Based on strategic data analysis, the company was able to justify marketing, training, and other initiatives that were previously difficult to justify on a financial basis. Strategic initiatives began to be focused on activities with the largest economic benefits (e.g., employee turnover and injuries), and the results provided a basis for selecting valid performance indicators for assessing store performance.

Target setting in a computer manufacturing firm

Any control system requires targets to determine success or failure. Many companies we studied followed a 'more is better' approach when setting targets for non-financial measures such as customer satisfaction. However, this assumption causes serious problems when the relation between the performance measure and strategic or economic performance is characterized by diminishing or negative returns. Without some analysis to determine where or if these inflection points occur, companies may be investing in improvement activities that yield little or no gain.

Such was the case with a leading personal computer manufacturer. Like many firms, the company used a five-point scale (1 = very dissatisfied to 5 = very satisfied) to measure customer satisfaction. One of the primary assumptions behind the use of this measure was that very satisfied customers would recommend their product to a larger number of potential purchasers, thereby increasing sales and profitability. Consequently, the performance target was 100 per cent of customers with a satisfaction score of 5.

This target was not supported by subsequent data analysis. Figure 4 shows the association between current customer satisfaction scores and the number of positive and negative recommendations in the future (obtained through follow-up surveys). The analysis found that the key distinction linking satisfaction scores and future recommendations was whether customers were very *dissatisfied*, not whether they were very *satisfied*. Customers giving the company satisfaction scores of 1 or 2 were far more likely to give negative recommendations and far less likely to give positive recommendations (if at all). Between satisfaction scores of 3 to 5 there was no statistical difference in either type of recommendation.

Figure 4 Computer manufacturer study linking customer satisfaction scores to subsequent product recommendations

The appropriate target was not moving 100 per cent of customers into the 5 (very satisfied) category, but removing all customers from the 1 or 2 categories, with the greatest potential gain coming from eliminating very dissatisfied customers (1 on the survey scale).

Value driver analysis in a financial services firm

One of the primary criticisms of traditional accounting-based control systems is that they provide little information on the underlying drivers or root causes of performance, making it difficult to identify the specific actions that can be taken to improve strategic results. Yet many non-financial measures used to assess strategic results are also outcome measures that shed little light on lower-level performance drivers. For example, a number of companies in our study found significant relations between customer or employee satisfaction measures and financial performance. But telling employees to 'go for customer satisfaction' is almost like saying 'go for profits'—it has little practical meaning in terms of the actions that actually drive these results. The question that remains is what actions can be taken to increase satisfaction. Unfortunately, many of these companies did not conduct any quantitative or qualitative analyses to help managers understand the factors that impact customer satisfaction or other higher-level non-financial measures. As a result, managers frequently became frustrated because they had little idea regarding how to improve a key measure in their performance evaluation. More importantly, the selection of action plans to improve higher-level measures continued to be based on management's intuition about the underlying drivers of non-financial performance, with little attempt to validate these perceptions.

Strategic data analysis can help uncover the underlying drivers of strategic success. A major financial services firm we studied sought to understand the key drivers of future financial performance in order to develop their strategy and select action plans and investment projects with the largest expected returns. In this business, increases in customer retention and assets invested (or 'under management') have a direct impact on current and future economic success. What this company lacked was a clear understanding of the drivers of retention and assets invested. Initial analysis found that retention and assets invested were positively associated with the customer's satisfaction with their investment adviser, but not with other satisfaction measures (e.g. overall satisfaction with the firm). Further analysis indicated that satisfaction with the investment adviser was highly related to investment adviser turnover—customers wanted to deal with the same person over time. Given these results, the firm next sought to identify the drivers of investment adviser voluntary turnover. The statistical analysis examining the drivers of adviser turnover is provided in Figure 5. The level of compensation and work environment (e.g. the availability of helpful and knowledgeable colleagues) were the strongest determinants of turnover. These analyses were used to develop action plans to reduce adviser voluntary turnover, and provided the basis for computing the expected net present value from these initiatives and the economic value of experienced investment advisers.

Predicting new product success in a consumer products firm

In the absence of any analysis of the relative importance of different strategic performance measures, companies in our study adopted a

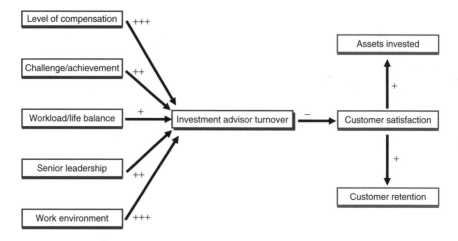

Notation: +/– refers to a strong statistical positive/negative link;
more +/– signs reflect stronger statistical associations
(precise numbers are not reported at company request)

Figure 5 Analysis linking employee-related measures to customer purchase behaviour in a financial services firm

variety of approaches for weighting their strategic performance measures when making decisions. A common method was to subjectively weight the various measures based on their assumed strategic importance. However, like all subjective assessments, this method can lead to considerable error. First, it is strongly influenced by the rater's intuition about what is most important, even though this intuition can be incorrect. Second, it introduces a strong political element into the decision-making process. For example, new product introductions were a key element of a leading consumer products manufacturer's strategy. To support this strategy, the company gathered a wide variety of measures on product introduction success, including hypothesized leading indicators such as pre-launch consumer surveys, focus group results, and test market outcomes, as well as lagging indicators related to whether the new product actually met its financial targets. However, the company never conducted any rigorous analysis to determine which, if any, of the perceived leading indicators were actually associated with greater probability of new product success.

An internal study by the company found that this process caused a number of serious problems. First, by not linking resource allocations to those pre-launch indicators that were actually predictive of new product success, resources went to the strongest advocates rather than to the managers with the most promising products. Second, because the leading indicators could be utilized or ignored at the manager's discretion and were not linked to financial results, the managers could accept any project that they liked or reject any project that they did not like by selectively using those measures that justified their decision. These consequences led the company's executives to institute a data-driven decision process that used analysis of the leading indicator measures to identify and allocate resources to a smaller set of projects offering the highest probability of financial success.

Barriers to strategic data analysis

Given the potential benefits from strategic data analysis, why is its use so limited? And, when it is performed, why do many firms find it extremely difficult to identify links between their strategic performance measures and economic results? Our research found that these questions are partially explained by technical and organizational barriers.

Technical barriers

Inadequate measures

One of the major limitations identified in our study was the difficulty of developing adequate measures for many non-financial performance dimensions. In many cases, the concepts being assessed using non-financial measures, such as management leadership or supplier relations, are more abstract or ambiguous than financial performance, and frequently are more qualitative in nature. In fact, 45 per cent of BSC users surveyed by Towers Perrin (1996) found the need to quantify qualitative results to be a major implementation problem. These problems are compounded by the lack of standardized, validated performance measures for many of these concepts. Instead, many organizations make up these measures as they go along.

The potential pitfalls from measurement limitations are numerous. One of the most significant is reliance on measures that lack statistical reliability. Reliability refers to the degree to which a measure captures random 'measurement error' rather than actual performance changes (i.e. high reliability occurs when measurement error is low). Many companies attempt to assess critical performance dimensions using simple non-financial measures that are based on surveys with only one or a few questions and a small number of scale points (e.g. 1 = low to 5 = high).[1] Statistical reliability is also likely to be low when measures are based on a small number of responses. For example, a large retail bank measured branch customer satisfaction each quarter using a sample of thirty customers per branch. With a sample size this small, only a few very good or very bad responses can lead to significantly different satisfaction scores from period to period. Not surprisingly, an individual branch could see its customer satisfaction levels randomly move up or down by 20 per cent or more from one quarter to the next.

Similarly, many companies base some of their non-financial measures on subjective or qualitative assessments of performance by one or a few senior managers. However, studies indicate that subjective and objective evaluations of the same performance dimension typically have only a small correlation, with the reliability of the subjective evaluations substantially lower when they are based on a single overall rating rather than on the aggregation of multiple subjective measures (Heneman 1986; Bommer et al. 1995). Subjective assessments are also subject to favouritism and bias by the evaluator, introducing another potential source of measurement error. The retail bank, for example, evaluated branch managers' 'people-related' performance (i.e. performance management, teamwork, training and development, and employee satisfaction) using a superior's single, subjective assessment of performance on this dimension. At the same time, a separate employee satisfaction survey was conducted in each branch. Subsequent analysis found no significant correlation between the superior's subjective assessment of 'people-related' performance and the employee satisfaction scores for the same branch manager.

A common response to these inadequacies is to avoid measuring non-financial performance dimensions that are more qualitative or difficult to measure. The Conference Board study of strategic performance measurement (Gates 1999), for example, found that the leading roadblock to implementing strategic performance measurement systems is avoiding the measurement of 'hard-to-measure' activities (55 per cent of respondents). Many companies in our study tracked the more qualitative measures, but de-emphasized or ignored them when making

---

[1] For discussions of issues related to the number of questions, scale points, or reliability in performance measurement, see Peter (1979) and Ryan et al. (1995).

decisions. When we asked managers why they ignored these measures, the typical response was lack of trust in measures that were unproven and subject to considerable favouritism and bias. Although these responses prevent companies from placing undue reliance on unreliable measures or measures that are overly susceptible to manipulation, they also focus managers' attention on the performance dimensions that are being measured or emphasized and away from dimensions that are not, even if this allocation of effort is detrimental to the firm. As a result, the performance measurement system has the potential to cause substantial damage if too much emphasis is placed on performance dimensions that are easy to measure at the expense of harder-to-measure dimensions that are key drivers of strategic success.

Information system problems

The first step in any strategic data analysis process is collecting data on the specific measures articulated in the business model. Most companies already track large numbers of non-financial measures in their day-to-day operations. However, these measures often reside in scattered databases, with no centralized means for determining what data are actually available. As a result, we found that measures that were predictive of strategic success often were not incorporated into BSCs or executive dashboards because the system designers were unaware of their availability.

The lack of centralized databases also made it difficult to gather the various types of strategic performance measures in an integrated format that facilitated data analysis. Gathering sufficient data from multiple, unlinked legacy systems often made ongoing data analysis of the hypothesized strategic relationships extremely difficult and time-consuming.

Data inconsistencies

While the increasing use of relational databases and enterprise resource planning systems can help minimize the information system problems identified in our research, a continuing barrier to strategic data analysis is likely to be data inconsistencies. Even within the same company, we found that employee turnover, quality measures, corporate image, and other similar strategic measures often were measured differently across business units. For example, some manufacturing plants of a leading consumer durables firm measured total employee turnover while others measured only voluntary turnover, some measured gross scrap costs (i.e. the total product costs incurred to produce the scrapped units) while others measured net scrap costs (i.e. total product costs less the money received from selling the scrapped units to a scrap dealer), and some included liability claims in reported external failure costs while others did not. Inconsistencies such as these not only made it difficult for companies to compare performance across units, but also made it difficult to assess progress when the measures provided inconsistent or conflicting information.

Inconsistencies in the timing of measurement can also occur. A leading department store's initial efforts to link employee and customer measures to store profitability were unsuccessful because different measures were misaligned by a quarter or more. Only after identifying this database problem was the company able to identify significant statistical relations among its measures. Similarly, a shoe retailer found that its weekly data ended on Saturdays for some measures and on Sundays for others. Since weekends are its primary selling days, this small misalignment made it difficult to identify relationships. Correcting measurement and data problems such as these was necessary before the companies could effectively use data analysis to validate their performance measures or modify their hypothesized business models.

A related issue is measures with different units of analysis or levels of aggregation. One service provider we studied had fewer than 1,000 large customers, and sought to determine whether customer-level profitability and contract renewal rates were related to the employee and customer measures it tracked in its executive dashboard. However, when it went to perform the analysis, the company found that the measures could not be matched up at the customer level. Although customer satisfaction survey results and operational statistics could be traced to each customer, employee opinion survey results were aggregated by region, and could not be linked to specific customers. The company also had no ability to link specific employees to a given customer, making it impossible to assess whether employee experience, training, or turnover affected customer results. Furthermore, the company did not track customer profitability, only revenues. To top it off, there was not even a consistent customer identification code to link these separate data files. Given these limitations, it was impossible to conduct a rigorous assessment of the links between these measures.

Organizational barriers

Lack of information sharing

A common organizational problem is 'data fiefdoms'. Relevant perform-ance data can be found in many different functional areas across the organization. Unfortunately, our research found that sharing data across functional areas was an extremely difficult task to implement, even when it was technically feasible. In many organizations, control over data provides power and job security, with 'owners' of the data reluctant to share these data with others. A typical example is an automobile manu-facturer that was attempting to estimate the economic relation between internal quality measures, external warranty claims, and self-reported customer satisfaction and loyalty. The marketing group collected exten-sive data on warranty claims and customer satisfaction while the oper-ations group collected comprehensive data on internal quality measures. Even though it was believed that internal quality measures were leading indicators of warranty claims, customer satisfaction levels, and future sales, the different functional areas would not share data with each other. Ultimately, a senior corporate executive needed to force the two func-tions to share the data so that each would have a broader view of the company's progress in meeting quality objectives.

Even more frequent was the reluctance of the accountants to share financial data with other functions. Typical objections were that other functions would not understand the data, or that the data were too confidential to allow broader distribution. However, our research found that one of the primary factors underlying these objections was the fear that sharing the data would cause the accounting function to lose its traditional role as the company's performance measurement centre and scorekeeper, thereby reducing its power.

Uncoordinated analyses

The lack of incentives to share data is compounded by the lack of incentives to coordinate data analysis efforts. Most companies perform at least some analyses of performance data, but these analyses are frequently done in a piecemeal fashion. For example, the marketing department may examine the drivers of customer satisfaction, the quality function may investigate the root causes of defects, and the human resource department may explore the causes of employee turnover, with little effort to integrate these analyses even though the company's strategic business model suggest they are interrelated. The lack of integrated analyses prevents the company from receiving a full picture of the strategic progress, and limits the ability of the analyses to increase organizational learning.

More problematically, the ability of different functions to conduct independent analyses frequently results in managers using their own studies to defend and enhance their personal position or to disparage someone else's. In these cases, the results of conflicting analyses are often challenged on the basis of flawed measurement and analysis. By not integrating the analyses, it is impossible to determine which of the conflicting studies are correct.

Fear of results

As the preceding examples suggest, performance measurement systems and strategic data analysis are not neutral; they have a significant influence on power distributions within the organization through their role in allocating resources, enhancing the legitimacy of activities, and determining career paths. As a result, some managers resist strategic data analysis to avoid being proved wrong in their strategic decisions. We found this to be particularly true of managers who were performing well under the current, underanalysed, strategic performance measurement system. While strategic data analysis could confirm or enhance the value of their strategic decisions, it could also show that their performance results were not as good as they originally appeared.

Organizational beliefs

Finally, more than a few of the organizations we studied had such strong beliefs that the expected relations between their strategic performance measures and strategic success existed that they completely dismissed the need to perform data analysis to confirm these assumptions. We repeatedly heard the comment that 'it must be true' that a key performance indicator such as customer satisfaction leads to higher financial returns. As our earlier examples indicated, these relationships frequently are not that straightforward. What often drives these strong beliefs is management intuition and past experience. However, even though management intuition and past history play important roles in strategic decision-making, the strategic control literature points out that competitive environments change and must be continually evaluated. Strategic choices and performance measures that were previously determinants of long-term economic success may no longer be valid. Strategic data analysis provides one mechanism to evaluate the ongoing validity of these organizational beliefs.

Conclusions

Recent discussions of strategic accounting and control systems have emphasized the development of new performance measurement systems that better reflect strategic objectives and their drivers. Our research indicates that the implementation of effective strategic performance measurement systems can be greatly enhanced by adding substantial sophistication to the choice and analysis of strategic performance measures and targets. This requires companies to move away from the overreliance on generic performance measurement frameworks and management intuition that currently guide many strategic performance measurement initiatives, and to place more emphasis on the use of quantitative and qualitative analysis techniques for selecting the measures that are actually leading indicators of strategic performance, determining the relative importance to be placed on the various measures based on their contribution to desired results, and assessing the measures' appropriate performance targets.

Even when data analysis indicates that the selected measures do not exhibit the expected relations, the results provide a mechanism for promoting the dialogue and debate that underlie effective strategic control. The contrary results can be due to incorrect assumptions in the strategic plan and business model, limitations in the measures, database problems, or organizational barriers that prevent improvements from reaching the bottom line. If managers strongly believe that hypothesized relations exist, efforts should be made to determine which of these explanations is true.

Finally, we found that successful data analysis and interpretation efforts require clear assignment of responsibilities for conducting analyses, strong executive support to ensure the availability of adequate resources and cross-functional cooperation, and regularly scheduled, ongoing reassessment of the results. The need for ongoing analysis is particularly important. Dynamic changes in a company's life cycle, corporate strategy, and competitive environment can change the relations in the strategic business model over time, or even make the entire business model obsolete. Regular, ongoing analyses allow the company to verify that the strategy, business model, and hypothesized linkages remain valid.

References

Ahrens, T. and Chapman, C. S. (2005). 'Management Control Systems and the Crafting of Strategy: A Practice-Based View', in C. S. Chapman (ed.), *Controlling Strategy: Management, Accounting and Performance Measurement*. Oxford: Oxford University Press.

Argyris, C. (1982). *Reasoning, Learning, and Action*. San Francisco: Jossey-Bass.

Bommer, W. H., Johnson, J. L., Rich, G. A., Podsakoff, P. M., and MacKenzie, S. B. (1995). 'On the Interchangeability of Objective and Subjective Measures of Employee Performance: A Meta-Analysis', *Personnel Psychology*, 48(3): 587–605.

Gates, S. (1999). *Aligning Strategic Performance Measures and Results*. New York: The Conference Board.

Hansen, A. and Mouritsen, J. (2005). 'Strategies and Organisational Problems: Constructing Corporate Value and Coherence in Balanced Scorecard Processes', in C. S. Chapman (ed.), *Controlling Strategy: Management, Accounting and Performance Measurement*. Oxford: Oxford University Press.

Hayes, R. H., Wheelwright, S. C., and Clark, K. B. (1988). *Dynamic Manufacturing: Creating the Learning Organization*. New York: Free Press.

Heneman, R. L., Moore, M. L., and Wexley, K. N. (1987). 'Performance-Rating Accuracy: A Critical Review', *Journal of Business Research*, 15(5): 431–48.

Ittner, C. D., and Larcker, D. F. (2003). 'Coming up Short on Nonfinancial Performance Measurement', *Harvard Business School Press*, 81(11): 88–95.

—— ——, and Randall, T. (2003). 'Performance Implications of Strategic Performance Measurement in Financial Services Firms', *Accounting, Organizations and Society*, 28(7/8): 715–41.

Julian, S. D. and Scifres, E. (2002). 'An Interpretive Perspective on the Role of Strategic Control in Triggering Strategic Change', *Journal of Business Strategies*, 19(2): 141–59.

Kaplan, R. S. and Norton, D. P. (1996). *The Balanced Scorecard: Translating Strategy Into Action*. Boston, MA: Harvard Business School Press.

Lorange, P., Scott Morton, M. F., and Ghoshal, S. (1986). *Strategic Control Systems*. St. Paul, MN: West Publishing Company.

Marr, B. (2004). *Business Performance Management: Current State of the Art*. Cranfield: Cranfield School of Management and Hyperion.

Miller, P. and O'Leary, T. (2005). 'Capital Budgeting, Coordination and Strategy: A Field Study of Interfirm and Intrafirm Mechanisms', in C. S. Chapman (ed.), *Controlling Strategy: Management, Accounting and Performance Measurement*. Oxford: Oxford University Press.

Muralidharan, R. (1997). 'Strategic Control for Fast-Moving Markets: Updating the Strategy and Monitoring Performance', *Long Range Planning*, 30(1): 64–73.

Peter, J. P. (1979). 'Reliability: A Review of Psychometric Basics and Recent Marketing Practices', *Journal of Marketing Research*, 16(1): 6–17.

Ryan, M. J., Buzas, T., and Ramaswamy, V. (1995). 'Making CSM a Power Tool', *Marketing Research*, 7(3): 10–16.

Sandt. J., Schaeffer, U., and Weber, J. (2001). 'Balanced Performance Measurement Systems and Manager Satisfaction—Empirical Evidence from a German Study'. Working paper, WHU—Otto Beisheim Graduate School of Management.

Schreyogg, G. and Steinmann, H. (1987). 'Strategic Control: A New Perspective', *Academy of Management Review*, 12(1): 91–103.

Simon, H. A., Kozmetsky, G., Guetzkow, H., and Tyndall, G. (1954). *Centralization Versus Decentralization in Organizing the Controller's Department*. New York: Controllership Foundation.

Towers Perrin (1996). *Compuscan Report*. New York: Towers Perrin.

Management Control Systems and the Crafting of Strategy: A Practice-Based View

Thomas Ahrens and Christopher S. Chapman

Managing their relationships with customers is a vital capability of organizations. Even though the role of accounting and management control systems (MCS) in this process has long been conceptualized under the label of strategic management accounting (Simmonds 1981, 1982), recent studies found it difficult to trace the influence of this concept on strategic organizational practices (Tomkins and Carr 1996, Guilding et al. 2000; Roslender and Hart 2003). This chapter draws on practice theory as a way of understanding the strategic potential of MCS. It focuses specifically on the day-to-day uses of MCS for the management of customer relationships in head office (HO) and local units.

In strategy literature, the relationship between strategy-making by senior management and the day-to-day activities of operational management is only beginning to be systematically explored (Whittington 2002; Johnson et al. 2003), despite the much earlier notion of 'crafting strategy' (Mintzberg 1987). The resource-based view of strategy has proved an important development in the attempt to relate organizational missions with organizational capabilities through the notion of routines (Johnson et al. 2003). Strategic capabilities and resources are thus grounded in day-to-day organizational action (Feldman 2004). In organization studies, the interest in hypercompetitive environments has resulted in a reconceptualization of the strategy-making process from an episodic to a continuous endeavour (Brown and Eisenhardt 1997).

In MCS literature we have witnessed two related developments. The balanced scorecard (BSC) originated as a relatively straightforward call for greater levels of non-financial performance measurement (Kaplan and Norton 1992). Subsequent developments sought to position the BSC at the heart of organizational strategy-making—in terms of strategy development, implementation, and refinement (Kaplan and Norton 1996, 2000). A difficulty in working with such ideas is the complex nature of the relationship between strategy, MCS, and operational management (e.g; Roberts 1990; Simons 1990; Ahrens 1997; Mouritsen 1999; Ahrens and Chapman 2002, 2004*a*, *b*).

In this chapter we suggest a form of analysis that may provide new insights into the nature of management control and strategy, and the relationship between the two. We seek to understand the relationship between management control and strategy through the detailed examination of management practice (Ahrens and Chapman 2004*b*). Practice theorists share a concern over the neglect of action in social theory (Schatzki et al. 2001). A practice perspective would seek to foreground the roles of individual organizational members in the context of the webs of organizational routines, none of which can typically pre-empt strategic choice (Child 1972).

In this way our practice perspective on the crafting of strategy through MCS can begin to address the ways in which the efforts of local managers might be harnessed to pursue continuously the agendas of the organizational centre. MCS hold out the promise of measuring out small achievable steps throughout an organization's operations that give local managers a sense of their contribution to organizational strategies. This is important because apart from very simple and stable situations, the conceptual linkages between organizational strategy and operational action cannot rely on mechanical cause-and-effect relationships. In relating MCS and strategy it would thus be important for the organizational centre to avoid simply replacing local efforts with their central instructions. In many organizations the significance of local information and local autonomy means that strategy as organizational practice only comes into its own through the day-to-day activities of individual managers. Whether the strategic tasks lie in customer selection and the active shaping of their preferences, or in identifying what the customer wants, the crafting of strategy benefits from a detailed understanding of the financial implications of strategic choices through MCS.

Practice theory

Even though there are almost as many practice theories as practice theorists, a shared concern has been the relationship between action and the systematic properties of its contexts (Schatzki et al. 2001). According to Ortner (1984) practice theory explains 'the relationship(s) that obtain between human action, on the one hand, and some global entity which we call "the system" on the other', where the system can be analysed as political, economic, cultural, or combinations between these.

Its concern with volition makes practice theory of immediate interest to strategy theorists. For practice theorists, as much as for other social scientists, volition is conditioned by aspects of 'the system' as well as by extant action, especially routines. Importantly, however, practice theory introduces a concern with the moment of action in which the actor is showing a certain knack, an immediate familiarity with the situation and the possibilities that it presents. For Bourdieu (1992) the 'sens pratique' shows itself for example in the timing of action to convey urgency, commitment, loyalty, distance, aloofness, etc., in just the right measures.

Compared with the actor's unspoken mastery of certain situations, explicit decision rules seem unwieldy and, very often, unrealistic. At the individual level, expert actors tend not to articulate explicit decision rules and 'apply' them to situations like a novice would (Dreyfus and Dreyfus 1988). Experienced drivers, for example, understand traffic situations holistically and act immediately. There is, literally, 'no time to think'. Novice drivers who get caught up in chains of reasoning lose control of the situation and crash. Novice management accountants tend to lack the ability to think through organizational situations with the conceptual schemes that they studied during their training (Ahrens and Chapman 2000). The usefulness of those schemes for practice only becomes apparent through experience.

Cognition in practice is thus not the application of 'thought tools' to certain situations to achieve certain ends, because in practice the processes in which situated actors come to know involves simultaneous changes of context, knowledge, and ends. Cognition becomes a process that is 'distributed—stretched over, not divided among—mind, body, activity and culturally organized settings (which include other actors)' (Lave 1988:1). It can generate new organizational strategies as much as it is informed by existing strategies that give it certain ends and context descriptions to work with. Conceptualized as distributed across different organizational elements, cognition is implicated in the ways in which the different ends of many actors intermingle with their various actions.

The notion of strategy as organizational practice is also highlighted in the dynamics between formal power and the resistance of those who are to be co-opted into an organizational strategy. de Certeau (1988) based his scheme of practices on the distinction between powerful actors who could rely on recognized power bases, such as governments, scientific institutions, wealthy corporations, etc., and the powerless to whom they addressed themselves through laws, scientific advice, consumer products, services, and advertisements. For de Certeau, strategy was the province of the powerful who could afford to develop and impress them on a public whose only recourse lay in mobile tactics to variously circumvent strategies or absorb them into temporary arrangements with the powers that be. An important implication of this distinction between strategy and tactics is to highlight the significance of the opportunities for adjustment and resistance within strategies and the manner in which those opportunities are seized by organizational members.

This is not to appeal to a stereotype of grass-roots resistance to top–down strategies but to open up for detailed investigation the spectrum of possible local responses and accommodations to central strategies, many of which may be spurred on by strategic ignorance of local circumstances and, conversely, local ignorance of central strategic priorities. Rather than see tactics as nested snugly within layers of overarching strategies, a practice view would emphasize the potential innovations of skilful situated actors and their subsequent impact on organizational strategy.

Research design

Our analysis is grounded in an in-depth longitudinal field study of MCS in Restaurant Division, a UK-based restaurant chain. In order to demonstrate the potential of a practice approach in helping to develop our understanding of the relationship between MCS and strategy, this chapter analyses the ways in which strategic resources for identifying, understanding, and satisfying the customer were constructed in Restaurant Division. First, we will analyse the ways in which customer relationships were analysed and managed in individual restaurants. We will then explore the ways in which HO marketing analysts and operations staff sought to draw on MCS as a way of engendering strategically informed routine behaviours in restaurants.

We approached fieldwork with the aim of developing a comprehensive view of the nature and role of MCS in one of the largest full-service restaurant chains in the UK. All restaurants were wholly owned by the company and were run by salaried managers. Restaurant Division had enjoyed substantial returns on sales and sales growth over a period of years. This growth had been attained partly through acquisition of smaller chains but mainly through addition of new units. More than 200 restaurants were organized as profit centres, which reported into areas and then regions of operational management. Restaurant Division was wholly owned by and reported to a leisure group quoted on the London Stock Exchange, but it was also registered as a company with limited liability and had its own board of directors (Figure 6).

Our fieldwork over a period of a little over two years involved interviews, examination of archival records, and direct observation of meetings and workshops. Table 3 details what might be thought of as formal data collection. Starting from a definition of MCS as 'the formal, information-based routines and procedures managers use to maintain or alter patterns in organizational activities' (Simons 1995: 5), we carried out a series of semi-structured interviews aimed at building a general picture of how the interviewees, from waiters to the managing director, thought about their roles, and what, if any, part was played by formal information and control systems in supporting these roles.

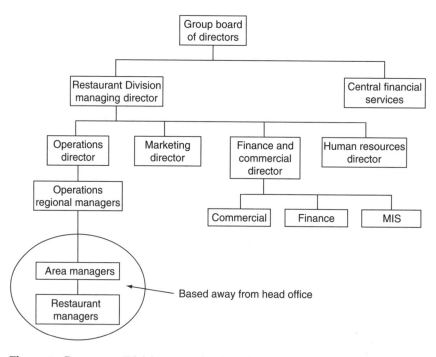

Figure 6 Restaurant Division organization chart

Table 3   Information on formal fieldwork activity

Functional breakdown of interviews carried out	
Central financial services	1
Head office—Commercial	6
Head office—Finance	11
Head office—HR	4
Head office—Managing Director	1
Head office—Marketing	5
Head office—MIS	2
Head office—Operations	4
Area managers	2
Restaurant managers	9
	45
Observations and attendance at meetings	
Area business development meetings	2
Cross-functional meeting to discuss the food margin	1
Eating of 'control' 3 course meals by both researchers	2
Area manager—restaurant manager performance reviews (held at individual restaurants)	6
Observation of kitchen operation	2
Residential control workshops	2
Various finance meetings	4
	19

These interviews lasted about seventy minutes on average. Most of them took place with both researchers present, were tape-recorded, and subsequently transcribed. Where this was not possible notes were taken during the interview, and more detailed notes were written up afterwards as soon as possible. Over the course of the study we interviewed the entire divisional board and executive committee, together with various other HO managers and staff specialists across all functions. In the operations hierarchy we interviewed both regional and area managers, and restaurant managers.

We reviewed internal planning, control and financial documents, materials used in internal training, computer data entry and reporting screens, etc. These materials were often presented and discussed during interviews, giving interviewees opportunities for talking to us through their work.

We carried out observations at the HO and in restaurants, as well as several residential training sessions. We made visits to fifteen restaurants, sometimes more than once, where we either observed performance reviews between restaurant managers and their area manager or interviewed restaurant managers and had shorter meetings with various assistant managers, chefs, and waiting staff. We also took the opportunity to observe restaurants (including kitchens) during opening hours. On two occasions we ordered the same three-course meals in order to assess the standardized nature of portions and presentation.

Informally, our presence at coffee breaks and meals during and after our formal observations and interviews meant that we could listen to participants' observations of, and, reactions to, the meetings. On such occasions we also learned about a rich stream of organizational gossip, jokes, and stories, which we used to test our developing understanding of the role of MCS in Restaurant Division.

An important issue in qualitative fieldwork is knowing when to exit the field (Miles and Huberman 1994). Qualitative research aims for deep contextual understanding of the kind that enables the researcher to gradually become able to predict organizational members' responses to certain kinds of issues. This is known as theoretical saturation (Glaser and Strauss 1967; Strauss and Corbin 1990). Depending on the issues under study and the complexity of the organization studied, saturation is achieved over varying lengths of time. We decided to terminate our fieldwork after we felt that we had developed a clear sense of the role of MCS within Restaurant Division. Formal feedback on our understanding was provided through discussions of a report on our findings with the divisional financial controller and the divisional finance director.

Analysis of rich field material is a creative ongoing process. As such various modes of analysis were overlapping and iterative (Ahrens and Dent 1998). Interview transcripts and field notes were organized chronologically, and the common issues in the material were analysed to understand areas of agreement and disagreement between organizational actors and groups. Findings that did not appear to fit emerging patterns identified in this process were marked for subsequent discussion as the research continued. Archival records were used to elaborate and confirm issues that arose in interviews and observations. We also dissected and reorganized the original transcripts around emerging issues of significance to our understanding of MCS.

The construction and management of the customer in restaurants

For the restaurant managers a key task was to mesh their understanding of customers with HO's strategy as communicated through MCS. The achievement of targets in individual restaurants required the continuous reconciliation of central expectations with the local situation. Customer satisfaction was a key non-financial performance measure for restaurants. Understanding how to achieve high customer satisfaction within budget constraints was an important skill of restaurant managers. For the individual managers this was not a matter of simply balancing satisfaction with costs. Rather, to make the central strategy work in their outlet they needed to understand the priorities of their particular clientele through their financial implications. MCS were used to structure the customer relationship in ways that allowed them to retain flexible control over it.

Taken together, Restaurant Division's performance measurement systems described a model of restaurant operation that balanced economic efficiency (such as customers per waiter or ingredients per dish) with service-level expectations according to centrally determined standards. Given this organizational set-up the overall balance of control in the organization might appear highly centralized, with restaurant managers expected to simply implement HO standards. This would however be too static a view. The implementation of standards in an actual restaurant required the continuous reconciliation of central expectations with the local situation. In the context of a full-service restaurant this turned out to be a complex task. In order to illustrate this point we offer the following stylization of the challenges of restaurant management during a single serving session.

Based on their current performance against budget, managers planned their restaurant's operational resources before each session. With a budget surplus, it would be possible to plan for generous staffing levels that might translate into improved customer service, greater customer satisfaction, and enhanced spend-per-head. Likewise, certain pre-prepared food items, e.g. baked potatoes, allowed for faster service, but might ultimately go to waste. A deficit against budget would suggest a different operational set-up. The restaurant manager might fill in as grill chef or help the waiting staff. There would be only minimal pre-preparation of food.

During each session these decisions could be finessed as the session unfolded. For instance, could the restaurant accommodate a large party without a reservation? The restaurant manager needed to consider the operational readiness of the restaurant. Was the kitchen in danger of getting overwhelmed by too many simultaneous orders? Were there too few waiting staff on shift? Did they have enough experience? Did kitchen and waiting cooperate or antagonize each other under pressure?

These questions of operational readiness were moderated by managers' perceptions of the characteristics of their guests. Would an arriving party be happy to have a drink in the bar before their meal? Did parties prefer a faster service to cover embarrassing lapses in conversation, or was a relaxed, slower service more appropriate? Could spending per head be increased by maintaining a constant supply of drinks to lively office parties? What concessions would restore customer satisfaction when a table had become dissatisfied?

Considerable effort and discussion went into constructing legitimate management as an ongoing dialogue between restaurant managers and their area managers (Ahrens and Chapman 2002). Central to this dialogue were these questions: 'What market are we in?', and 'Who are our customers?'. At the restaurant level they had obvious answers—whoever walks through the door. From the point of view of the strategists at the HO, the answers were much more complicated because they were tied up with more general processes of strategizing. For HO these questions formed the starting point for detailed processes through which various managers and directors sought to develop the strategic resources of Restaurant Division such that the overall strategy of growth might be systematically supported without ignoring the skills, experience, and knowledge of the local staff who ultimately would serve their particular customers.

The construction and management of the customer in the HO

The newly appointed marketing director was very clear that her role and that of her team was to enhance the financial performance of Restaurant Division, supporting the strategy of growth.

I see the role of the marketing department in driving the sales, driving the top line—inevitably making sure whatever we do, it doesn't drive the top line to the detriment of profit. (Marketing Director)

The starting point in achieving this goal was to establish agreement on Restaurant Division's brand. It was well understood that the restaurant business involved managing certain key hygiene factors.

Any piece of market research will tell you customer wants high standards, safe, clean. (HR Director)

Long-term success, however, depended on the development of a distinctive brand.

The brand's important at the moment because it gives the customer a certain minimum standard and a reassurance of what they're gonna get when they go through the door. (Regional General Manager)

...you come into a [Restaurant Division restaurant], you feel, immediately the anxiety is de-stressed from you by the way that we're going to deal with you as you come through the door. And you sit down and you get an informal, quality meal, which is our brand position. We're not there yet, that's the big task for next year. (Marketing Director)

But beyond being 'relaxing', 'informal', 'accommodating', and 'friendly', what should be key to the vision of Restaurant Division's brand image? There was agreement amongst senior management that without a more distinctive customer proposition Restaurant Division's growth strategy would be difficult to achieve.

I mean we are perceived as an undifferentiated brand in an undifferentiated market. So, you know, I mean you could ask anybody what we were about [laughs] they wouldn't answer in a line. I couldn't find anything, in any document I read, I couldn't find a succinct line. I could find a mission statement which was...I think it was '[to be] the first choice in every local area for a proper restaurant.' [...] but we don't have anything that's consumer orientated at all. (Marketing Director)

The marketing director's frustration with the mission statement was driven by the fundamental problem of aligning strategic and operational management. How could she harness the efforts of local managers without a brand vision that was more clearly related to the day-to-day management of restaurants? And how could she do so without stifling restaurant managers' desire to contribute their specific knowledge and experience? The mission statement as it stood struck a balance that placed the emphasis firmly at the local level. 'How to make each individual restaurant first choice in its own area' opened up a very large range of equally valid actions, and the mission statement itself provided little guidance for choosing between alternatives. In the eyes of the marketing director the brand value of informality was convenient for an organization with restaurants all over the country, but it did not offer a coherent concept.

For a chain organization, the absence of some central theme to the mission was particularly vexing because it undermined the potential advantages that Restaurant Division could derive from its size. How exactly were HO's considerable conceptual and technical resources to be deployed for the practical tasks of addressing and attracting new and repeat customers?

So on the one hand we, we've got to retain a national identity to get the benefit out of things like TV advertising, but at the same time research is telling us that people want it to be less formal as a brand, in other words, more informal and with more local taste, so there'll be certain elements of the brand that are fixed and they tend to be the things you can't touch really. (Operations Director)

Despite this trend towards the flexible and less uniform, the marketing director was at pains to point out that developing the brand concept and then fostering appropriate local actions required a significant analytical effort at the HO. She related the processes of strategic analysis and communication to key financial and non-financial information. Such information was a central plank in developing a sense of accountability for the actions of her subordinates and herself.

I want [my marketing analyst's work] to be measurable, I want to be able to turn round at the end of every piece of activity and say 'this has worked or it hasn't worked and this is why.' And you can't do that if you don't set yourself proper objectives in the first place. (Marketing Director)

[Corporate head office executive] said to me yesterday 'Okay, Judy, if I gave you a million pounds can you do some marketing activity which would give me two million pounds?' And I had to say, 'No I can't.' Now I'd like to be able to turn round and say, 'Yes I can, and it's this, and this is why I know'—and I can't. So I find that frustrating. (Marketing Director)

But as well as fostering a greater sense of accountability the marketing team clearly felt that better management information would play a vital role in developing practical lines of action to support the divisional strategy. For example, it might help decide which groups of existing customers and non-users to target with what kinds of one-off or long-term discount schemes, as well as which categories of restaurants to earmark for different kinds of refurbishment and alterations.

I think you've got to clearly define who you're targeting towards and you, you can either target people who are currently going in there [the restaurants], but they know you anyway and are turning up, so the cost effectiveness of that would be questionable [...] Or you can target people who, who have maybe not any perception of what you're about. But if you do that you've got to give them a reason to turn up, a reason to re-evaluate, and a reason to say, well, why didn't you go somewhere else. And that's the trick in getting that mix right basically. (Marketing Analyst)

You know, nineteen per cent of our family users never go back. They've got the [family discount] card, [but] never go back in because they haven't got [an outlet] near them, 'cos they've been travelling or whatever. And so we were just giving away discount on them and, and you know it should be an incentive for people to come back again. (Marketing Director)

[Better information would] enable me to understand what percentage of our market would be using it how often. And [...] if it's easier to get people moving from two to four [restaurant visits per year], or is it easier for some people to move from four to eight? And I don't know that. Then I could say, 'All right, well, the easiest to get my first slot of activity would be to get people to move from four to six visits a year, right.' Well, I can mail them and I know that a mailing is going to cost me 48 pence. I know their names and addresses and I can target my offer to them, 'cos I know they like this, um, I can say, you know, 'If you spend ten pounds you get this,' you know. I can do all sorts. (Marketing Director)

I'd like to have some more segmentation by [restaurant], so, you know, I'd like to be saying with all the restaurants with gardens in summer, which ones aren't performing? Of those where we've just done refurbishment, which ones aren't and which ones are, which ones do we need to do activity and which ones don't need to do activity. And I'd like the regional marketing manager to take responsibility for being able to be proactive and analysing the information. (Marketing Director)

What connected those ideas for the management of marketing activity was that they relied on strategic uses of financial and non-financial management information.

The marketing director regarded more detailed management information as absolutely essential to her work. She felt that restaurant managers based their judgements all too often on 'anecdotal' information and might be dismissive of requests she might make of them to systematically collect more reliable information. Nevertheless, she and other senior HO managers were keen to avoid constructing analytical models of restaurant operations that sought to simply overwrite local knowledge and conditions.

I see next year very much about national activity [...] establishing what the brand is about, which is run by my trial group [...] and then underneath we've got, and quite down near the bottom we've got a whole load of local activity, which is the manager knowing his area, knowing the garages, knowing the schools, knowing the cubs,[1] knowing the scouts, and building from the local information base around his [restaurant], direct mail, um, doing local promo-

---

[1] Junior scouts.

tions with local papers, um, and then tailoring his outlook much more to a local community. And that's in terms of how the [restaurant] looks and in terms of what he actually does. (Marketing Director)

On the brand positioning? [. . .] it's being led by our marketing department. I've got two of my area managers sitting on the working parties 'cos their areas will be in the trial for it, so they will have some influence on what goes into that in the detailed stuff rather than the directional stuff. The directional stuff is coming from the marketing department supported by the board. The detailed stuff's coming into the sub-working parties which will have operational representatives on, and assistant people on and HR people on, to try and give it real flesh around the bones. (Regional General Manager)

In relation to the brand value of informality the operations director explained how this process of giving it 'real flesh', or introducing it to specific restaurant contexts, worked in relation to a particular aspect of service standards for waiting staff.

We have a thing called a check-back, in other words within two minutes a waitress has to check-back with the customer on the main course: 'Is everything all right, Sir?' That will be measured if the mystery diner goes in. Now that, that is a good example of formality, so you and I could be talking like this, obviously we're happy because we're talking and she'll come up, interrupt you . . . Now what we really want them to do is to just look and observe, and you can, if you and I sat there like this, you know [leans forward, frowns], she, she, she'll know there's an issue, assuming it's not an argument. But if you say that to a waitress 'Well you know, show your own judgement,' so what you're actually doing is looking to catch my eye and going, 'Okay?' before long, because we've got ten thousand people in our business, it's becoming that when two guys come in in a suit, obviously talking about business, you don't need to check-back. And that is the challenge. How do we not lose all that good work . . . Very difficult and I don't know the answer other than through education. And of course everybody will say, 'Well that's easy. It's obvious'. But in reality, I promise you now, it won't be long before that's what would happen: You don't need to check-back if it's two guys in a suit [. . .] The way we build up all these things is to involve waitresses, managers. Umpteen people now have been put together in groups to describe how best we do it [. . .] There's got to be some system but at the same time it's not got to appear as formal as you [as a customer] feel like you're being processed. (Operations Director)

Discussion

In Restaurant Division, MCS informed various processes of strategizing. To achieve the targets for its strategy of growth, the marketing director sought to develop an initially undifferentiated brand concept in ways that would enable her to harness the efforts of individual restaurant managers for specific HO initiatives, each one of which would be targeted at specific strategic objectives. For example, with respect to the management of customers, she systematically segmented customers into groups with specific consumption profiles for whom particular offerings, membership cards, and other incentive schemes were designed to increase customer spending. Spending increase was analysed as a combination of repeat custom and spending per visit. This allowed not only for the evaluation of operational management but also generated information that could be used to refine the customer profiles. With respect to the management of restaurants she categorized them according to the facilities that they offered to customers and the revenue effects of different kinds of enhancements to those facilities.

From a marketing point of view MCS was thus central to enabling the marketing department to work towards Restaurant Division's strategy of growth through small measurable steps. In this way, the growth strategy could be related to specific marketing activities intended to link to patterned but not predetermined local activity in restaurants. The strategy of trying to be the 'first choice in every local area', left the marketing team initially frustrated because it simply sought to leave the local local, and did not provide a brief for HO marketing. It gave no direction for action. The tailoring of local offerings in terms of service or marketing incentives was regarded as important, but it was also acknowledged that it ought to be based on some core strategic proposition without, importantly, simply replacing local efforts with central instructions. The examples of the working parties on brand positioning and the checkback initiative showed the perceived advantages of seeking to develop service elements jointly between the HO and restaurants in order to achieve the desired effects on restaurant operations.

Herein, we believe, lies an important contribution of a practice perspective on MCS and strategy. Traditionally, management control studies have highlighted the problems arising from local resistance to HO strategies, or contrasted HO with grass-roots strategies. Vaivio (1999) for example, emphasized the initially disciplining effects of central financial and non-financial management information on local sales managers and the subsequent reinterpretation of that information in an emerging sales discourse that placed local over central insights. By contrast, a practice perspective makes visible the potential for management control information to become tied up in a productive local–central interaction. Strategy formulation becomes a process that reckons with local resistance (de Certeau 1988). Management control information offers a way of not only gauging the effects of different strategic designs but also pursuing different degrees of flexibility enjoyed by restaurants that operate within that overall design (Ahrens and Chapman 2004*a*).

Our analysis of managers in Restaurant Division recognized that strategy as an encompassing organizational phenomenon ultimately comes to life in the actions of individual managers (Ortner 1984), which would suggest that management control as a practice is far from the exclusive domain of accountants. In this chapter we sought to explore the ways in which HO marketing staff and various managers from the operations hierarchy sought to draw on performance information in their efforts to draw together diverse facts, aspirations, and routine actions in the construction of Restaurant Division's strategy. Managers throughout the organization sought to distribute the cognitive processes of strategy formation across the organization rather than centralize them at the HO (Lave 1988). The processes of management control—the collection of information for mapping organizational action as well as the dissemination of performance information—formed one of the ways in which they sought to bring about this 'distribution-across'.

In this sense our analysis connects with process-oriented strategy studies. What we seek to add is an understanding of how processes of strategizing come to be constructed through MCS as well as non-financial management information. For example, in terms of Restaurant Division's relationship with its customers, the strategic task lay as much in customer selection and moulding as in identifying what the customer wants. With the help of different kinds of management information the process of strategizing became a process of discovering what the company wanted the customer to want and develop processes to deliver according to those aspirations.

Our study of the practices surrounding the strategic uses of management control information in Restaurant Division thus occupies a middle ground between emphasizing the structuring powers of MCS and their deconstruction into the actions of networks of individuals. Management control as 'action at a distance' emphasizes its colonizing qualities, the ways in which the uses of MCS are meant to reproduce centrally conceived designs of operation across diverse locales (Robson 1992). Actor-network theory, by contrast, emphasizes the constitution of management control and other organizational systems through networks of individuals (and non-humans) (e.g. Briers and Chua 2001; Jones and

Dugdale 2002; Dechow and Mouritsen 2003; Quattrone and Hopper, In Press). The shifting nature of those networks opens up the possibility of deconstructing management control, through either change or disintegration, because the networks tend to be characterized by a lack of durable and overarching motives, such as the commercial motive in the case of Restaurant Division. Our study emphasizes the ongoing construction of the commercial motive through highly varied uses of MCS. Rather than an instrument of power at a distance or the seed of organizational deconstruction, MCS functioned as an interactive bridge between diverse operational and strategic resources.

Conclusions

By focusing on the routines and practices surrounding the strategic uses of performance information both in the HO and in restaurants we were able to more clearly demonstrate the ways in which strategy and operational management interact. This relationship lies at the heart of what makes the functioning of MCS so hard to understand. It frequently appears that all the finely designed 'tie-ins' between high-level strategic planning and detailed operational control seem to disintegrate as soon as a large organization tries to actually use its MCS. Complex management control innovations that promised to 'drill down' corporate objectives into the last manufacturing cost centre and the farthest sales district end up falling into disuse.

In the past, the response from the proponents of activity-based costing (ABC), the BSC, or Economic Value Added to critics of those systems was simple: Use it more strategically! ABC becomes activity-based management. The BSC stops being a high-level performance measurement system for non-financial performance measures and becomes instead a cornerstone of strategic management—as does Economic Value Added. However, understanding the implications of such exhortations requires a more detailed understanding of the ways in which MCS might support the crafting of strategy (Mintzberg 1987).

In practice, the usefulness of MCS depends on whether managers with sufficient experience of their organization and industry are given the time to model the interdependencies between organizational processes, strategic priorities, and financial outcomes. In our case organization we observed the ways in which this process of modelling became a routine part of day-to-day management, spilling over into attempts to engender the development of new ways of interacting with customers. Performance information was to play a central role in shaping wide-ranging discussions that drew together many interfunctional relationships (Chapman 1998).

We saw, however, that performance information was not in and of itself strategic, but opened up possibilities for managers to model the business for themselves. The emphasis was not on MCS and techniques as such but on the ways in which they were linked to operational and strategic issues. This was because, apart from very simple and stable situations, the conceptual linkages between organizational strategy and operational action cannot rely on mechanical cause-and-effect relationships. In competitive markets such relationships are short-lived.

For management control to function strategically it is best used as a framing device, not an 'answer machine' (Burchell et al. 1980). Otherwise strategy mapping may come to be mistaken for the organization's 'actual' business model rather than a process that was meant to support modelling the business. In this sense the criticisms that are often levelled at MCS with strategic potential, such as the BSC or ABC, are confusing the systems design with its use. When the causal maps on which those systems are based are not updated, financial analysis easily ossifies into a routine of its own, instead of engendering routines of financial analysis for better understanding the organization.

References

Ahrens, T. (1997). 'Strategic Interventions of Management Accountants: Everyday Practice of British and German Brewers,' *European Accounting Review*, 6(4): 557–88.
—— and Chapman, C. S. (2000). 'Occupational Identity of Management Accountants in Britain and Germany', *European Accounting Review*, 9(4): 477–98.
—— —— (2002). 'The Structuration of Legitimate Performance Measures and Management: Day-to-day Contests of Accountability in a U.K. Restaurant Chain', *Management Accounting Research*, 13(2): 1–21.
—— —— (2004a). 'Accounting for Flexibility and Efficiency: A Field Study of Management Control Systems in a Restaurant Chain', *Contemporary Accounting Research*, 21(2): 271–301.
—— —— (2004b, 5–6 June). 'Management Accounting as Practice and Process'. Paper presented at the Global Management Accounting Research Symposium, Lansing, MI.
—— and Dent, J. F. (1998). 'Accounting and Organizations: Realizing the Richness of Field Research', *Journal of Management Accounting Research*, 10: 1–39.
Bourdieu, P. (1992). *The Logic of Practice*. Cambridge: Polity Press.
Briers, M. and Chua, W. F. (2001). 'The Role of Actor Networks and Boundary Objects in Management Accounting Change. A Field Study of an Implementation of Activity-Based Costing', *Accounting, Organizations and Society*, 26(3): 237–69.

Brown, S. and Eisenhardt, K. M. (1997). 'The Art of Continuous Change: Linking Complexity Theory and Time-Paced Evolution in Relentlessly Shifting Organizations', *Administrative Science Quarterly*, 42(1): 1–34.

Burchell, S., Clubb, C., Hopwood, A. G., Hughes, J., and Nahapiet, J. (1980). 'The Roles of Accounting in Organizations and Society', *Accounting, Organizations and Society*, 5(1): 5–27.

Chapman, C. S. (1998). 'Accountants in Organizational Networks', *Accounting, Organizations and Society*, 23(8): 737–66.

Child, J. (1972). 'Organizational Structure, Environment and Performance: The Role of Strategic Choice', *Sociology*, 6: 1–22.

de Certeau, M. (1988). *The Practice of Everyday Life*. Berkeley, CA: University of California Press.

Dechow, N. and Mouritsen, J. (2003). 'Enterprise Wide Resource Planning Systems and the Quest for Integration and Management Control'. Paper presented at the Global Management Accounting Research Symposium, Lansing, MI. www.bus.msu.edu/acc/gmars/papers.html.

Dreyfus, H. and Dreyfus, S. (1988). *Mind over Machine: The Power of Human Intuition and Expertise in the Era of the Computer*, 2nd edn. New York: Free Press.

Feldman, M. S. (2004). 'Resources in Emerging Structures and Processes of Change', *Organization Science*, 15(3): 295–309.

Glaser, B. and Strauss, A. (1967). *The Discovery of Grounded Theory: Strategies for Qualitative Research*. Chicago, IL: Aldine.

Guilding, C., Cravens, K. S., and Tayles, M. (2000). 'An International Comparison of Strategic Management Accounting Practices', *Management Accounting Research*, 11(1): 113–35.

Johnson, G., Melin, L., and Whittington, R. (2003). 'Guest Editors' Introduction: Micro Strategy and Strategizing: Towards an Activity-Based View', *Journal of Management Studies*, 40(1): 3–22.

Jones, T. C. and Dugdale, D. (2002). 'The ABC Bandwagon and the Juggernaut of Modernity', *Accounting, Organizations and Society*, 27(1/2): 121–63.

Kaplan, R. S. and Norton, D. P. (1992). 'The Balanced Scorecard—Measures that Drive Performance', *Harvard Business Review* (Jan.–Feb.): 71–79.

—— —— (1996). *The Balanced Scorecard: Translating Strategy into Action*. Boston, MA: Harvard Business School Press.

—— —— (2000). 'Having Trouble with Your Strategy? Then Map It', *Harvard Business Review* (Sept./Oct.): 167–77.

Lave, J. (1988). *Cognition in Practice*. Cambridge: Cambridge University Press.

Miles, M. and Huberman, A. (1994). *Qualitative Data Analysis*, 2nd edn. London and New Delhi: Sage.

Mintzberg, H. (1987). 'Crafting Strategy', *Harvard Business Review*, 65(4): 66–75.

Mouritsen, J. (1999). 'The Flexible Firm: Strategies for a Subcontractor's Management Control', *Accounting, Organizations and Society*, 24(1): 31–56.

Ortner, S. B. (1984). 'Theory in Anthropology since the Sixties', *Comparative Studies in Society and History*, 26(1): 126–66.

Quattrone, P. and Hopper, T. 'A "Time-Space Odyssey": Management Control Systems in Two Multinational Organisations', *Accounting, Organizations and Society*. (In Press.)

Roberts, J. (1990). 'Strategy and Accounting in a U.K. Conglomerate', *Accounting, Organizations and Society*, 15: 107–26.

Robson, K. (1992). 'Accounting Numbers as "Inscription": Action at a Distance and the Development of Accounting', *Accounting, Organizations and Society*, 17(7): 685–708.

Roslender, R. and Hart, S. J. (2003). 'In Search of Strategic Management Accounting: Theoretical and Field Study Perspectives', *Management Accounting Research*, 14(3): 255–79.

Schatzki, T. R., Knorr Cetina, K., and von Savigny, E. (eds.) (2001). *The Practice Turn in Contemporary Theory*. London and New York: Routledge.

Simmonds, K. (1981). 'Strategic Management Accounting', *Management Accounting*, 59(4): 26–29.

—— (1982). 'Strategic Management Accounting for Pricing: A Case Example', *Accounting and Business Research*, 47, 206–14.

Simons, R. (1990). 'The Role of Management Control Systems in Creating Competitive Advantage: New Perspectives', *Accounting, Organizations and Society*, 15(1/2): 127–43.

—— (1995). *Levers of Control*. Boston, MA: Harvard Business School Press.

Strauss, A. and Corbin, L. (1990). *Basics of Qualitative Research: Grounded Theory Procedures and Techniques*. London and New Delhi: Sage.

Tomkins, C. and Carr, C. (1996). 'Reflections on the Papers in This Issue and a Commentary on the State of Strategic Management Accounting', *Management Accounting Research*, 7(2): 271–80.

Vaivio, J. (1999). 'Examining "the Quantified Customer" ', *Accounting, Organizations and Society*, 24(8): 689–715.

Whittington, R. (2002). 'The Practice Perspective on Strategy: Unifying and Developing a Field'. Paper presented at the Academy of Management, Denver, CO.

Strategies and Organizational Problems: Constructing Corporate Value and Coherence in Balanced Scorecard Processes

Allan Hansen and Jan Mouritsen

What is strategy? Management accounting researchers have often ignored this question when they say that management accounting is for implementing rather than formulating strategy. Inspired by Anthony's seminal work (1965), where management controls and strategic planning were separated, management accounting researchers have often treated strategy as a 'black box'. However, recent debates have paid more attention to strategy. The debates in the 1990s, for example, emphasized that the future of management accounting (e.g. Bromwich and Bhimani 1994; Ittner and Larcker 1998) is dependent on whether it can frame and conceptualize strategic issues in organizations; to articulate strategy is a way to regain the lost relevance of management accounting (Johnson and Kaplan 1987). These thoughts have also been reflected in management accounting innovations. In strategic cost management the value chain (Shank and Govindarajan 1993), product attributes (Bromwich 1990), and customer functionality and quality (Cooper and Slagmulder 1997) have been mobilized and strategic performance measurements systems take a point of departure in customers' value proposition (Kaplan and Norton 1996, 2001). Strategy is put forward in management accounting in order to illuminate what corporate value and coherence is about (e.g. Chenhall and Langfield-Smith 1998; Langfield-Smith 1997) and management accounting is no longer neutral as Anthony (1965) suggested. Strategic management accounting is involved in mobilizing objects and logic that seek to encapsulate what strategy is. Here management accounting enters a complex field because it has to navigate between multiple, heterogeneous, and even competing representations of what corporate value and coherence mean.

In this chapter we study processes of constructing corporate value and coherence in organizational practices. Thus, we do not consider corporate value and coherence to be pre-defined. On the contrary we consider them to be phenomena that are constantly retranslated in organizational practices. We contend that interpretations of corporate value and coherence are ingredients in any strategy formulation and consequently also in any strategic conceptualization in management accounting. However, we also claim that the conceptualizations from strategic management accounting might be challenged by what we call organizational problems, which we see as situated manifestations of pressures to act in organizational settings. Organizational problems translate, and problematization 'describes systems of alliances, or associations between entities, thereby defining the identity and what they "want"'(Callon 1986: 206).[1]

We explore these issues through four firms' mobilization of the balanced scorecard (BSC). The BSC is a well-known example of strategic management accounting in which 'pre-made' conceptualizations of corporate value and coherence can be found. Even though Kaplan and Norton (1996: 37–8) note that other conceptualizations of strategy may be used, it is primarily the 'Porterian' framing of strategy (Porter 1980) that lasts as the strategic conceptualization in the BSC (Kaplan and Norton 1996: 37, 2001: 89). Thus, the 'pre-made' conceptualization of strategy in the BSC is that first, environment and customers have to be considered and understood, and then it is possible to develop internal processes and investments in learning and growth activities. But when firms mobilize the BSC, other conceptualizations of strategy may emerge, and, as we will show, such other conceptualizations can be found in organizational problems that are internal to the firm and exist as local pressures act. This approach assumes that organizational action exists prior to the work to develop strategy and that therefore strategy is not before organizational action and problems but part of organizational action and problems. Strategy is one of the operations of organizational action. Thus, we suggest, like others, that strategic management accounting should be studied in the context in which it operates (Burchell et al. 1980; Hopwood 1983).

If strategy is one of the operations of ongoing organizational action, the possible effects of a BSC probably are not only to implement a strategy designed around Porter's strategic opportunities. It is related to the specific organizational problems that inform the design and mobilization of the BSC. In our four cases we found that Porterian

---

[1] We recognize that in this chapter all the facets of translations as described by Callon (1986) have not been addressed. In addition to problematization he also discusses interressement, enrolment, and mobilization. We pay only scant attention to the three latter processes in this chapter; however, we still have the possibility to illustrate the fluid character of corporate value and coherence and consequently strategy in practical settings.

strategy was a weak element in the implementation of the BSC and the strong elements were organizational problems such as planning systems, cross-functional integration, internal benchmarking, and business process reengineering (BPR). These problems framed the justification of the BSC in the four firms—one in each of the firms. Planning, cross-functional integration internal benchmarking, and reengineering are 'internal' problems rather than market strategies. These internal problems then coloured the mode in which value and coherence were debated, and they thus framed the concerns labelled strategy.

We analyse how four firms brought the BSC into practice and discuss what purposes and concerns it was related to. Our aim is not to examine how strategy should have been formulated in relation to the BSC but rather to analyse how the firms did discuss strategy. Some may suggest that managers in the companies misunderstood what strategy and the BSC were all about. We do not think so and we argue that studies of processes of developing BSC can enlighten us about what strategy formulation is as in practice. This persuades us that in our examples concrete problems of internal production processes rather than notions of the customer or the market facilitate the discussion of value and coherence in the company, ending in propositions of strategy. This does not imply that customers and markets were absent in the strategies of the companies, but they were not the point of departure in formulating what value and coherence were to the companies. There was a way from internal production issues to a strategy in the companies. This way was developed in the four firms, and what seemed to be narrow and particular or internal turned out to be inclusive and general.

Our exploration of BSC processes may add to our understanding of what implementation of strategic management accounting is about. We supplement studies of implementation, which have provided important insight into the general factors at stake when implementing new management control and performance measurement systems (e.g. Anderson 1995; Shields 1995; Anderson and Young 1999; Cavalluzzo and Ittner 2004), showing how selection and interpretation of metrics, decision-making authority, training, etc. affect their implementation. In contrast, we attempt to conduct a 'performative' study where we focus on how elements come into being and create the meaning of BSC in the specific situations in which they are located. The objects for analysis are the singular *translation processes* of value, coherence, and strategic management accounting/performance measurement (see also Preston et al. 1992; Chua 1995; Briers and Chua 2001). The analysis refrains from seeing strategy as a black box and attempts to see and illuminate its adoption to and fluidity compared with local conditions and concerns (see also Roberts 1990; Miller and O'Leary 1993; Mouritsen 1999).

Strategy and the BSC

Strategy has many faces (Mintzberg 1987; Mintzberg et al. 1998). Numerous dichotomies have been mobilized in order to cope with the complexity of the concept. Is strategy a top–down or a bottom–up process (Goold and Campbell 1987)? Is strategy emergent or deliberate (Mintzberg and Waters 1985)? Is strategy outside–in (Porter 1980) or inside–out (Prahalad and Hamel 1990)? In this chapter we ask how strategies require organizational problems to respond to and thus how strategies get form and content. This may be an awkward discussion for those blinded by the separation between formulation and implementation of strategy. However, as we try to make sense of the four cases we present hereafter, it appears to us that emergent strategy is part of (strategic) management accounting because, seen as practice, strategy often starts as a discussion of organizational problems, and (strategic) management accounting is involved in developing and responding to organizational problems. Kaplan and Norton's conceptualization (2001: 89) of strategy starts with 'the value proposition [that] enables companies to define their targeted customers', which informs the selection of target customers and a positioning of one self in the market. They (e.g. Kaplan and Norton 2001: 75) draw on Porter's conceptualization (1980) of strategy so that a company 'selects the value proposition at which it will excel, a company also selects the customer segment or segments for whom that value proposition will be the differentiator, causing them to do business with the company. It is important to identify clearly the company's targeted customers' (Kaplan and Norton 2001: 89). This is a 'positioning perspective' on strategy (Mintzberg 1987) and three generic value propositions are possible: product leadership, customer intimacy, and operational excellence (Treacy and Wiersema 1995). To Kaplan and Norton, strategy is 'a means of locating an organization in what organisation theorists like to call an "environment"... Strategy becomes a "niche", in economic terms, a place that generates "rent"' (Mintzberg 1987: 15).

The value proposition embedded in target customers represents an *outside–in* logic as the value proposition is considered to 'describe the context' (Kaplan and Norton 2001: 11) for the internal processes and intangible assets within the company. The job of realizing strategy becomes one of 'ensuring alignment between an organization's internal activities and its customer value proposition' (Kaplan and Norton 2001: 90). However, the outside–in logic may be challenged with an inside–out logic (e.g. Johnson and Scholes 2002), where strategy begins by appointing internal competencies and routines (e.g. Prahalad and Hamel 1990; Grant 1991). One might say that these challenges are symptoms of the multiple and heterogeneous character of strategy which Kaplan and Norton (1996: 38) seem to recognize implicitly, as they say—even if they do not analyse how—that BSC may accommodate an 'inside–out' or other perspectives on strategy. All in all, these reopenings of the strategy black box must intensify the call made by management accountants for insight to the processes of construction of strategic issues in practice; if there is no grand scheme of strategy or corporate value and coherence what is it then that constitutes the ideas that prevail in practice?

To study the implementation of BSC, we draw on a constructivist or performative perspective on action (Latour 1986, Callon 1986), where strategy—and corporate value and coherence—is constructed or performed by actors. In this chapter we analyse the BSC as what Star and Griesemer (1989: 393) call a boundary object: 'Boundary objects are objects which are both plastic enough to adapt to local needs and the constraints of the several parties employing them, yet robust enough to maintain a common identity across sites.' The BSC is to us an open concept, which can take a series of different forms, and yet it is also robust (which we consider to be the distinction between non-financial and financial numbers—leading and lagging indicators—organized and balanced in several perspectives and with a relation to strategy implementation. There is, however, a considerable space for local adaptations and innovations.

In our conceptualization of the construction of corporate value and coherence we draw on the notion of translation (Latour 1986, Callon 1986), and the significance of phenomena will be performed rather than found in the phenomena themselves since 'everything . . . is uncertain and reversible, at least in principle. It is never given in the order of things . . . ' (Law 1999: 4). Accordingly, the BSC is given content and identity via the relations it entertains with other entities in practice. This theoretical position is one that tells that entities take their form and acquire their attributes as 'a result of their relations with other entities' (Law 1999: 3, italics in original). In principle, any entity and relations can play; they are heterogeneous rather than pure (Law 1999: 5), and it is not possible a priori to point out the relations that will be decisive for translations of corporate value and coherence. This approach contrasts with other theories of strategic management accounting, which assume that by definition we know what items such as strategy and performance are a priori.

In this chapter we challenge whether strategy in relation to the BSC is in fact (always) deliberate and builds on an outside–in logic. We suggest that realized strategy in relation to the BSC emerges from particular organizational problems. The entities constituting strategy are different from those suggested in strategic management accounting because the notions of the market and the customer were distant in formulating the objective of the BSC in our empirical situations. Rather, organizational problems that developed over time in the firms constituted the interests that BSC was to bend around. In effect, if this is true, this means that the presumptions and articulations of strategy in much strategic management accounting literature can be challenged. It may be that the answers to the question of what strategy is are too institutionalized in the academic debate on strategy and management accounting and that new possibilities of their relationships and practical constitution have to be considered.

The cases

The four cases are all well known in the Danish debate on the BSC, and they all used external consultants to help in their implementation. Table 4 summarizes understandings (translations) of corporate value and coherence in the four companies. These particular translations were formulated in fairly early stages of the implementation of the BSC in companies. Other translations have emerged since but these early stages hold interesting insights because propositions about what value and coherence in respect to strategic performance measurement are much debated in these stages. No particular translation was stabilized or institutionalized. Things were in the process of becoming.

The table depicts the organizational problem related to the implementation of BSC in each company. This problem was the barrier to the development of corporate value and coherence and was an input to staging the concerns and justifications about what the BSC was supposed to achieve for the firms. The table also summarizes the role of performance measurement in the firms.

Table 4 Corporate value, coherence, and strategic performance measurement in four cases

Company name	ErcoPharm	Kvadrat	Columbus IT Partner	BRFkredit
Industry	Pharmaceuticals	Textile	IT	Mortgage credit
Problem	Corridor thinking—suboptimization due to functional orientation. The solution is cross-functional integration.	The innovative and creative culture is a barrier for growth. Demand for a planning culture.	Growth and heterogeneity in the sales divisions A need to standardize the sales divisions.	Cost full and slow order expedition within the company—there is a need to reengineer certain processes within the company.
Value proposition	Cross-functional integration	Planning	Internal benchmarking	Reengineering
The role of performance measurements	Performance measurement accounts for mutual dependency between the functions.	Performance measurement initiates individual goal setting and planning.	Performance measurement enables comparison of process and performance in different sales divisions.	Performance measurement facilitates control of reengineered processes and possibility to document success.

We may add that the customer was not absent in discussions related to the BSC, but it was not the point of departure to propose what value was to the firm or what corporate challenges were. Customers and markets were mobilized as appendices to the central purposes of the BSC in the firms, but only after organizational problems were addressed. This makes strategic logic into something that is embedded in particular organizational problems rather than in the target customer's value proposition, as suggested by Porter.

The cases illustrate how the BSC can be justified by entities other than the customer and the market. A broad set of possible purposes is in place, and the BSC is spacious enough to accommodate them all without losing its appeal as a strategic management accounting system. We present the cases as illustrations of four distinctly different/singular purposes in each of the firms. This is clearly a simplification. In each of the firms there were undoubtedly more propositions about the problems to be negotiated and handled through the BSC as the firm's problems could be conceptualized differently—they were not fixed but negotiable.

This perspective that the BSC can be understood as an object with many possible functions and effects has not been addressed much in the literature. Literature on the BSC illustrates its possibility as a strategic management accounting system, either as a causal business model or as a communication device. We suggest an addition, namely, to study it as a *boundary object* (Star and Griesemer 1989) that is filled with purpose and function as an effect of particular organizational problems mobilized in the implementation process.

We learned about the four firms through visits and interviews with key persons involved in BSC *projects*. The interviews were semi-structured, lasted for about two hours, and dealt with questions related to strategy formulation, the functionality of the BSC, choice of performance measurement, and the conditions for and effects of implementing the BSC in the particular organizations. These interviews allowed us to explore the process of identifying how the BSC was equipped (in this phase of the project) with purpose and ambition. In the subsequent sections of the chapter we present the four cases one by one.

ErcoPharm: BSC for cross-functional integration

ErcoPharm is a production division of OrionPharma based in Denmark. OrionPharma is an R&D-oriented pharmaceutical division of the OrionGroup, a Finnish company specializing in health care products.

Pharmaceutical R&D at OrionPharma focuses on three therapy areas: central nervous system disorders, cardiology and critical care, and hormonal therapies related to both human and animal health. The company globally employed more than 5,800 people with R&D, sales, and production in both sales and product divisions all over the world in 2002, and OrionPharma's net sales were €483 million.

The implementation of the BSC in ErcoPharm was a local implementation as it was carried out before the BSC became an official management control system (MCS) in the OrionGroup. Yet the local implementation in ErcoPharm played a role in the overall implementation of the BSC in the group through its learning effects as a pilot project.

The recurrent concern in our interviews was cross-functional integration, which tied concerns of strategy and performance measurement to the firms' (important, strategic, and problematic) issues. A systematic effort to establish coordination between functional entities was a crucial problematization towards improving the performance of the firm. To go through a BSC process was considered as a means to address this problem. The chief controller explained:

People's mindset was at that time, when we discussed balanced scorecard for the first time, embedded in 'corridors'. At that time the cross-functional integration in the company was poor. We experienced solid boundaries between production, sales/marketing, clinical testing etc. and even competition between the functions. They simply did not communicate with each other. Not because they did not want to, but because they could not see the interdependence between the functions. It meant that each function became isolated and sub-optimised. So one of the reasons that we considered balanced scorecard was—and I guess the most important reason—that it could help us to facilitate a better co-ordination between the entities. I guess you can say that in the process of developing balanced scorecard, cross-functional integration was the point of departure.

The value attached to the BSC was a capability to speak for cross-functional, sequentially dependent processes and to create attention to their synchronization. The business controller argued:

Cross-functional integration is very much what strategy and balanced scorecard is all about in our company

The BSC was envisaged as a mechanism that could give visibility to the interdependence between organizational entities. For example, the manager for clinical testing emphasized as follows:

As we see it, we have got a chain of processes that are connected. Through balanced scorecard it is possible to directly address the question of what each function expects from others. What does clinical testing expect from sales/ marketing, sales/marketing from production etc. We set up goals and measurement for all that in the balanced scorecard process. We've got everything on print now—what it is that we expect from each other now—an understanding of what it is that we can do for each other. When we start to measure the key processes in each functional area and start to talk about the possibilities to control it, the interdependence between the functional areas becomes clear. And we can begin to optimise overall. This is why balanced scorecard and the process we have been through have been so important to us. We can now easily see when things are interconnected. And when there is a point in discussing things with other functional areas.

So, to create value, attention had to be related to the linkages between operational processes, and thus the problem was to synchronize functional processes. The customer and the market position were considered secondary, or at least taken for granted, as the business controller stated:

We all know who the customer is. The thing that really matters to our company is to get the integration between the different functions right. This is the issue that has to be the point of departure when we develop strategic performance measurements.

The BSC was adequately spacious to inscribe this concern and hence contribute to functional integration. It allowed the problems encountered in the firm to be stronger than its own design principles, but it also maintained its status as an organizing element in developing the responses to organizational problems. The BSC maintained its identity in

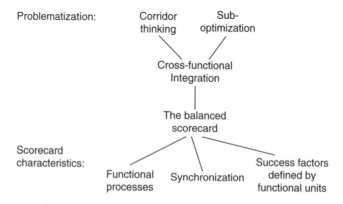

Figure 7 Organizational problems and the BSC in ErcoPharm

the image of four dimensions of performance measurement, and it allowed a local interpretation of what strategy was about, namely the local problematization of cross-functional integration. Figure 7 illustrates how the BSC gained its initial characteristics in ErcoPharm.

Kvadrat: BSC for planning

Kvadrat develops and markets modern soft furnishing designs and curtains to the contract market and selected segments of the retail market. Today, Kvadrat is a brand name in a professional market where quality and design are vital parameters. Production takes place in twenty-eight textile factories and print-works in Western Europe. In 2001/2002, with the combined effort of some 160 employees, Kvadrat achieved a turnover of approximately €50 million. Exports account for 80 per cent of the turnover.

The rationale behind the development of BSC in Kvadrat was enhanced integration of planning activities. At the time when the BSC was mentioned as a solution, the firm saw itself as overly creative and innovative. The chief controller explained the rationale of the then possible implementation as follows:

Our most important reason for implementing balanced scorecard was that we needed a planning culture at that time. The employees are not good at writing down what they wanted and committing themselves to what they have planned. If plans are written, like in BSC, you can actually check whether you have done it or not afterwards. Kvadrat is a creative company and we think it is important that we've got the spirit—creativity—in the air. However, the creative culture can be hard to handle. It cost a lot of money and can be a problem when we want to produce things and get them out of the door. We simply have to plan in order to survive. People have to commit themselves.

In Kvadrat the BSC was mobilized as a means to promote a planning culture, which stood in contrast to the reliance on the power of individuals' pursuance of creativity and innovation. The BSC was presented as a mechanism to express goals, ambition, and measures so that reporting and evaluation could be performed. The notion of performance came into light as accountability to plans. This was the basis for developing a planning culture, it was argued.

The BSC was launched as a tool to be used by the individual employee for his or her own planning. The process was centred on 'mini-scorecards'—personal BSC where each employee had drawn up his or her own quantified goals related to the work process. The chief controller explained:

The planning our employees carry out now is framed by balanced scorecard. They plan through their 'mini-scorecard'. They set up goals and measures for their plans and relate them to specific activities. They explicate activities, time them and reflect upon what the realisation might be dependent upon—interdependencies and so on. Of course they also address issues of performance directly because they commit themselves to a target.

A powerful aspect of the BSC, according to the CEO, was that it drew on a non-financial language. This helped make the creative culture a planned one, because this language was direct and about the activities performed by employees. They could better identify themselves with goals and measures when the terminology was a non-financial language about activities.

As employees recorded their own goals individually, a high number of performance measures were incorporated in the BSC and it was developed as a planning tool, because it detailed the actions and effects to be expected from the organization's members. This use of the BSC was at odds with the idea of BSC as a means for implementing market strategy, the chief controller underlined, where the ambition was to involve a much smaller number of measures. The chief controller elaborated:

The consultants that helped us implement balanced scorecard had a special idea about how the scorecard should be and how the measures should be structured. They began the process elsewhere. They began with the customer. In our mini-scorecard everything is filed—all the things that the employees plan, all the plans, goals and measures. If you for instance have an area where employees have outlined six goals and related measures, then we think we should include them all unless they overlap. According to the consultants you should take another point of departure. We argued these issues with the consultant. However, we think that we use balanced scorecard for something special in our organisation. We would like to teach people how to plan.

The chief controller contended that the BSC as a means to constitute a planning culture did not necessarily match the concern for implementing the customer value proposition through the BSC. In Kvadrat the aim was to use the BSC to develop measures and goals for the individual employee and groups, and the input for setting up measures and goals was less a general business model than the experience of individual labour processes.

The customer was not absent in Kvadrat's discussions, but it was not a problem. It was obviously important but since it was no problem there was no reason to design and develop strategic management accounting around the customer.

The pursuance of a planning culture affected the identity of the BSC in Kvadrat. The issue was to get the employees to think about how they could plan in relation to their own personal processes and how their plans could benefit Kvadrat. Individualizing the planning process, or perhaps more clearly adding planning and communication of objectives to the individual's activities, the effect was more a reflection of internal concerns than an implementation of the customer's value proposition. The 'bottom–up' planning process was not to accommodate the customer but to teach the employee to plan. The development of planning capabilities was singled out to be the problem, which—if solved—would have important ('strategic') implications for how the firm would conduct its affairs. The drive towards planning, irrespective of their knowledge that the BSC was about the customer (it was claimed), was a big issue that was seen to transform the identities of employees and thus construct a completely new company where the path into the future was laid out much more coherently (and also linearly) than before.

In this sense Kvadrat's BSC resembles a conventional BSC, but it looks different because the ambition is to use it to inscribe all employees and make the sum of employee goals the firm's goals. Among managers there was an understanding that employees were capable and resourceful and therefore that in a sense the capabilities of employees were such that they could override the specific concern for the customer. The collective of creative individuals could even know more about the customers'

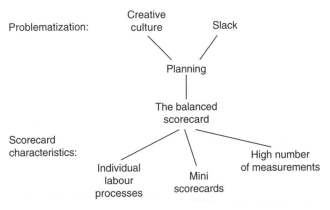

Figure 8 Organizational problems and the BSC in Kvadrat

needs than customers would themselves know, and possibly therefore the initial marginalization of the customer comes back in another way, not through the wants expressed by customers, but perhaps via the coherence of the capabilities that increased planning could do for the development of interesting actions—also for customers. The problem of a creative culture was mitigated via a BSC, and the resulting planning culture would have lasting ('strategic') effects on the operations of the firm. Figure 8 illustrates the role of BSC in Kvadrat.

Columbus IT Partner: BSC for benchmarking

Columbus IT Partner, founded in 1989, is a leading supplier of business management systems for the mid-market, and a global partner of Microsoft Business Solutions. Columbus IT Partner had in 2001 approximately a turnover of €100 million and more than 850 employees in twenty-six countries. Headquartered in Copenhagen, Denmark, the Columbus network of strategically located subsidiaries in Europe, Africa, Asia, and the Americas ensures customers an integrated standard approach worldwide, supported by local knowledge.

Since it started, Columbus has experienced high growth and in parallel with its increasing size it has faced a problem of controlling expansion. Particularly, there was an increasing problematization of the variation in the execution of key processes, and the claim that standardization was needed was increasingly aired. Through standardized processes the expectation was that sales divisions around Europe could transfer knowledge among each other. The chief controller described growth and the problem of lack of standards and structure as follows:

What happened was that the sales divisions were too much alone. It was clear during the period with high growth. It was harder and harder to obtain synergy between the different divisions unless more administrative procedures were installed. 250 new people were employed last year. With a growth like that we needed more structure and principles. Things do not just happen by mouth-to-mouth. At the same time we could see that if we wanted to be aggressive and be 200 in England and 200 in Germany, there was no reason to learn the same thing twice in each country. In addition we have learned a lot in Denmark and these experiences had to be transferred.

The BSC was related to the salient demand for more control. At the time, to Columbus, standardization concerned the numerous sales divisions that were deemed to be largely similar production systems. This was the reason that standardization could be contemplated. In Columbus the BSC was related to the problem of benchmarking. It became a tool for standardization. The chief controller explained:

Balanced scorecard was warmly welcomed in the sales divisions because they saw something useful. They could also use it in the interaction with us. They could ask: how should I do this or do you have anything in relation to this issue? It became possible to compare Austria, US, England, etc. Some were good at something, others at other things. They learned how to do things in respect to all the measures in balanced scorecard, which we tried to relate to best practices. I think that is the reason why balanced scorecard was so well accepted. The balanced scorecard is not just a strategic measurement system, it is a short way to do things better.

The measurements in the BSC were seen as resources for comparing sales divisions; it was possible to compare a process in one division with the same process in another. To facilitate comparison between sales divisions, Columbus developed distinctions between different stages in the development of the sales divisions; a sales division could be a support office, a mainstream entity, or an integrator. For each of these different organizational forms a series of key processes were set-up, and related goals and measurements followed:

It was more a matter of comparing processes rather than talking about customers. It was another point of departure but nevertheless crucial at that point of time.

It was a conscious decision to make the BSC different from its stipulated procedures. The customer had no priority in the narrative of the BSC, and learning through benchmarking was favoured, which was an effect of the internal problem of growth:

The basic reason why we implemented balanced scorecard was that we had grown so much, and that it was recognized by top management that the 20 countries we were in and the new ones that were yet to come were making or would make the same mistakes. Of course they make mistakes, but there has to be a medium to report the mistakes and initiate a learning process and communicate standards for all the things that we do and the things that create value to our organisation.

The inside was made up of operational issues and concerns of learning from each other. Problematizing through benchmarking was an impetus for making organizational strategy a mechanism to build efficiency into

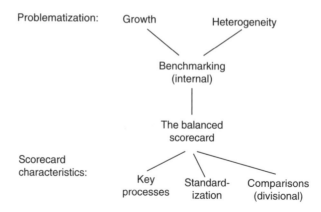

Figure 9   Organizational problems and the BSC in Columbus IT

operations and allow growth to happen simultaneously. Figure 9 illustrates the character of the BSC in Columbus IT.

BRFkredit: BSC for Business Process Reengineering

BRFkredit is an independent mortgage credit institution that offers financial solutions and other services related to real estate and property. BRFkredit offers loans against a mortgage on owner-occupied homes, commercial properties, and subsidized housing. In the corporate lending segment, BRFkredit focuses on loans for office and business properties and for private rental and cooperative housing. Loans for residential purposes account for almost 90 per cent of the total lending, whereas office and business properties make up less than 10 per cent. Being owned by a foundation, BRFkredit is under no pressure to pay dividends or increase share prices. Hence, BRFkredit has its focus on providing bondholder value rather than shareholder value. The company administered in 2001 loans for approximately €20 billion and its equity was valued €1.2 billion.

The BSC was implemented in BRFkredit in parallel to a BPR project. The financial manager explained about the BPR project:

> At that time we decided to change our organisation. The reason was that we recognised that we didn't perform well enough: too high process time and costs.

Consequently, BRFkredit initiated two BPR projects:

The first reengineering project was about improving the efficiency in the loan processing process. The target was shorter process time, professionalism, improved communication, and a higher success rate (offer vs. contract). The second reengineering project was about the distribution channel for the private sector, primarily the estate agents. We thought we could get more loans out here—there was a high potential, but we really didn't exploit our possibilities. We also looked at other channels and also the communication between the estate agents and BRFkredit.

To monitor BPR projects, a control system was needed, the financial controller explained. The BPR process was extensive and complex and a formal goal setting system was needed. The BSC became the resource here and it was closely linked with the BPR process. The financial manager explained:

When we started with balanced scorecard it was with a point of departure in two BPR-processes. We found that the philosophy behind balanced scorecard easily could be used as a tool to manage the input and the output related to the BPR processes. When we started to use balanced scorecard the theory behind it was quite new and we gave it our own touch. However, I think the way we used it was powerful.

The BSC was presented as an MCS, which could control the process of reengineering. The financial manager, and with him other top managers, used the BSC to outline goals and measures and to formalize the evaluation of the processes. They sought to grasp the change of the processes, and the BSC gave them a framework for converting success factors into measures and wrapping them in systems of accountability:

We have used balanced scorecard to control the processes. For all the input and output we had in the BPR process we evaluated critically the question of Critical Performance Indicators. We went thoroughly through the two processes with senior management and asked: what is it that we want to contribute with and what are the results? In addition we asked: does it work? And we measured the effects. It was the reason why we got success with balanced scorecard, I guess, we could see what worked and what did not. We spend a lot of time deciding in what way we should measure the effects of the reengineering work.

The construction of this BSC was built on an inside–out logic. The processes needing revitalization were catalysts for developing strategic performance measurements and the scorecard played a role in

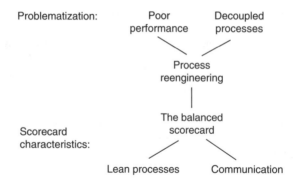

Figure 10   Organizational problems and the BSC in BRFkredit

conceptualizing and understanding the organizational change initiated by the reengineering projects. This combination between measurement and process development was characterized as crucial by the financial manager. He suggested:

We worked with processes and reporting simultaneously. We developed the processes and documented the result via the numbers. The scorecard actually reveals the way we have organised our BPR-process. These are the background for our measures—for example: reduce our portfolio exit by xx. Now we have set-up some five years measures based upon these criteria. We use them in our strategy process now, and they provide the managers with some good input for discussion.

When the BSC was implemented in BRFkredit it took its character from the reengineering processes. Later, its identity also came from other sources, among other things from the development of a new market strategy. But in this initial stage the point of departure was the two reengineered processes: loan processing and distribution. Figure 10 illustrates the characteristics of BSC in BRFkredit.

Discussion

The four examples presented above suggest that BSCs are mobilized vis-à-vis organizational problems that colour the scorecards' identity. In these cases, the BSC came from important yet distinct organizational problems, and in its association with these problems, it gained character. It surveyed the implementation of cross-functional integration, introduction of a planning culture, the use of benchmarking, and the development of BPR. The BSC was bent around organizational problems, and the role of strategic performance measurement—the representation of corporate value and coherence—in the four firms differed dramatically. In ErcoPharm, measurements were used to link organizational entities, and therefore the attempt was to develop measurements 'between' the processes that the representations were to integrate, while in Kvadrat the ambition was to make individuals disclose their ambitions so that some form of coherence between people could be developed via visibility into goals and objectives. In Columbus IT the concern was to compare processes by measurement, and for BRFkredit, the measurements were used to signify the effect of a new and transformed process.

The situated logic of the process of developing strategic management accounting

The specific or situated logic that guided the development of the BSC in the four companies varied from case to case and its role was flexible as it was related to particular organizational problems in the companies. This tells us something about what it means to implement strategic management accounting in general and develop a BSC in particular.

First, there is a question about what corporate value and coherence are. Often in the strategic management accounting literature, conceptualizations are extrovert and oriented towards locating the firm in its environment. Our cases illustrate that these might be challenged because translations of value and coherence also emerge from particular organizational problems and these problems seem to be developing situated logic and justification of the BSC project and thus also the role accorded to it.

Second, the implementation of a BSC is itself a process that involves complements, overlaps, and conflicts between various articulations of what its purpose is to be. In the cases we found a discussion of what the BSC could achieve by itself and what it was supposed to do in the firms. This included an explicit discussion of what parts of the BSC were not relevant. It appeared, at least, that project managers were conscious of possible differences between what they would term the 'theory of the BSC' and the way they wished to draw it into their firms. They realized that BSC could be used for many other things and have very different presentations from what they considered to be the norm of a BSC. To project managers this did not invalidate the BSC; it gave it new power. It could be bent towards purposes so that a local identity could be upheld and yet, at the same time, the notion that BSC was implemented, and not something else, could be also be upheld.

Third, as a mechanism for strategic management accounting in the cases the BSC safeguarded the notion of strategy so that it partly came to refer to what was *important and problematic* in a firm rather than any distinct object like the market, the competition, or the customer, which appear to be favoured in texts of the BSC. This did not restrain the companies from using it liberally, but they added to it and made it perform distinctly in relation to the emerging concerns of their firms rather than vis-à-vis a preordained object in the environment. We saw that strategy, as practice, is a fragile and dynamic thing, which is bound to organizational problems, and it may not be possible a priori to define how these look. Does the BSC look for strategy and find organizational problems, or will organizational problems look for an implementation device and find the BSC? In both situations, the BSC only performs in settings; it performs by allowing additional complements to colour its identity.

Yet the BSC is also strong because it adds to the locality. It presents a strategic discourse where value, coherence, and measurement are tied together. It allows firms to develop closure around complex projects that reorient their identities because it helps frame connections that were not readily available beforehand. Notably, by insisting on goal-directed measurement that translates more or less vague ambitions and goals into measurements, it justifies a debate on connections and how such connections are part of the firm. The BSC in general allows 'grand ambitions' and 'reporting systems' to be talked about simultaneously. In addition, it is probably no disadvantage that the BSC also has a reputation in business; that it helps define what 'modern management' is about. It is an institutionalized object that is very difficult to be against, and therefore it also has power in particular settings and can be used to transform them.

A strategic management accounting system such as the BSC is one input into organizational action and it contributes to developing a situated logic around particular organizational problems. In their meeting points, strategies will emerge. Emerging strategies develop through inputs, many of which are intended strategies, but intentions cannot govern the development of actual strategies alone, because they have

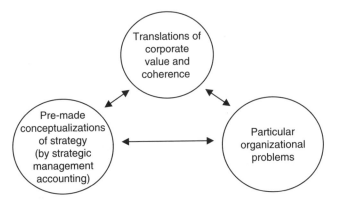

Figure 11   Components in translations of corporate value and coherence

to respond to organizational problems as they have sedimented themselves. Therefore, new strategic management accounting intervenes into existing organizational arrangements, but can only be strong if it adopts viewpoints parallel to those that emerge as organizational problems.

Thus, Figure 11 depicts our point that translations of corporate value and coherence relate not only to pre-made conceptualizations of strategy (for instance as suggested by Kaplan and Norton) but also to particular organizational problems (corridor thinking, lack of planning, heterogeneity, underperformance); the issue of corporate value and coherence is not given a priori. The four cases we have introduced portray the pre-made conceptualizations as marginalized. However, it may not always be so. Pre-made conceptualizations may interact more or 'fit' better into other settings; however, they can never make it alone. Particularities will always present themselves. Organizational problems hold significant insight into what is at stake in the individual organization, and therefore—in relation to strategic management accounting—a certain dose of modesty is welcome because there will be leaks in the pre-made conceptualizations of what it is that might generate value and coherence in the particular organizational setting. Thus, we suggest that we stop and reflect.

This chapter has called for pluralism. It suggests that theory about strategic management accounting should be concerned with the role of the specific resources that are present in practice in the form of particular organizational problems as they influence the translation of corporate value and coherence.

Organizational problems and the 'functionality' of strategic management accounting systems

To understand the juxtaposition between organizational problems and strategic management accounting systems generally is partly to engage in what Ahrens and Chapman (2004) term the enabling side of (strategic) management accounting system emphasizing their role in the process of learning and building competencies in organizations. They note that management accounting systems can have a very active and influential role in intervening in small and big decision-making processes. We may add that this is exactly because they are introduced and operated in view of organizational problems so that there is an interest in manoeuvring the management accounting systems towards decision-making. But this is hardly the effect merely of a 'good' management accounting system. It is because an effort has been made to tie the management accounting system with a context that a priori is only loosely coupled with this context, but it gains connectivity in the mobilization of the organizational process.

Organizational problems are thus not 'negative'—they are ongoing problematizations that continue to develop an appreciation of where the firm would go among the numerous paths that could have been followed. Organizational problems are 'positive' in the sense that they seek to engage the future of the firm. They are 'in action' because they respond to the history of the firm and develop alternatives to feelings of misalignment that push unintended consequences forward; at least they identify effects that are unbearable and therefore somehow need to be rectified. Organizational problems are—as part of emerging strategy—always a problematization that engages the future.

In the translation processes the problems and solutions were closely related; the problems were connected to a method of their rectification. In all our cases this method of rectification involved performance (which justified the problem), delegation (that makes things happen), and coordination (how elements are related). The solution—the counterpart to the problem—was an 'administrative' procedure that embedded organizational decision-making. This is where the BSC came in as a mechanism to tie together performance, delegation, and coordination and express them coherently; it helped create this integration. Here, the BSC was 'functional' as it devised a procedure to put the problems of benchmarking, cross-functional integration, individual goal setting, and process reengineering into solutions of decentralization, planning, control, performance, and change. It actually helped integrate various singular management areas such as marketing and production and intertwined them through a representational space where 'administrative' obligations and duties were drawn up.

The action between strategic management accounting systems and organizational problems is not only a discussion of the outside versus the inside, which has been the case in this chapter. Yet in our analysis of the four firms it was exactly the confrontation between the internal and the external that included the tension between BSC articulations and practical articulations.

Conclusions

Often, the idea of strategy has been left unproblematized in strategic management accounting debates. In this chapter we have found that the rhetoric and conceptualizations of corporate value and coherence made by strategic management accounting systems may not always be reflective of practice. We suggest that organizational problems are central aspects of a going concern where the firm is already in an operating mode and has a history so that strategy becomes emerging rather than pre-definable. The history is where organizational problems are and these attach to new strategic management accounting systems and provide them with identity and purposes, which in some situations are very far from the rhetorical functioning of such new systems. At the same time, however, new strategic management accounting systems also exist as entities that can function as a BSC in all four firms even if their local characteristics vary.

When Kaplan and Norton (2001: 104) precisely note in respect to their conceptualization of strategy that '[W]e do not claim to have made a science of strategy.... The description of strategy, however, should not be an art. If we can describe strategy in a more disciplined way, we increase the likelihood of successful implementation', they make an understandable distinction. The challenge is, however, that organizational problems are not easily inscribed and disciplined and they seem to have particular roles in terms of translating value and coherence in firms. As organizational problems are located in the history of the firm, they are also part of the emerging strategies of the firm. As illustrated in the cases, the strategic management accounting tool cannot be separated from the problem it is seen to negotiate, and, suddenly, how strategic management accounting can remain outside the realm of strategy formulation is difficult to see.

The BSC is analysed here as a boundary object (Star and Griesemer 1989). As a boundary object, BSC is plastic enough to appeal distinctly to a local situation where its identity is moulded through the specific network of affairs that make it up. This is why it can 'stand for' cross-functional integration, planning culture, benchmarking, and BPR. Its association with organizational problems forces it to attain colour from the specific situation. However, it is also plastic enough to keep an identity that traverses between the contexts of its application. It has an imagery with four dimensions and some relation between strategy and indicators that can be identified across contexts and can provide a blueprint of 'modern management'. The BSC does not encapsulate all activities in local situations, as the four firms knew they were not just applying the BSC. The global character is more an imagery that provides a form into which management practices can be put and which combine what may be shorthand for any conceivable concern that a management of a firm may have.

References

Ahrens, T. and Chapman, C. (2004). 'Accounting for Flexibility and Efficiency: A Field Study of Management Control Systems in a Restaurant Chain', *Contemporary Accounting Research*, 21(2): 271–302.

Anderson, S. W. (1995). 'A Framework for Assessing Cost Management System Change: The Case of Activity-Based Costing Implementation at General Motors, 1986–1993', *Journal of Management Accounting Research*, 7(Fall): 1–51.

—— and Young, S. M. (1999). 'The Impact of Contextual and Process Factors on the Evaluation of Activity-Based Costing Systems', *Accounting, Organizations and Society*, 24(7): 525–59.

Anthony, R. N. (1965). *Planning and Control Systems: A Framework for Analysis*. Boston, MA: Harvard University.

Briers, M. and Chua, W. F. (2001). 'The Role of Actor-Networks and Boundary Objects in Management Accounting Change: A Field Study of an Implementation of Activity-Based Costing', *Accounting, Organizations and Society*, 26(3): 237–69.

Bromwich, M. (1990). 'The Case for Strategic Management Accounting: The Role of Accounting Information for Strategy in Competitive Markets', *Accounting, Organizations and Society*, 15(1/2): 27–46.

—— and Bhimani, A. (1994). *Management Accounting Pathways to Progress*. London: The Chartered Institute of Management Accountants.

Burchell, S., Clubb, C., Hopwood, A. G., Hughes, J., and Nahapiet, J. (1980). 'The Role of Accounting in Organizations and Society', *Accounting, Organizations and Society*, 5(1): 5–27.

Callon, M. (1986). 'Some Elements of a Sociology of Translation: Domestication of the Scallops and the Fishermen of St. Brieuc Bay', in J. Law (ed.), *Power, Action and Belief: A New Sociology of Knowledge? Sociological Review Monograph: 32*. London: Routledge & Kegan Paul, 196–233.

Cavalluzzo, K. S. and Ittner, C. D. (2004). 'Implementing Performance Measurement Innovations: Evidence from Government', *Accounting, Organization and Society*, 29(3/4): 243–67.

Chenhall, R. H. and Langfield-Smith, K. (1998). 'The Relationship between Strategic Priorities, Management Techniques and Management Accounting: An Empirical Investigation Using a Systems Approach', *Accounting, Organizations and Society*, 23(3): 243–64.

Chua, W. F. (1995). 'Experts, Networks and Inscriptions in the Fabrication of Accounting Images: A Story of the Representation of Three Public Hospitals', *Accounting, Organizations and Society*, 20(2/3): 111–45.

Cooper, R. and Slagmulder, R. (1997). *Target Costing and Value Engineering*. Portland, OR: Productivity Press.

Goold, M. and Campbell, A. (1987). *Strategies and Styles: The Role of the Centre in Managing Diversified Corporations*. Oxford: Blackwell.

Grant, R. M. (1991). 'The Resource-Based Theory of Competitive Advantage: Implications for Strategy Formulation', *California Management Review*, 33(3): 114–35.

Hopwood, A. G. (1983). 'On Trying to Study Accounting in the Contexts in Which It Operates', *Accounting, Organizations and Society*, 8(2/3): 287–306.

Ittner, C. D. and Larcker, D. F. (1998). 'Innovations in Performance Measurement: Trends and Research Implications', *Journal of Management Accounting Research*, 10: 205–38.

Johnson, G. and Scholes, K. (2002). *Exploring Corporate Strategy*. London: Pearson Higher Education.

Johnson, T. H. and Kaplan, R. S. (1987). *Relevance Lost: The Rise and Fall of Management Accounting*. Boston, MA: Harvard University Press.

Kaplan, R. S. and Norton, D. P. (1996). *The Balanced Scorecard: Translating Strategy into Action*. Boston, MA: Harvard Business School Press.

—— and Norton, D. P. (2001). *The Strategy-Focused Organization: How Balanced Scorecard Companies Thrive in the New Business Environment*. Boston, MA: Harvard Business School Press.

Langfield-Smith, K. (1997). 'Management Control Systems and Strategy: A Critical Review', *Accounting, Organizations and Society*, 22(2): 207–32.

Latour, B. (1986). 'The Power of Associations', in J. Law (ed.), *Power, Action and Belief*. London: Routledge & Kegan Paul, 264–80.

Law, J. (1999). 'After ANT: Complexity, Naming and Topology', in J. Law and J. Hassard (eds.), *Actor Network Theory and After*. Oxford: Blackwell, 1–15.

Miller, P. and O'Leary, T. (1993). 'Accounting, "Economic Citizenship", and the Spatial Reordering of Manufacture', *Accounting, Organizations and Society*, 19(1): 12–43.

Mintzberg, H. (1987). 'The Strategy Concept I: Five Ps for Strategy', *California Management Review*, 30(Fall): 11–24.

—— and Waters, J. A. (1985). 'Of Strategies, Deliberate and Emergent', *Strategic Management Journal*, 6(3): 257–72.

—— Ahlstrand, B., and Lampel, J. (1998). *Strategy Safari: A Guided Tour through the Wilds of Strategic Management*. Hemel Hempstead, UK: Prentice-Hall.

Mouritsen, J. (1999). 'The Flexible Firm: Strategies for a Subcontractor's Management Control', *Accounting, Organizations and Society*, 24(1): 31–55.

Porter, M. E. (1980). *Competitive Strategy*. New York: Free Press.

Prahalad, C. K. and Hamel, G. (1990). 'The Core Competence of the Corporation', *Harvard Business Review*, 68(3): 79–91.

Preston, A. M., Cooper, D. J., and Coombs, R. W. (1992). 'Fabricating Budgets: A Study of the Production of Management Budgeting in the National Health Service', *Accounting, Organizations and Society,* 17(6): 561–93.

Roberts, J. (1990). 'Strategy and Accounting in a U.K. Conglomerate', *Accounting, Organizations and Society,* 15(1/2): 107–26.

Shank, J. K. and Govindarajan, V. (1993). *Strategic Cost Management: The New Tool for Competitive Advantage.* New York: Free Press.

Shields, M. D. (1995). 'An Empirical Analysis of Firm's Implementation Experiences with Activity-Based Costing', *Journal of Management Accounting Research,* 7(Fall): 1–28.

Star, S. L. and Griesemer, J. R. (1989). 'Institutional Ecology, "Translations" and Boundary Objects: Amateurs and Professionals in Berkeley's Museum of Vertebrate Zoology', *Social Studies of Science,* 19: 387–420.

Treacy, M. and Wiersema, F. (1995). *The Discipline of Market Leaders: Choose Your Customers, Narrow Your Focus, Dominate Your Market.* Reading, MA: Addison-Wesley.

Capital Budgeting, Coordination, and Strategy: A Field Study of Interfirm and Intrafirm Mechanisms[1]

Peter B. Miller and Ted O'Leary

Introduction

There has been remarkably little systematic study of the processes and practices through which capital budgeting decisions are made within and between organizations. The complex strategic and organizational phenomena created by capital budgeting have been similarly neglected. Such issues have fallen between the gaps that separate the distinct yet related literatures of accounting, finance, and strategy. Recent large-scale surveys of practice have demonstrated trends in the use of particular valuation techniques, and advances in real-options modelling have identified ways in which valuation practices might be modified and extended. Despite such research, our understanding of investment appraisal processes is seriously inadequate, as scholars in accounting and finance have acknowledged. In particular, little is known of how organizations may seek to establish congruence between individual investment decisions made in many different sub-units, and articulations of overall organizational strategy. The ways in which investments can build organizational distinctiveness have scarcely been addressed. Also, the capital budgeting literature has remained impervious to the rise in network forms of organization, which may call for processes of

[1] This study was made possible by the support and cooperation of many employees of Intel Corporation. We are indebted particularly to Andy Bryant, Gerry Parker, and Mike Splinter for granting permission for the study, and to David Layzell for his support and encouragement throughout. We are grateful for comments received from participants in research colloquia at INSEAD, the London School of Economics and Political Science, Michigan State University, University College Dublin, the University of Manchester, the University of Southern California, and the University of Ulster at Jordanstown. We are grateful also for comments received from Christoph Drechsler, Ian Garrett, Sue Haka, Bob Kaplan, Joan Luft, Mike Newman, Brian Pentland, Mike Power, John Roberts, Geoff Sprinkle, Norman Strong, Lenos Trigeorgis, and Yanling Zhang. The financial support of the British Design Council, the Centre for Analysis of Risk and Regulation, and PriceWaterhouseCoopers is gratefully acknowledged.

investment coordination between legally separate entities and the pursuit of strategies at interorganizational levels. This chapter reports the results of a four-year longitudinal field study conducted at executive office levels in Intel Corporation. It seeks to remedy the neglect of firm-level empirical analyses of capital budgeting, and of the mechanisms used to coordinate investment decisions and associated expectations in a manner consistent with overall organizational strategy. More specifically, it examines whether managers at Intel systematically coordinate investments in a manner consistent with the theory of complementarities.

The importance of coordinating individual capital investment decisions to produce the benefits of complementarity relations has been examined in several recent studies. As Milgrom and Roberts (1995a,b) note, such relations arise when additional investment in any one component of a system increases the returns to additional investment in the others. They have argued that, where extensive complementarities are present, value-maximizing results may be achieved only by coordinated change in all the components of a system—such as novel marketing policies, products, production processes and manufacturing capabilities—and not by altering one of these elements in isolation from shifts in the others. Brennan and Trigeorgis (2000), among others, have sought to promote real-options analyses to enable a firm's managers to formally appraise the value of such inter-related investments. At the interfirm level, Dyer and Singh (1998) have sought to elaborate the ways in which a firm may secure 'relational rents' through the creation of complementary assets with other corporations.

However, as several authors have noted, the significance of complementarity relations may extend far beyond the direct realization of increased profits from a particular set of investments. The identification and production of such relations may be central to the enactment of wider organizational strategies, as Roberts (2004), Siggelkow (2001) and Whittington and Pettigrew (2003) have argued. On this view, the pursuit of comparative advantage involves forming cross-sectional and time-series relations between investments, over a long period of time. Investments in a firm's unique elements of intellectual property and skill are thus to be combined with one another, and with other, more generic types of resources. This allows the formation of systems of mutually reinforcing assets that are distinct, and that may be difficult for competitors to replicate.

Despite the formal modelling of complementarity relations, and theoretical and empirical studies of their significance in the formation of corporate strategies (Siggelkow 2001), there remains an empirical deficit in the study of the actual capital budgetting and investment coordination practices that are used by firms (Jensen 1993; Graham and Harvey 2002). This is particularly so with respect to field-based research that looks intensively at the investment appraisal practices of a single firm using a wide variety of data. More specifically, despite intuition and casual observation, little is known about the mechanisms (other than competitive markets) through which the coordination of investments and related expectations is achieved within and among firms (Miller and O'Leary 1997). Also, little is known about how the coordination mechanisms used by firms relate overall organizational strategy to financial evaluation techniques, such as net present value (NPV), payback, and return on investment (ROI), that form the core of traditional capital budgeting practices. While Graham and Harvey's recent survey of capital budgeting (2001) polls a large set of firms, poses a broad range of questions concerning whether and when particular valuation techniques are used, and provides unique information on the financing policies of firms, issues of investment coordination are not addressed specifically. For instance, their questionnaire does not ask whether managers consider the scope of an investment decision, what mechanisms enable them to define this scope, and, if there are complementarities to be economized upon, what practices are used to coordinate investments within and among firms and to value the set of synergistic assets.

To analyse the implications of interfirm and intrafirm investment coordination for overall organizational strategy, we focus on a hitherto neglected mechanism—the technology roadmap—which is an important part of Intel's capital budgeting process. While the existence of roadmapping practices has been noted in the literature outside accounting, their role in investment appraisal has not been explored to date. Technology roadmaps are used to ensure that large-scale capital investments made by sub-units of the firm (in assets such as new processes, microprocessor products, and manufacturing capacity) are coordinated with one another, and that they are aligned, also, with investments in enabling and related technologies on the part of a wide range of other firms, including those in Intel's supplier base, its OEM customers, and developers of operating systems, software, and communication infrastructures. We describe the technology roadmap mechanism, and we examine how it integrates with discounted cash flow (DCF) analyses to permit an individual capital spending proposal, such as in a new microprocessor product, to be valued within the system of complementary investments of which it is a part. We examine also the role

of industry-level technology roadmaps produced by the Semiconductor Manufacturing Technology (SEMATECH) consortium, and
how these support firm-level coordination of investments and related
expectations.

There has been some prior attention to the technology roadmap
mechanism in the practitioner literature. Willyard and McClees (1989)
have offered a short and purely descriptive treatment of its use within
individual business units of Motorola. Spencer and Seidel (1995) have
recounted the early stages of adoption of roadmap practices by the
SEMATECH consortium, drawing on the first author's recollections as
CEO of that body. In academic literature, Browning and Shetler's history
(2000) of SEMATECH notes briefly how roadmap practices helped the
consortium to supplant its early (and controversial) role as builder of
globally competitive US firms with the seemingly more neutral one of
aligning technology development plans. This chapter differs from the
existing literature on roadmap practices in providing a detailed empirical analysis of how they enable the coordination of capital spending
decisions at intra- and interfirm levels, and how this is relevant for
accounting research.

The chapter contributes to research on managerial accounting, capital budgeting, and strategy in two key respects. First, and in contrast to
existing studies that operate only at the intrafirm level (Miller and
O'Leary 1997), it provides a detailed description and analysis of a set of
practices that are largely unreported within the accounting literature. It
examines the roles of technology roadmap practices in aligning capital
spending decisions across sub-units of the firm and across firms. Particular attention is paid to how roadmap practices enable such decisions
to be coordinated on a dynamic basis, thus facilitating the 'active management' of investment programmes that has become a key concern in
recent theoretical and normative literatures on the capital budgeting
process (Trigeorgis 1996; Brennan and Trigeorgis 2000).

Second, there is a contribution to the literature on the design of
accounting control systems, and strategy at the interfirm level. What
Doz (1996) terms 'initial complementarity', the prospect of synergies
from interfirm investment coordination, may fail to give rise to actual
or 'revealed complementarities' because the resources in a network of
firms co-evolve in ways that 'lock [individual partners] into unproduct-
ive relationships or preclude partnering with other viable firms' (Gulati
et al. 2000). Calling for research to examine 'the factors that impede the
realization of relational rents' at the interfirm level, Dyer and Singh
(1998) suggest, as a starting point, that each firm should consider the

potential for loss of flexibility at the time a network is formed. Our analysis of technology roadmapping practices shows how the problem of lock-in may also be addressed at an earlier stage in the technology development process. In particular, we demonstrate how the roadmap provides a mechanism for stimulating and monitoring competition in component and technology development before specific networks are formed. Such a mechanism complements the kinds of 'interfirm design instruments' or control systems that are more usually studied and that focus on organizational and information-sharing arrangements as partners enact a particular long-term alliance (Baiman and Rajan 2002).

The remainder of the chapter is organized as follows. Section 2 describes our field research methods. Section 3 analyses the structure of the complementarity relations available to Intel. Section 4 examines the roles of technology roadmaps in coordinating investments at inter- and intrafirm levels. Section 5 provides implications for future research and conclusions.

Method

Permission to undertake research within Intel was sought initially in negotiations with an executive vice-president of the firm. Approval was granted subject to signing a formal non-disclosure agreement. This allowed the researchers to gain access to private information, and to study the application of the firm's investment coordination and appraisal practices to a particular technology generation during the period May 1996 to June 2000. Release from the non-disclosure agreement was secured at the conclusion of the research, so that the firm's identity could be revealed. This process did not constrain the arguments and evidence presented in this chapter, and Intel did not require any particular items of data, analysis, or argument to be included in the manuscript or excised from it.

By negotiating access to the most senior managerial levels of Intel, and conducting a multi-year study, it was possible to identify sources of data and to examine materials relating to the firm's actual capital budgeting process that are inaccessible to survey-based and large sample studies (Graham and Harvey 2001). Such a detailed and extensive piece of field research is unusual in the literature. However, any such study has the inherent limits of a small sample, with the inevitable constraint that its results may be sample specific. This may be overcome in subsequent research, in particular by utilizing the detailed empirical description provided for theory development and communication.

Four research methods were used to compile a substantive database. These were interviews with key decision-makers, the manual collection and analysis of internal documents, first-hand observation of processes, and the collection and analysis of the public record concerning the firm and the industry.

Given the concern to study the coordination of major capital investments, interviews were sought with many of the firm's most senior officers. Interviews were requested with thirty-three executives and managers, selected for their roles in making investment decisions and in developing and extending the firm's capital budgeting practices. All of those approached agreed to be interviewed. All interviews were conducted by the authors. Most of these were at Intel's corporate offices in Santa Clara (California), and at its facilities in Chandler (Arizona), Albuquerque (New Mexico), and Hillsboro (Oregon), and the remaining were at one of the firm's manufacturing facilities in Leixlip (Ireland). Those interviewed included: the president and CEO; the chief financial officer; vice-presidents for technology development, manufacturing, microprocessor product design, and marketing; the director of technology strategy; and managers and engineers in R&D facilities and high-volume factories. In addition, interviews were conducted with three technical analysts who focus exclusively on examining the semiconductor industry for the primary trade publications. They were asked to describe their understanding of Intel's coordination practices. All interviews were semi-structured and lasted a minimum of one hour. All but three of the interviews were tape-recorded.

The researchers gained access to and analysed a range of documents confidential to Intel. These included the firm's capital investment manual, engineering and technical manuals, and the proceedings of intra-firm conferences that describe how investment appraisal and coordination practices were devised and how they have been modified and extended in use. Intel fabrication facilities in Ocotillo (Arizona), Rio Rancho (New Mexico), and Leixlip (Ireland) were visited, to gain a first-hand understanding of the firm's technology development and manufacturing processes.

Internal data sources were complemented by analyses of the public record concerning the firm and the industry. Press releases and press coverage were studied, as well as speeches by Intel executives, the proceedings of trade conferences, technical and trade journals, and the reports of technical and financial analysts.

The firm and its complementarity structure

Intel designs and manufactures microprocessors, the logic devices that enable computers to execute instructions.[2] Throughout the 1990s, its share of the worldwide market for PC microprocessors exceeded 70 per cent of units shipped. During the same period, the firm's ratios of gross profit and operating profit to net revenues generally exceeded 50 per cent and 30 per cent, respectively. The ratio of operating profit to total assets generally exceeded 20 per cent, such that key analysts ranked Intel the world's most profitable microprocessor producer.[3] A key element in the firm's strategy has been to invest, at frequent intervals and in a coordinated manner, in improved fabrication processes, new products, and enhanced manufacturing practices.

Since the mid-1980s, Intel has invested in an improved process for fabricating microprocessors, termed process generation, at intervals of approximately three years. In addition, and at comparable intervals, it has designed at least one new family of microprocessor products, and commenced manufacture in three to six geographically dispersed factories, each of them incorporating improvements in layout, operating policies, training, and other procedures. This process of recurrent investment in both products and processes requires substantial levels of intra- and interfirm coordination. Developers of Intel's proprietary process generations collaborate closely with a range of suppliers such as Silicon Valley Group and Nikon that are investing concurrently to design more advanced equipment sets and materials. Without corresponding advances in lithographic equipment sets manufactured by those firms occurring at defined moments, Intel would be unable to operationalize its successive generations of process technologies. The value of advances in microprocessor design would thus be substantially reduced. Also, Intel's microprocessor architects seek to coordinate their designs with those of customers and firms that are investing in complementary products. These include computing devices by Dell, Compaq, Fujitsu, and others, operating systems by developers such as Microsoft and Linux, database management systems, and extensive sets of application software programmes. Again, without these complementary investments being made by other firms, and their timing being carefully and

---

[2] The firm also manufactures hardware and software products for Internet-based and local-area networking, as well as chip-sets, motherboards, flash-memories, and other 'building blocks' for computing and Internet-based communication.

[3] M. Slater, 'Profits Elude Intel's Competitors', *Microprocessor Report*, 10 May 1999.

accurately synchronized, the financial gain to Intel of improvements in the speed of microprocessors arising from process and product advances would be substantially less.

Through the coordination of investments within the firm, and with both upstream and downstream firms, Intel's executives seek to economize on what Milgrom and Roberts (1995b) have termed a 'complementarity structure'. In this section, we set out the components of this complementarity structure, as a prelude to examining in Section 4 the mechanisms that are used to coordinate them. In the three subsections that follow, we examine the separate sets of relations comprising that structure. First, we examine how they may arise when a new process generation is developed and operationalized concurrently with new microprocessor products. Second, we look at the benefits available when new microprocessor product designs align with complementary computing, operating system, and software products. Third, we consider how complements may be achieved when a new process generation is accompanied by advances in the designs of Intel's high-volume factories. To illustrate the importance of successful coordination, and how critical timing is, the fourth and final subsection illustrates the costs to the firm of failing to align successfully the overall set of complementary assets.

Coordinated process generation and microprocessor designs

The aim of investing in each new process generation is to reduce the minimum linear feature size of an electronic element, such as a transistor, so that more of them can be formed on a silicon wafer.[4] This increase in transistor density has two main effects. First, it increases the yield of good microprocessor die per silicon wafer (die-yield). Second, it improves the speed at which a microprocessor can execute instructions (clock-speed).[5]

Intel's executives seek to establish and optimize complementarity relations by coordinating incremental investments in a process generation that increases transistor density, and incremental investments in

---

[4] At present, electronic elements below 0.09 micron in length are being patterned on wafers and, historically, the length has been reducing by a factor of ~0.7 per process generation. A micron equals 1/1,000,000 of a metre.

[5] As feature-sizes are reduced, electrons take less time to complete an electronic circuit, thus enhancing the clock-speed of the microprocessor.

new products. The design of a new product generally consists of exten-
sions to an architecture, so that the microprocessor can execute an
enhanced set of functions at a faster clock-speed. A typical effect is to
increase the number of electronic elements on the microprocessor die,
thus increasing its area and reducing die-yield per wafer on a given
fabrication process (see Appendix). The returns to coordinated introduction of a new process generation and a new microprocessor are
generally higher than to both changes made independently. The increased transistor density of the process at least partially offsets the
larger die-size of the product, resulting in lower unit costs of manufacture. It also boosts the clock-speed increases that are achieved by improvements to the product architecture. The coordination of investment
in process generation and microprocessor design forms the initial step
in the production of complementarity relations. A second step is to seek
to align the designs of the microprocessor products with those of complementary products.

Coordinated microprocessor and complementary product designs

Intel's strategy is to lead competitors in introducing new microprocessor products, and to coordinate the launch of each one with the introduction of more advanced computing devices, operating systems, and
application software designed by other firms. To achieve this, timing is
critical. An executive board member and president of Intel Capital
commented that his main concern was to achieve two things: first, to
ensure 'that our strategies are aligned with our complementors', and
second, to speed up the programmes of complementors if necessary to
make sure that 'when their product gets to the market, it is pretty much
in-time with our product, not a year or two years later...'.[6] The benefit
to Intel in both cases is to increase the speed at which high volumes can
be achieved with a new generation of technology. With a market share in
excess of 70 per cent, the firm's revenue growth rate was seen to depend
increasingly upon the formation and expansion of markets rather than
an increase in market share. As the manager responsible for Technical
Analyst Relations commented: 'We started moving into a mentality that
went along the lines: if we can do things that stimulate the market

---

[6] Interview, executive board member and president of Intel Capital, 28 July 1998.

growth, we will assume that we are going to take our fair share of that position.'[7]

From its dominant position within the microprocessor market, Intel aims to produce complementarities that are available through coordinating investments at the interfirm level. The timing of the launch of a new microprocessor is critical, since Intel usually introduces a new microprocessor at a relatively high price, which is then reduced significantly during the product's short life cycle. The aim is to secure product acceptance on the part of the most demanding users initially, while the product is still manufactured in low volumes in the development factory, and then to stimulate demand growth by lowering prices as additional factories are brought on-stream. Life cycle revenue is thus significantly higher for Intel when its product investments are coordinated successfully and precisely with those of related firms, such that a new microprocessor, enhanced operating systems, improved Internet infrastructures, and novel software applications are all available from the outset of a given generation.

Coordinated process generation and factory designs

The third element in the complementarity structure involves the coordination of investment in each process generation with investment to enhance Intel's high-volume manufacturing capabilities.

While successive process generations offer increases in die-yield and clock-speed, each one also involves working to finer tolerances, across a greater number of manufacturing steps, using several equipment types and materials that are new to the firm and to the industry. Performance levels achieved in the development factory become more difficult to sustain as successive process generations are transferred to high-volume manufacturing facilities, whose personnel have to learn the parameters of increasingly complex systems. Lower performance levels during the learning period could require investment in excess capacity to achieve a given level of output, thus diminishing the benefits Intel gains from stimulating high-priced, early-period demand for new microprocessors.[8]

---

[7] Interview, Manager, Technical Analyst Relations, 24 August 1998.
[8] Interview, Director of Technology Strategy, 11 December 1996.

The firm seeks complementarities by coordinating the introduction of each process generation, offering enhanced die-yields and clock-speeds, with advances in factory design aimed at reducing the time to learn new system parameters. Since the early 1990s, and to combat the so-called 'Intel-U',[9] the firm has sought closer integration of its development site and high-volume factories, using 'virtual factory' control practices. The intent has been to engineer each generation of high-volume factories so that it more closely copies and reflects the exact layouts, equipment sets, operating procedures, and intervention policies established in the development site. The trajectory of improved performance in the development site is thus to be continued within each of the high-volume factories, as though the network as a whole comprised a single manufacturing entity.

Costs of a coordination failure

There are costs of coordinating investments in process, product, and factory designs with one another internally, and with those of suppliers, complementors, and customers externally. They include the expense of the organization structures and systems by which various groups align their design decisions. Also, there are costs of rendering product development resources fungible, so that, for instance, groups of architects may be re-assigned to develop a particular microprocessor more quickly to synchronize with the earlier availability of a process generation. Historically, Intel executives have found such expense to be substantially lower than the benefits. As the Chief Financial Officer remarked: 'We will take a new process [generation] as soon as we can get one, and we will put as many products on the new process as we can, and incur any [incremental] cost necessary.'[10] The returns from a new process are considered to be so great that the limiting factor is regarded as technological rather than financial.

Table 5 estimates the manufacturing costs of one hypothetical coordination failure, in which the 0.25-micron process generation becomes

---

[9] The phrase is part of Intel folklore. It refers to the early history of process transfers, when product yield would decline significantly each time a process generation was transferred from development to high-volume factories, and would remain depressed for several months, resulting in a U-shaped yield curve.

[10] Interview, Chief Financial Officer, Intel Corporation, 26 August 1998.

available one quarter later than the Pentium II microprocessor product. It is assumed that volume of sales for the quarter remains unchanged, but in the absence of newer fabrication technology Pentium II would continue to be manufactured on the earlier 0.35-micron process generation. As a consequence, the product's die-size is larger and the yield of good die is lower. Each wafer produces only 58 good dies, compared with 120 if the newer fabrication process were available. The net effect of the delay is excess manufacturing cost of $480 million, almost 6 per cent of Intel's operating income for the year 1998. Even relatively short lags between the arrival of a fabrication process and a product may thus result in significant diminution in Intel's operating income.

Table 5 Estimated manufacturing cost of a failure to coordinate process generation and product designs

Condition	Process lags product by three months	Synchronized designs
Process Generation (micron)	0.35	0.25
Product	Pentium II	Pentium II
Die-size and yield data		
Microprocessor die-size (mm^2)	203	131
Yield of good die per silicon wafer	58	120
Estimated manufacturing costs per good die ($)		
Fabrication	49	28
Package	16	16
Packaging and testing	15	12
Module parts and assembly	14	14
Total manufacturing cost per good die ($)	94	70
Manufacturing cost of coordination failure		
Unit cost difference ($94 − $70)	24	
Volume (first quarter, 1998 estimated unit shipments of Pentium II)	20 million	
Estimated total cost of coordination failure ($)	480 million	
Excess cost as % (1998) operating income ($8,379,000,000)	5.7	

Note: Intel Corp., Microprocessor Reference Guide (2000) and press releases; L. Gwennap and M. Thomsen, *Intel Microprocessor Forecast* (Sebastopol, CA: Micro Design Resources, 1998).

In the following section, we analyse how Intel seeks to avoid such costs, and to realize the benefits available from the complementarity structure, through practices of intra- and interfirm investment coordination.

Technology roadmaps

Consistent with the large-scale firms surveyed by Graham and Harvey (2001), Intel's capital budgeting process requires discounted cash flow (DCF) analyses. Net present values (NPVs) are calculated for proposed new microprocessors within the product development groups, for instance.[11] Net present cost analyses are used extensively, as when factory planners are choosing between capacity installation alternatives, such as whether to refit an existing facility for a new process generation or build from a greenfield site, or whether to expand production in one country rather than another.[12]

In light of the extensive set of complementarities available to the firm, however, the capital budgeting process restricts the right of sub-units to evaluate investments 'independently at each of several margins', in Milgrom and Roberts' phrase (1990: 513). To be approved, an investment proposal must not only promise a positive return, but also align with a technology roadmap.[13]

A technology roadmap sets out the shared expectations of the various groups that invest to design components, as to when these will be available, and how they will interoperate technically and economically, to achieve system-wide innovation. Typically, it will address each of several future coordination points, defined by a year or quarter-year. The groups involved in preparing it may include sub-units of a firm, as well as suppliers, complementors, and OEM customers. A roadmap is an inherently tentative and revisable agreement, one of whose key roles is to enable design groups to assess the system-level implications of advances, delays, or difficulties in bringing investments in new component

---

[11] Interview, Vice-President, Microprocessor Products Group, 25 July 1996.

[12] Interview, Chief Financial Officer, Intel Corporation, 26 August 1998. Net present cost analyses establish discounted cost differentials, taking revenue to be the same across alternatives.

[13] Intel Corporate Finance, *Capital Project Authorization* (1998) (internal document); Interview, Corporate Capital Controller, 23 July 1996.

designs to fruition.[14] Equally, the expectations reflected in a technology roadmap may require fundamental revision if there are indications of insufficient demand for the end-user products to which the system of component innovations is expected to give rise. A roadmap thus provides a mechanism for the dynamic coordination of expectations where there is recurrent intra- and interfirm investment.

Through linking an investment explicitly with a technology roadmap, the proponent is required to demonstrate that it synchronizes and fits with related and complementary investments within and beyond the firm. Ensuring that individual investment decisions are congruent with the relevant roadmap is afforded the highest priority by Intel's executive officers. The complementarity structure is considered to be of such importance that it is addressed directly by the president and CEO. As he remarked: 'We obviously do ROIs on products and things of that sort, but the core decisions the company makes, the core decisions are basically technology roadmap decisions...'[15]

In the subsections that follow, we analyse and illustrate how a technology roadmap is prepared and the roles it plays in investment coordination. We follow the chronology of roadmap preparation, beginning with the alignment of investment decisions between Intel and firms in its supplier base.

Coordination with suppliers' innovations

Intel depends upon innovations by suppliers of equipment sets and materials to operationalize each of its new process generations, and thus begin its cycles of complementary investment in process, product, and factory designs. The firm regards such innovations on the part of

---

[14] However, the costs of revision to individual sub-units and firms may increase as a particular coordination node approaches, because each will have invested in the expectation of system-wide success.

[15] Interview, President and CEO, Intel Corporation, 17 December 1998. By 'ROIs', the CEO means summary financial statistics, including NPV and net present cost, as mandated by Intel's Capital Project Authorization manual. 'Moore's law' is named for Intel co-founder and chairman-emeritus Gordon Moore, who noted in 1975, and on the basis of empirical observations extending across fifteen years, that the semiconductor industry seemed capable of doubling the number of electronic elements on a memory device every eighteen months. See Moore (1975).

suppliers as benefiting the industry as a whole, and cooperates with other semiconductor manufacturers to specify collective design needs and time-lines. As the president and CEO of Intel remarked, it is 'much more economical for our industry to work as a whole to create some base technology, and the real intellectual property, the real value-added, comes not from creating a stand-alone piece of lithographic equipment, or a stand-alone piece of ion implanter [equipment]; it comes from the integration of those into a total process'.[16] This means that Intel is able to work with competitors in creating stand-alone pieces of technology, while seeking to gain a competitive advantage from the integration of the different components.

Coordination of investments by semiconductor firms and their supplier base is facilitated by a technology roadmap that is prepared under the auspices of the SEMATECH consortium. Table 6 shows top-level statistics from such a roadmap that was published in 1994. It was prepared by delegates from each of the thirteen firms comprising the consortium, including Intel, which accounted collectively for over 80 per cent of the US output of semiconductor devices. They collaborated with trade associations representing supplier firms through joint working groups and conferences, and liaised also with relevant US federal and university laboratories. The resultant roadmap indicated the design requirements for equipment sets and materials at each of five future coordination points.

The preparation of the technology roadmap may be divided for analytical purposes into three steps. The first step was to specify rates and directions of change in individual design variables to achieve coordinated results at each point or node (Table 6). The intention was to indicate to suppliers when the US semiconductor industry would demand novel equipment sets and materials of particular tolerances and capabilities, in sufficient quantities for high-volume manufacture. The changes in design variables were specified by extrapolation from historical performance levels, specifically, by assuming that the innovative conditions under which Moore's law had been achieved in the past could be made to persist. As the Manager of Lithography Process Equipment Development commented, while Moore's law is not a law of physics, 'it's a pretty strong economic law because once the industry deviates from Moore's law, then the rate of investment is going to

---

[16] Interview, President and CEO, Intel Corporation, 17 December 1998.

Table 6 Required rates and directions of change in individual design variables to achieve coordinated and system-wide innovation as specified in National Technology Roadmap for Semiconductors (1994)

Technology node	Current			Future		
	(N_0) 1995	(N_1) 1998	(N_2) 2001	(N_3) 2004	(N_4) 2007	(N_5) 2010
Suppliers' innovations in equipment sets and materials[a]						
Lithography						
Minimum feature size (μm)	0.35	0.25	0.18	0.13	0.10	0.07
Scaling factor per generation		~0.7	~0.7	~0.7	~0.7	~0.7
Silicon wafers						
Wafer diameter (mm)	200	200	300	300	400	400
Increase per two generations (mm)		100	100		100	
Advances in semiconductor product designs						
Memories						
Bits per die (millions)	64	256	1,000	4,000	16,000	64,000
Multiple per generation		4	~4	4	4	4
Cost/bit (thousands of a cent)	0.017	0.007	0.003	0.001	0.0005	0.0002
Scaling/reduction factor		~0.45	0.5	~0.5	0.5	~0.5
Microprocessors						
Transistors per die (millions)	12	28	64	150	350	800
Multiple		~2.3	~2.3	~2.3	~2.3	~2.3
Cost/transistor (thousands of a cent)	1	0.5	0.2	0.1	0.05	0.02
Scaling/reduction factor		0.5	~0.5	0.5	0.5	~0.5

[a]For brevity of exposition, only two types of components whose designs are coordinated are included here; the full version of the roadmap includes many others, such as deposition and implantation equipment, mask technologies, etc.

Note: Adapted from Semiconductor Industry Association, *National Technology Roadmap for Semiconductors* (San Jose, CA: SIA, 1994: B-2).

change, and the whole structure will change...'.[17] Were that to happen, it would indicate that the industry as a whole was maturing.

It was anticipated that electronic feature sizes could continue to be reduced at a rate of 0.7 per coordination point due to investments in innovation by lithography suppliers, and that this would combine with certain minimum rates of increase in wafer diameter achieved by silicon suppliers (Table 6). Coordinated availability of these and other newly developed components would permit semiconductor firms to continue to operationalize new process generations that would increase the number of bits on a memory product by a factor of four,[18] and the number of transistors on a microprocessor die by a multiple of ~2.3. While the roadmap thus indicated when the US semiconductor industry expected to demand components of given capability, it deliberately avoided 'specifying preferred technology solutions or specific agendas that particular organizations should follow'.[19] The intention was that suppliers should compete to establish the most effective technologies for meeting demand at various coordination nodes.

The second step was to provide an intensive, industry-wide assessment of the state of component R&D, so as to focus the attention and the investments of suppliers on the most promising technology alternatives. In the case of the later coordination points particularly, a number of alternative technologies were identified in each of several critical areas that might meet the industry's requirements if further researched and developed. The aim in clearly identifying them was to bring about a form of coordinated competition on the part of suppliers, so that they would concentrate investment on the commercialization of alternatives regarded as most likely to succeed for a given coordination node by the consensus of industry experts.

For the case of lithographic equipment, the roadmap identified three potential technologies—proximity X-ray, e-beam projection, and extreme ultraviolet (EUV)—for patterning electronic features of 0.1-micron and below. Each of them had proponents among semiconductor firms and within the supply base. IBM and others contended that X-ray machines would be superior, and invested accordingly, whereas Lucent

[17] Interview, Manager of Lithography Process Equipment Development, 3 November 1997.

[18] This is the rate of increase in electronic elements on a memory device that Moore's law calls for, viz. a multiple of four per three years, or two per eighteen months (Moore 1975). The industry established a different constant for increases in microprocessor functionality, viz. a rise in the number of transistors per die by a multiple of ~2.3 every three years.

[19] Semiconductor Industry Association, *National Technology Roadmap for Semiconductors* (San Jose, CA: SIA, 1994: 1).

expended significant R&D on e-beam projection. Other suppliers, supported by Intel, proposed development of EUV machines.[20] The roadmap anticipated that semiconductor firms would select only one of the technologies for use in high-volume production, thus enabling them to share the high costs of R&D. The successful technology could thus enjoy industry-wide demand for several coordination nodes.

During 1997, Intel formed a private industry consortium with two other semiconductor firms, AMD and Motorola, to accelerate the development of EUV lithography. The consortium invested $250 million of venture capital in EUV projects at three US Department of Defence laboratories. The intent was to leverage the R&D programmes of suppliers committed to EUV. They could delay substantial investment in its commercialization until the laboratories, which had pioneered the early stages of EUV technology, had pilot-tested its ability to pattern electronic features reliably. Equally, the consortium's approach enabled Intel, AMD, and Motorola to delay lock-in to a long-term design and supply relationship with the EUV suppliers, until after 'proof of concept' had been established. The manager of Technical Analyst Relations commented, with respect to the three different forms of advanced lithography under consideration at the time, '[W]e think the industry will only support one of these three, and Intel has said, up front, if somebody else comes up with a better idea, we are not going to be proud, we are going to adopt it. We'll go whichever way.'[21] So, while Intel might invest in one particular technology, it will also observe closely developments in other substitute and competitor technologies, and make prototype machines available on the open market so as to encourage competition.

The third and final step in the SEMATECH roadmapping process was for the consortium to agree to revisit the feasibility of projections in a series of frequent update meetings. These may consider arguments from members to alter conditions such as the frequency with which the industry will shift to novel sets of technologies. During 1994, for instance, Intel executives concluded that two-year innovation cycles were more likely to be optimal for the firm than the historical three-year cycle. The decision was based on a DCF analysis of whether more frequent increments in transistor density and microprocessor clock-speed, available from two-year cycles, would outweigh such costs as faster obsolescence of process generations and products.[22] In extensive negotiations with consortium

---

[20] C. Fasca, 'Litho Powerhouse Formed', *Electronic News*, 15 September 1997.

[21] Interview, Manager of Technical Analyst Relations, 24 August 1998.

[22] Interview, Chief Financial Officer, Intel Corporation, 26 August 1998.

members and the supply industry, a temporary shift to two-year cycles was agreed with respect to the 0.25-, 0.18-, and 0.13-micron nodes, with a reversion to three-year cycles thereafter (Table 6).[23] Also, the revision meetings are used to monitor whether the development of alternative component technologies is proceeding as anticipated. In the case of lithography, SEMATECH members concluded during the late 1990s that enhancements to an established technology—deep ultraviolet—would serve the industry for patterning feature sizes of 0.1-micron and smaller. As a consequence, investments in the commercialization of X-ray, e-beam, and EUV technologies were further deferred.

The SEMATECH technology roadmap thus provides a mechanism for coordinating expectations and investments among a set of firms and its supplier base in a key sector of the modern economy where there is recurrent and system-wide innovation. In addressing design requirements comprehensively for all core types of components, it reflects the dependence of investment returns to any one specialized firm on close coordination with the design plans of others. All the technology elements need to be in place before a transition can be achieved to the next generation.[24]

Partial coordination of a system of investments may not come close to producing optimal returns in this industry, an observation consistent with the implication that Milgrom and Roberts (1995*b*) derive from their models of complementarity relations. By establishing where design lags are most likely to occur at each of several future nodes, and then identifying and monitoring promising alternative lines of technology development, the roadmap may enable firms to avoid premature commitment to any one particular technology and set of interfirm relations. And by affording opportunity to lobby for changes in the roadmap, the SEMATECH process acknowledges the inherently high levels of uncertainty affecting all parties, and the need to focus attention and resources on any unexpected technical and financial difficulties affecting particular firms or sectors.

Intrafirm coordination

In light of the shared expectations formed with suppliers, Intel managers continue the roadmap preparation procedure inside the firm. They plan

---

[23] A revised version of the SEMATECH roadmap incorporating the changes was published during 1997.

[24] Semiconductor Industry Association, *National Technology Roadmap for Semiconductors* (San Jose, CA: SIA, 1994: 27).

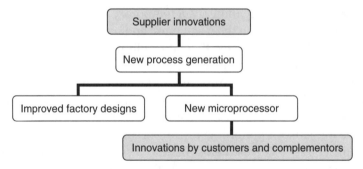

Figure 12   Components of the 0.25-micron technology generation whose design Intel sought to coordinate at intra- and interfirm levels. Components developed by other firms are indicated by shaded boxes.

several future process generations to coincide with the availability of more advanced equipment sets and materials. Three primary pieces of data are recorded in the intrafirm roadmap with respect to each generation: when it is expected to be available for test production and high-volume manufacture; the key technical changes it is to introduce, particularly with respect to additional transistor density; and the expected capital investment to install a unit of capacity utilizing the new process.[25] The data are communicated to Intel's factory design group and microprocessor architects, so that they may extend the intrafirm roadmap to show the combined financial effects of aligning the introduction of each process generation with that of more advanced manufacturing practices and new products.

In 1994, for instance, the intrafirm roadmap showed the planned availability during 1997 of a process generation to pattern 0.25-micron transistors on silicon wafers (Figure 12). To partially offset the rise in investment per unit of capacity associated with the more advanced process, factory designers sought to coordinate its introduction with that of improved manufacturing layouts and operating policies in high-volume factories:

I am designing policies hand-in-hand with the people who are currently developing [a process generation]. So it is meant to be a continuum.... [We] design a continuum of policies, so that we have a set of policies that's intended to maximize information turns in a technology development factory, and in early

[25] A unit of capacity is measured as a given number of wafers introduced into production in a week (e.g. 5,000 wafer-starts-per-week). Capital investment data are only communicated selectively within the firm, to senior managers who require it as input to their investment proposals.

high-volume factory to maximize output, late high-volume to minimize cost, ramping to maximize the ramp velocity. We need—in a factory, at a given snapshot in time—a WIP policy, an equipment maintenance policy, a cross training policy, etc., etc., that fit together.[26]

Of particular concern was the need to increase ramp-velocity by altering factory layouts and equipment installation, staffing, and operating policies. Ramp-velocity is a measure of how quickly a new process generation can be 'copied' from its development site to high-volume factories without impairing a given level of die-yield. The faster this is achieved, the lower the total investment needed to meet a given volume of demand, and the greater the financial benefits of a new process generation.

Microprocessor architects extended the intrafirm roadmap still further, by planning the investment schedules and time-lines of several new product families to coincide with the availability of the new process. By examining this alignment, we demonstrate the roles of a technology roadmap in permitting capital spending on new products to be appraised within the system of complementary assets of which they are to form a part.

Capital spending on a new microprocessor is typically proposed in stages, during a period of four or more years. Early investment is aimed at deriving a general model of the enhanced capabilities the new product might deliver for particular market segments, without commitment to a precise time-frame for execution or to manufacture on a given process generation. But, as architects move from that model to instantiating the new product as a set of circuits, layouts, and masks necessary for manufacture, returns to additional investment come to depend significantly on coordinating product design closely with that of a particular process generation. The investments needed to achieve this are substantial. As the vice-president of the Microprocessor Products Group commented, 'I may spend in the order of a hundred-engineer-years of creating a physical layout only to find that I have to re-do it for the next generation [process] technology.'[27]

A technology roadmap provides a mechanism for appraising whether such irreversible investment is justifiable in light of the investment time-lines and expected capabilities of complementary components. During the early 1990s, for instance, Intel executives decided that, in addition to designing further products within its 32-bit architecture, the

[26] Interview, Principal Scientist, Manufacturing Systems, 22 August 1997.
[27] Interview, Vice-President, Microprocessor Products Group, 25 July 1996.

firm would also develop a line of new 64-bit microprocessors aimed at higher-end workstation and server markets. A processor code-named Merced, devised jointly by Intel and H-P, was planned as the first instantiation of the new architecture. By consulting the technology roadmap, product architects sought to align their investment in the new product with the availability of a suitable new process generation:

[The technology development] organisation is very good at putting out a roadmap internally as to when they expect a certain process generation to arrive. It is based on history of how often we have been able to increment the process generations, and based on a forecast by some people in [the] organisation that are continually looking at where they expect, for example, lithography to evolve [by] a certain point of time. So, the [product] design group and myself, or general manager at the time, would have access to this technology roadmap . . . that says, basically, as a function of time, this is the beginning point of the ramp of the .35-micron generation, for example, this is the entry point of the .25-micron generation, this is the entry point of the next generation that will follow that. . . . The decision [on coordinating] a high-end product like this Merced [with a particular process generation] . . . is actually very easy, in the sense that your product is oriented for performance. There is only one promise that you have [for customers] on this product, and that is that you'll offer the highest performance capability at the time for these high-end systems. So, you want to implement that on the most advanced [process] technology that would be available for manufacturing at the time the product would come out.[28]

The initial decision of the product architects was that the Merced should be introduced during the life cycle of the 0.25-micron process generation during 1998 or early 1999 (Figure 12). They believed that the product time-line could be made to align with that of the process, that the size of the product would permit an acceptable die-yield per wafer using transistors of 0.25-micron in length, and, generally, that an acceptable NPV would result from such a coordination.

The decision to launch a powerful and large die-sized product such as the Merced on the 0.25-micron process was based on a key assumption that the product would quickly be shifted to the newer 0.18-micron process generation. Not only was that generation expected to offer a further increase in transistor density, it was also anticipated that it would operate on larger, 300-mm silicon wafers, which were in the course of being developed by suppliers. As a consequence, the relatively large die-size of a product such as Merced would quickly be offset by process generation advances, such that an acceptable long-run yield of

---

[28] Interview, Vice-President, Microprocessor Products Group, 25 July 1996.

good die per wafer could be achieved. However, unexpected revisions to the process roadmap in October 1997 led to a fundamental revision of such expectations.[29]

The expectation that suppliers could develop and supply the larger wafers in time for the 0.18-micron generation had proven to be incorrect. In addition, as Merced's designers sought to perfect the new 64-bit architecture, they found during 1997 that the die-size of the product would be significantly larger than had been anticipated.[30] A key role of the technology roadmap mechanism is to convey such shifts in expectations, which may arise inside or outside the firm, to product developers to inform their capital investment decisions. Influenced by the delay in arrival of the larger wafer size, and also by difficulties in perfecting the Merced's instruction set, Intel's executive officers decided during 1997 to defer its launch, and the product's development time-line was reset so as to coincide with a later process generation.

However, the time-line and technical attributes of the 0.25-micron process were found to be fully aligned with those for a second family of new microprocessors, the Pentium II. As the general manager responsible commented: 'Pentium II was clearly the flagship product of our 0.25-micron technology. I want to make sure that the 0.25-micron technology is well suited for this product.'[31] This involved close collaboration between process engineers and product architects so that, as the Pentium II instruction set was refined and as its circuits and layouts were completed during 1996 and 1997, the emerging 0.25-micron process generation was adjusted to support features critical to its performance. Intel personnel thus sought to maximize the clock-speed of the new product while keeping its die-size sufficiently small for economic manufacture. The Pentium II contained 7.5 million transistors, 36 per cent more than its direct predecessor, the Pentium Pro. But coordination of decisions on the part of product architects and process engineers resulted in a die-size for the new product that was actually 33 per cent smaller than that of the Pentium Pro (Table 7). Also, whereas architec-

[29] Interview, Manager of Lithography Process Equipment Development, 3 November 1997.

[30] Interview, Chief Financial Officer, Intel Corporation, 26 August 1998; L. Gwennap. Intel's Two-Track Strategy Re-routed, *Microprocessor Report*, 4 August 1997. To correct for such unanticipated delays in completing any one microprocessor, Intel's policy is to design several new products in parallel design groups. Development of an alternative product may thus be accelerated through transfers of architectural skills and other resources, to protect the firm's competitive position in given market segments.

[31] Interview, General Manager, California Technology and Manufacturing, 17 December 1998.

Table 7   Relative performance indicators for the Pentium II microprocessor

Process generation			
Minimum feature-size (microns)	0.35	0.35	0.25
Products			
Brand name	Pentium Pro	Pentium II	
Version	Redesign	Original	Redesign
Date of first shipment	Second quarter, 1996	Second quarter, 1997	Fourth quarter, 1997
Performance indicators			
Die size			
Transistors per microprocessor (millions)	5.5	7.5	7.5
Increase on Pentium Pro product (%)		~36	
Microprocessor die-size (mm^2)	196	203	131
Die size *increase* due to architecture enhancement (%)		~4	
Die size *reduction* due to process generation shift (%)			~35
Die size *reduction* on joint product & process changes			~33
Clock-speed			
Maximum product clock-speed (MHz)	200	300	450
Speed increment due to product architecture improvement (%)		50	
Speed increment due to process generation shift (%)			50
Speed increment on joint product and process changes (%)			125

Note: Intel Corp., *Microprocessor Reference Guide* (2000) and press releases; L. Gwennap and M. Thomsen, *Intel Microprocessor Forecast* (Sebastopol, CA: Micro Design Resources, 1998).

tural improvements alone would have boosted the clock-speed of the Pentium II by ~50 per cent, closely aligning its development and that of the 0.25-micron process resulted in a speed increase of 125 per cent. Complementarities are thus sought through coordinated product and process designs that combine improvements in clock-speed, which increase the marketability of a product, with combined reductions in its die-size that reduce fabrication cost.

However, realizing the incipient benefits of new process and micro-processor generations depends on whether other firms devise more advanced end-user computing devices, and markets for them, so as to accelerate the high-volume deployment of Intel's products. To that end, the firm's executives seek to ensure that their technology roadmap is aligned with those of OEM customers and complementors. It is to these issues that we now turn.

Coordination with customers' and complementors' designs

Since the early 1990s, Intel has taken a direct interest in the formation of end markets for the varied types of products that incorporate its micro-processors. For instance, in the case of a particular version of the Pentium II, the Xeon processor, Intel coordinated its development with that of other firms' workstation and server computers, operating systems, database management systems, and an extensive range of applications software, in such areas as electronic commerce, supply chain management, and mechanical design automation. The aim was to ensure that these firms would invest to 'integrate, tune, and optimize [their] solutions around this new microprocessor',[32] thus expanding Intel's market shares in the enterprise computing segment.

In seeking to align its plans with those of downstream firms, Intel shares elements of its technology roadmap with them, on a reciprocal basis and under non-disclosure agreements, for a period of up to two years prior to the planned product launch dates:

So, about the time that we are freezing on the product that we want to design, and looking forward to two years of design for its introduction, we have to take that to the software community and say 'Fine, here are the 70 new instructions that this processor has which will make [for example] your multi-media appli-cations better', under non-disclosure agreement. 'Here they are, start designing the product'. So, [we take that data to] the software community, and the hard-ware community, and you also get the [technical analyst] people who make a living out of following our industry...telling them 'this is the direction that Intel's going in'.[33]

The sharing of roadmap data with technical analysts, thus going beyond the firms that are directly involved in product development, is integral

---

[32] Intel Corporation press release, 'Intel Pentium II Xeon processor launch', 29 June 1998.
[33] Interview, Chief Executive Officer, Intel Corporation, 17 December 1998.

to the coordination of investments at the interfirm level. Bringing about complementary investments at the interfirm level may depend on whether the parties have means of attesting the reliability of each others' claims and promises. In particular, smaller software vendors may be unwilling to invest if they lack confidence in the claims that Intel makes for its future microprocessor generations. As one means of addressing such issues, Intel sometimes provides support in the form of technical assistance and venture capital to such firms.

But, since about 1993, and also to assuage such concerns on the part of downstream firms, Intel has availed of the services of a small number of independent technical analyst firms. One such firm is Micro Design Resources. As its President remarked, 'We are the community organizer. We have brought together this community of people which cares about microprocessors.'[34] What is meant by this is that Micro Design Resources collects information from various parties involved in the production of microprocessors, and disseminates it to the entire network, thus permitting information exchange and informed interaction. Intel informs Micro Design Resources of key technical changes that it plans to incorporate in each of several future products, indicating also the particular market segment to which each one is being addressed, and its expected price point. The analyst firm's income stream depends significantly on the perceived objectivity and accuracy of its appraisals of such microprocessors on the part of customers who buy its newsletters, which include firms throughout the semiconductor, hardware, and software industries, as well as stock analysts. Equally, Intel's willingness to continue sharing data with the analyst firm depends on the latter's adherence to product appraisals that, while they may on occasion be critical, nevertheless adhere to non-disclosure agreements with respect to proprietary data. A technology roadmap thus provides a mechanism for the coordination of investment decisions throughout a design network, extending from suppliers to various sub-units within a firm and to its OEM customers and complementors.

Conclusions

This chapter has examined the link between capital budgeting and complex organizational strategies. In reporting the results of a field

---

[34] Interview, President, Micro Design Resources, 7 July 1998.

study of how a major firm in the microprocessor industry coordinates and appraises investments in systems of complementary assets, it has sought to help remedy the deficit in firm-level studies of such issues. We have examined whether managers at Intel systematically coordinate investments in a manner consistent with the theory of complementarities. We have considered the coordination processes and practices that allow integration across sub-units within the firm, and across stages in the design, manufacturing, and marketing processes. We have also shown that capital budgeting and coordination processes can extend beyond the firm in the modern economy. Capital budgeting, we argue, needs to be extended to include a much broader set of processes and issues than has been the case to date. Rather than view this extension as a matter of simply refining valuation methods, the capital budgeting literature needs to accord a central place to the roles of intra- and interorganizational coordination processes in linking the evaluation and management of investment proposals with corporate strategies. The links between investment appraisal and strategy, we argue, need to be taken more seriously by researchers, and their implications for intra- and interorganizational coordination mechanisms considered more extensively.

We have examined a coordination mechanism that has been neglected in the investment appraisal literature in accounting. We have described the overall complementarity structure within which Intel operates, both intra- and interfirm, and demonstrated the costs of failing to coordinate successfully the sets of complementary assets. The role of technology roadmaps in coordinating both investments and expectations has been documented for the sub-units of Intel, and for the relations among Intel and its suppliers, complementors, and OEM customers. The links between roadmaps as coordination mechanisms and traditional capital budgeting practices have also been analysed. We argue that the chapter makes the following three contributions.

First, our findings provide strong firm-level evidence supporting the arguments of Trigeorgis (1995, 1996) and of Milgrom and Roberts (1995a, 1995b) that the system of assets, rather than the individual investment decision, may often be the critical unit of analysis and decision for managers. This is consistent with intuition and casual observation, and of considerable importance for overall firm strategies. In the case of Intel, analysing 'synergies among parallel projects undertaken simultaneously' (Trigeorgis 1996: 257) is the aspect of investment appraisal that is always considered at the highest levels in the firm because, as we have demonstrated, the costs of failing to coordinate such complementary investments may be very high. Our findings thus provide support for the extension of theoretical and empirical analyses to incorporate systems of parallel and interacting investment decisions that occur across units within the firm and among firms.

Second, we find that value-maximizing investments in systems of complementary assets require coordination mechanisms that are largely overlooked in recent theoretical literature. In particular, the role of top-level executives extends far beyond Milgrom and Roberts' claim (1995*b*) that they 'need only identify the relevant complementarity structure in order to recommend a "fruitful" direction for coordinated search' to lower-levels in the hierarchy. At Intel, executives have collaborated with peers in supplier, customer, and complementor firms to develop and operationalize a technology roadmap mechanism. We examine how this is used to establish, coordinate, and revise expectations, within and between firms, as to when the components of an asset system should be made available and how they should interoperate to enable system-wide innovation.

In contexts where innovation is widely distributed across sub-units and across firms, the benefits of such a coordination mechanism for dynamically adjusting expectations are particularly significant. As we demonstrate for the case of Intel, decisions on accelerating or postponing investments such as in a new microprocessor are embedded in what one executive termed an 'ecosystem' (Miller and O'Leary 2000). Optimal results may be secured only through awareness of proposed shifts in the time-lines and anticipated outcomes of many other investment decisions, such as made by fabrication process developers within the firm, lithography firms in the supply base, or a set of independent software vendors designing complementary products. To avoid lock-in to an inferior source of component designs, as well as misappropriation of intellectual property, mechanisms for monitoring and evaluating technology development programmes of alternative suppliers are needed. The significance of complementarity relations among investments is widely recognized in the literature, and the merits of identifying such relations at intra- and interfirm levels is also acknowledged. It is important now for researchers to identify and analyse empirically the mechanisms that allow firms to realize the benefits of complementarities.

Third, this study enables us to identify issues for investigation in future large-sample surveys and field-based analyses of the capital budgeting process. In particular, we suggest investigating whether there are systematic differences between industries in the effectiveness with which interdependent investments are planned and coordinated across firm boundaries. For instance, anecdotal evidence indicates that firms in the telecommunications industry have found it very difficult to align investments in the components of advanced telephony, with significant negative returns to investment as a consequence (Grove 2001). A number of specific research questions follow. For instance, if there are such differences across industries, why do they arise? Are the differences due, for instance, to the absence of appropriate institutional arrangements such as those provided by SEMATECH, or is it attributable to the lack of a norm such as Moore's law, through which initial expectations are formed? Or is it a function of the differing rate and nature of technological progress, such that in one industry (e.g. microprocessors) innovation is relatively predictable and incremental, and in another (e.g. biotechnology) it is highly uncertain and fundamental? Further research should focus on such questions to enable us to ascertain whether there are systematic differences across industries with respect to mechanisms for forming, revising, and enacting expectations, such that some industries are better able to achieve systemic and interfirm innovation than others.

As a result of Graham and Harvey's recent survey (2001), we now have a comprehensive and detailed understanding of the utilization of particular investment valuation practices on the part of large and small firms in a variety of industries. It is important to build upon this information by asking managers whether synergies or complements are addressed formally as part of the capital budgeting process and, if they are, what formal mechanisms are used to achieve this. Our clinical study suggests the widespread use of technology roadmap practices in the computing and microelectronics industries. At Intel, the CEO and other executive officers pay particular attention to investment coordination as a key driver of NPV. This suggests that it is now appropriate for survey researchers to pose questions relating to how the relevant unit of investment analysis and appraisal is arrived at. For instance, a roadmap may offer a robust mechanism for articulating possible responses to the uncertainties of intra- and interfirm coordination. This may be preferable to arbitrarily adjusting the cash flow forecasts or discount rates of individual investment decisions, an approach which Graham and Harvey (2001) observe is presumed in the existing literature. Systematic investigation of these issues, through fieldwork and survey research, would be of considerable benefit.

Additional field studies of the explicit use of formal coordination mechanisms in other industries such as automobile and airplane manufacture would be extremely valuable. It would be of interest to learn whether mechanisms similar to those observed in the microprocessor industry, which allow for the optimizing of complementary investments, exist in other industries. It would also be of interest to learn how the coordination of expectations is achieved in other industries. While 'Moore's law' sets out a time-line and a corresponding cost improvement for advances in process technology that is specific to the semiconductor industry, it would be helpful to know whether comparable ways of coordinating expectations with respect to investment decisions exist in other industries.

Appendix

Effects of coordinating a process generation shift with introduction of a new product

Panel A	Panel B	Panel C
Process generation (x)	Process generation (x)	Process generation ($x + 1$)
Product generation (y)	Product generation ($y + 1$)	Product generation ($y + 1$)

A microprocessor is fabricated by forming electronic elements, such as transistors, on a square of silicon wafer. The elements are connected by layers of metal traces to form a set of integrated circuits. The finished product is a square of silicon embedded with electronic circuitry, termed a die.

Each square on the circles above represents a microprocessor die fabricated on a silicon wafer, and the black dots represent particles that contaminate the wafer during processing, rendering a microprocessor unusable. It is assumed that the number of particles is a function of imperfections in the fabrication process, and independent of the number of die. Each of the three panels shows a total of five fatal defects in identical locations.

The shift from panel A to panel B shows the effects of introducing a new microprocessor product without a corresponding change in process generation. The die-size of product $(y + 1)$ in panel B is larger than that of its predecessor, (y) in panel A, because the new microprocessor contains more transistors and circuits to give it added power and functionality. The yield of good-die per wafer is reduced as a consequence: there are fewer dies per wafer, and a greater proportion of them are destroyed by the contaminant particles. Fabrication cost per good (or usable) die will rise as a consequence. Also, the clock-speed of product $(y + 1)$ may be impaired, because the larger die-size results in electrons travelling longer distances to complete a circuit.

The introduction of the new product $(y + 1)$ may be more economic if it is coordinated with a process generation change, from (x) to $(x + 1)$, as represented in the shift from panel B to panel C. The increased transistor density provided by the new process will at least partially offset the increased die-size of the new product, such that the yield of good (or usable) die per wafer and the clock-speed of the device are both increased.

References

Baiman, S. and Rajan, M. (2002). 'Incentive Issues in Inter-firm Relationships', *Accounting, Organizations and Society*, 27(3): 213–38.

Brennan, M. and Trigeorgis, L. (2000). 'Real Options', in M. Brennan and L. Trigeorgis (eds.), *Project Flexibility, Agency and Competition*. Oxford: Oxford University Press.

Browning, L. and Shetler, J. (2000). *Sematech*. College Station, TX: Texas A&M University Press.

Doz, Y. (1996). 'Evolution of Cooperation in Strategic Alliances', *Strategic Management Journal*, 17(4): 55–83.

Dyer, J. and Singh, H. (1998). 'The Relational View: Cooperative Strategy and Sources of Interorganizational Competitive Advantage', *Academy of Management Review*, 23(4): 660–79.

Graham, J. and Harvey, C. (2001). 'The Theory and Practice of Corporate Finance: Evidence from the Field', *Journal of Financial Economics*, 60(2/3): 187–243.

—— —— (2002). 'How do CFOs Make Capital Budgeting and Capital Structure Decisions?', *Journal of Applied Corporate Finance*, 15(1): 1–36.

Grove, A. (2001). 'Communications Strategy and the Nation's New Agenda', Strategic Management Society Annual International Conference.

Gulati, R., Nohria, N., and Zaheer, A. (2000). 'Strategic Networks', *Strategic Management Journal*, 21(3): 203–15.

Jensen, M. (1993). 'The Modern Industrial Revolution, Exit, and the Failure of Internal Control Systems', *Journal of Finance*, 48(3): 831–80.

Milgrom, P. and Roberts, J. (1990). 'The Economics of Modern Manufacturing: Technology, Strategy and Organization', *American Economic Review*, 80(3): 511–28.

Milgrom, P. and Roberts, J. (1995a). 'Continuous Adjustment and Fundamental Change in Business Strategy and Organization', in H. Siebert (ed.), *Trends in Business Organization*. Tubingen: J. C. B. Mohr.

—— —— (1995b). 'Complementarities and Fit: Strategy, Structure and Organizational Change in Manufacturing', *Journal of Accounting and Economics*, 19(2/3): 179–208.

Miller, P. and O'Leary, T. (1997). 'Capital Budgeting Practices and Complementarity Relations in the Transition to Modern Manufacture: A Field-Based Analysis', *Journal of Accounting Research*, 35(2): 257–71.

—— —— (2000). *Value Reporting and the Information Ecosystem*. London: PriceWaterhouseCoopers.

Moore, G. (1975). 'Progress in Digital Integrated Electronics', in *International Electron Devices Meeting Technical Digest*. Piscataway, NJ: Institution of Electrical and Electronic Engineers.

Roberts, J. (2004). *The Modern Firm*. Oxford: Oxford University Press.

Siggekow, N. (2001). 'Change in the Presence of Fit: the Rise, the Fall and the Renaissance of Liz Claiborne', *Academy of Management Journal*, 44(4): 838–57.

Spencer, W. and Seidel, T. (1995). 'National Technology Roadmaps: The US Experience', in *Proceedings of the 4th International Conference on Solid State and Integrated Circuit Technologies*. Piscataway, NJ: Institution of Electrical and Electronic Engineers.

Trigeorgis, L. (1995). *Real Options in Capital Investment*. London: Praeger.

—— (1996). *Real Options*. Cambridge, MA: MIT Press.

Whittington, R. and Pettigrew, A. (2003). 'Complementarities Thinking', in A. Pettigrew, R. Whittington, L. Melin, C. Sanchez-Runde, F. Van Den Bosch, W. Ruigrok and T. Numagami (eds.), *Innovative Forms of Organizing*. London: Sage.

Willyard, C. and McClees, C. (1989). 'Motorola's technology roadmap process', *Research Management*, 30(5): 13–19.

INDEX